DEDICATION

Special thanks to our First Responders who train hard, work hard, and rush into harm's way to keep us safe.

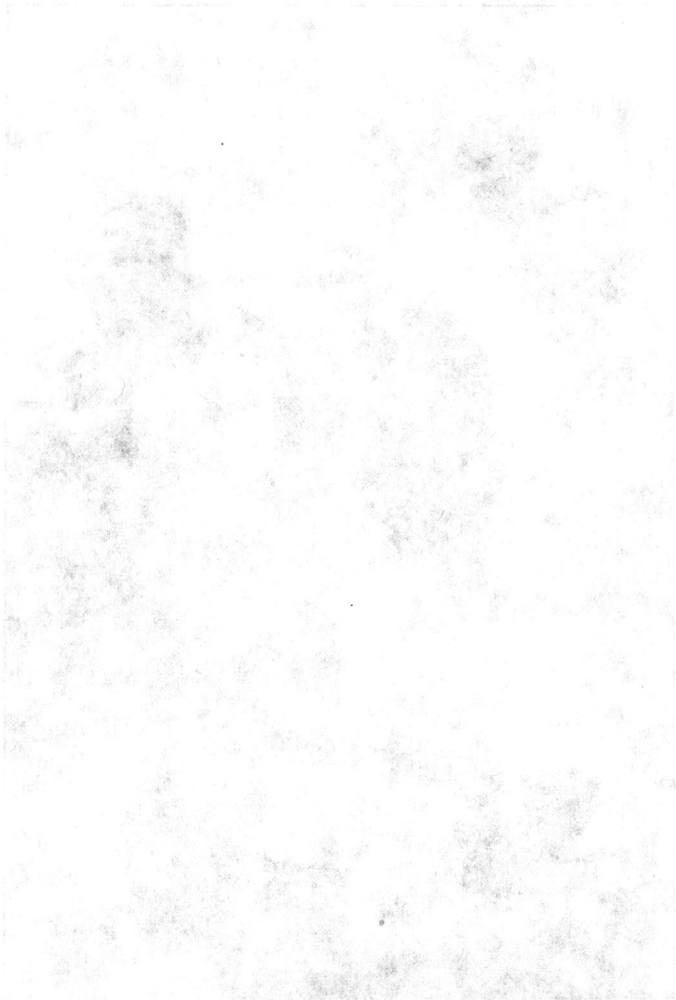

EXPLOSIVES, IEDS AND BREACHING FOR LAW ENFORCEMENT

Jack W. Peters
Duane R. Mattson

Matt A. Byers, Tyson Krieger & Garrett Shannon

Editor: Joan Raymond
Joanraymondwriting.com

Official Training Guide for

American Explosives Group, Inc.
www.americanexplosivesgroup.com

Published by Do North Media
PO Box 52, Walterville, Oregon 97489
jack@donorthmedia.com
(541) 541 554-6720
www.donorthmedia.com

Do North Media.com

Third Edition September 2020

Special thanks for expert consultation by:

Tyson Krieger, Gold Beach FD Chief, Associate Instructor

Garret Shannon, USMC, Retired, Associate Instructor

Matt Byers, Elemental Explosives Corp.

Katie E. DeKoker, USAF, USA, 3ID, Combat Veteran

Kevin Bourgault, US Army, 10 Mt. Div. Retired

Ray Murphy, US Army EOD, Retired

Daniel Tanner, Tannerite Sports, LLC.

Rick Foster, Rick Foster Construction

Rick E. Eilers, U.S. Air Force EOD, Retired

Cover photo by Marcio Jose Sanchez, Associated Press.

Most photos, video, and illustrations by Jack W. Peters

Special thanks to other photo and video contributors:

Desiree Stratford

Josh Morell

John Janzen

Ryan Niemi

Ray Poppeck

Jeff Johnston

ISBN Number 978-0-9719814-8-5

DISCLOSURE

Explosive materials can be extremely dangerous. Homemade explosives and Improvised Explosive Devices (IEDs) are very unpredictable, which makes them even more hazardous. Never handle explosive materials without proper training, licensing, or authority to do so.

This book is designed to be a valuable resource tool, but it will not make you a bomb technician. Anyone in the business of explosives and blasting, must assume responsibility to acquire proper knowledge and experience first. Additionally, they must abide by their own agency's operating procedures, as well as federal laws and regulations.

Breaching activities that require detonating explosives around people and buildings can be extremely dangerous, with the potential of legal liabilities for officers and the departments they represent. Use extreme caution, common sense, and follow your departmental protocols and procedures for the necessary guidelines to ensure every mission is as safe and successful as possible.

Every effort has been made to establish the accuracy of this information. The author and publisher assume no liability or loss caused by errors and/or omissions.

RESTRICTED MATERIAL

This manual is intended for use by law enforcement, first responders, emergency personnel, security agencies, U.S. military, and allied units.

Due to the sensitive nature of this material, we recommend that it remain secured to prevent it from being compromised, misused, mishandled, or shared by those that are not authorized to receive or control this information.

TABLE OF CONTENTS

1.	Explosives and Public Safety	P. 11
2.	Explosives Regulation	P. 15
3.	Storage and Transportation	P. 27
4.	Explosive Characteristics	P. 37
5.	Binaries & Blasting Agents	P. 49
6.	Commercial Explosives	P. 53
7.	Military Explosives	P. 65
8.	Homemade Explosives	P. 77
9.	Blasting Caps and Fuses	P. 91
10.	Preparing Explosive Charges	P. 105
11.	Special Blasting Techniques	P. 127
12.	Safety and Security	P. 135
13.	Explosive Ordinance Disposal	P. 139
14.	Homemade Explosives Labs	P. 145
15.	Improvised Explosive Devices	P. 151
16.	IED Scenario Locations	P. 169
17.	IEDs used with Active Shooters and Riots	P. 179
18.	United States IED Case Study	P. 199
19.	Explosives Door Breaching	P. 213
20.	Explosives Obstacle Breaching	P. 229
21.	Breaching Standoff and Reports	P. 243
22.	IED Bomb Water Disrupters	P. 259
23.	Index	P. 265

Appendix

A	Video links from QR codes to scan by phone	P. 270
B	ATF's List of Explosive Materials	P. 271
C	Breaching MSD K Factor Chart	P. 278
D	List of Important Contact Information	P. 279
E	AEG Author, Team Profile	P. 280

I. EXPLOSIVES AND PUBLIC SAFETY

Chapter Topics:

- Why First Responders need to understand explosives.
- Understand why criminals and terrorists will use explosives.
- Understand the frequency of explosive materials and IEDs are found in the United States alone.

The idea of this book is to help you understand and de-mystify the use of explosives, both legally and criminally. It will also introduce you to a variety of explosive materials ranging from Commercial, Homemade, Military and IEDs.

Why do First Responders need to understand explosives?

We believe every First Responder should have a basic understanding of explosive materials including IEDs, their precursors, components and possible responses to these threats. Why? Because your agency will fall within one of two categories - one that deals with these issues on a constant basis, or one that will eventually.

Yes, larger police departments have EOD bomb techs and SWAT teams, but these specialists are not typically the ones that find the explosive materials or devices. It's the front-line police officers, firefighters or security officers that first notice something just doesn't look right.

Why do criminals and terrorists use explosives?

They are very effective! As lethal as explosives are, terrorists do not have to create mass casualties, they just need to scare people. The threat of explosives accomplishes that. They frighten people.

In Iraq and Afghanistan, IEDs are responsible for the majority of troop deaths and injuries. In Iraq in 2009, IEDs were responsible for 59% of deaths and injuries with an increase to 63% in 2011 (Inter Press Service News Agency).

Explosives are reasonably inexpensive and easy to make out of a variety of materials. In civilian areas, they could be made from household and industrial materials. In military conflict areas, they could primarily be made from military munitions.

Furthermore, terrorists can reduce their exposure through remote, timed, victim activated, or timed fused initiation systems. This leaves them free from being amidst combat action or shooting scenarios. Explosive devices can let them stay in the shadows and call the shots. It is this kind of power that inspires the sickest minds to build the next bomb.

Explosive related incidents in the United States

Bomb squads are called out many times every day in the United States. For everything from the family finding Vet souvenirs from previous wars to investigating suspicious packages and bomb threats. The exact number per year is difficult to pin down, but it is thousands. The ATF has in its official record 5,909 for 2013.

Here are some statistics from the ***ATF US Bomb Data Center***:

Explosives Incidents in the United States

The following statistics are based upon explosives incidents reported to the USBDC, including bombings, attempted bombings, incendiary bombings, stolen explosives and other categories.

Year	No. of Explosives Incidents	No. of Injuries	No. of Fatalities
2013*	5,909	390	31
2012	5,815	159	21
2011	5,219	36	5
2010	4,897	99	22
2009	3,886	57	4
2008	4,198	97	15
2007	3,143	60	15
2006	3,797	135	14
2005	4,031	148	19
2004	3,919	263	36

*The number of injuries reported for 2013 is elevated due to the Boston Marathon Bombing that occurred on April 15, 2013.

Keep in mind also, that the use of explosives in the US and worldwide, both legally and illegally, will only continue to expand.

The legal use primarily falls within two areas of business, mining, and fireworks, both growing industries.
On the illegal or criminal front, there are a number of Islamic organizations that are waging war against the west, such as *Al-Qaeda, the Taliban, Al-Shabaab, Boko Haram* and *ISIS*.

These groups are busy competing with each other to see how much death, destruction and fear they can create.

When they cannot officially operate in a country, there seems to be no shortage of so-called 'Lone Wolf' operatives willing to take up the cause. Since 2014, there has been a noticeable increase in these types of attacks in the United States, as well as other countries where terrorism events are more unlikely, such as in Canada and Australia.

However, before we give all the credit to the Islamic groups, you will see in our U.S. IED Case Study, that terrorists come in any nationality and under any political or religious brand. The bottom line is, now is the time to keep your eyes open and understand how to respond to this increasing threat.

2. EXPLOSIVES REGULATION

Chapter Topics:

- U.S. Federal law, and agencies regulating explosives, mining, and transport.
- ATF licensing requirements for lawful blasters.
- Canadian Federal agencies for regulating explosives and transport.
- Understand that state and local agencies may have regulator authority.

We first want to you to understand legal explosives use. By understanding the basics of licensing and regulation, you will be able to more effectively know if someone is licensed to help determine whether any explosives or blasting activity is lawful or not.

U.S. Federal Law

In the United States, explosives related definitions, laws and regulations are covered by the ***Code of Federal Regulations, (CFR)***. This includes the following Titles:

The following CFR Title information is located in the ATF Orange Book:

CFR Title 18. Sec. 1102, Chapter 40 – Importation, Manufacture, Distribution and Storage of Explosive Materials

CFR Title 27, Part 555 – Commerce in Explosives

CFR Title 29, Part 1910.109 - Explosives and Blasting Agents

The following CFR Title is located in Department of Transpiration publications.
CFR Title 49, Part 171, 172, 173 - Transportation

In the United States, the primary regulative agency for explosive materials is the Federal Department of Treasury's **Bureau of Alcohol, Tobacco, Firearms and Explosives** (**BATFE**), typically referred to as the ***ATF***.

The ATF is a Federal Agency that has three primary functions:

- Grant a license or permit to persons or companies that use explosives.

- Maintain and update regulations and laws for the use of explosives.
- A law enforcement agency that investigates and prosecutes suspects involved in explosives related crimes.

ATF website www.atf.gov

They publish their ***Orange Book*** titled **Federal Explosives Law and Regulations**. Quotes and section references in this book are made from the Orange Book, ATF publication number 5400.7, revised June 2012.

An online PDF file of the *Orange Book* can be found at the ATF website or at the American Explosives Group website.

Note that U.S. Agencies and the Military are exempt from ATF regulations.

Employee Safety Agencies

In the United States, work site safety regulation is managed by the **Occupational Safety and Health Administration (OSHA)**.
They have jurisdiction over non-mining explosives and blasting activity such as demolitions, logging and fireworks companies.
In the United States, commercial mining and aggregate operations, both surface and underground is regulated by the **Mine Safety and Health Administration (MSHA)**. Pronounced (M-Shaw), the agency enforces compliance with health and safety standards based upon the *Federal Mine Safety and Health Act of 1977*.

Commercial mines include mineral and non-mineral lode or placer operations where there are employees or heavy equipment used in the mining process. Mine operators review and file a safety plan of operation and miners receive specified training for surface or underground operations. This includes use of all safety equipment from respirators to emergency self-rescue devices. Underground operations also must have access to a mine rescue team in the event of a cave-in emergency.

Note that through an interagency agreement, MSHA officers also represent the ATF in the field to ensure safety and compliance with the use of explosive materials.

OSHA website www.osha.gov

MSHA website www.msha.gov

Transportation Agency

The commercial transporting explosives within the United States is controlled by the **U.S. Department of Transportation** (**US DOT**). This agency has jurisdiction of all commercial or "in-commerce" explosive material transportation. This includes by roadway, railway, water or air. They provide all transpiration, hazmat related regulation and safety procedures such as the requirement to post hazard class placard signs.

DOT Website www.dot.gov

US Federal ATF Licensing

From the *Safe Explosives Act* of 2002, legal use of explosives in the United States requires a license or permit issued by the Bureau of Alcohol, Tobacco, Firearms and Explosives. The following information is based upon the requirements upon the January 2010 publication date.

A U.S. citizen engaged in the following explosives-based activity will require a license:

To import, manufacture, deal in (wholesale or retail), receive and transport for any interstate or foreign commerce.

Types of licenses include:

Type 20	Manufacturer of High Explosives
Type 23	Importer of High Explosives
Type 26	Dealer in High Explosives
Type 53	Dealer in Fireworks (Display)

A U.S. citizen engaged in the following explosive based activity will require a permit:

To purchase, receive, possess, transport, use and store.

Types of permits include:

Type 33	User of High Explosives
Type 53	User of Fireworks (Display)

A licensee has the same privileges as a permittee, so they are not required to also obtain a permit.

ATF Orange Book definitions, section 841

> (j) "Permittee" means any user of explosives for a lawful purpose, who has obtained either a user permit or limited permit under the provisions of this chapter.

Also see section 555.41 (3)

> (m) "Licensee" means any importer, manufacturer, or dealer licensed under the provisions of this chapter.

Also see section 555.41 (2)

There is also an option for a **Limited Permit,** that allows the receipt and use of explosive materials from a licensee or permittee for no more than six occasions during a 12-month period.

Obtaining a License or Permit

To obtain a license or a permit, the applicant needs to meet the following criteria:

- Over the age of 21 (although persons under the age of 21 maybe legally employed in licensed or permitted businesses).
- No convictions or under indictment for a criminal felony charge.
- Must not be a fugitive from justice.
- Must not be a user or addicted to a any controlled substance.
- Must not be mentally defective.
- Must not be an illegal alien.
- Must not have been dishonorably discharged from the U.S. armed forces.
- Must not have renounced their U.S. citizenship.

To obtain a license or a permit, the applicant needs to complete the following:

- An application is submitted on ATF form 5400.13/5400.16
- "Has not knowingly withheld information or has not made any false or fictitious statement intended or likely to deceive, in connection with the application."
- The person filing the application has premises in the state they intend to conduct business from.

- The person filing the application has met the storage requirements for the class of explosives they wish to possess" (If you have magazine storage, provide information on location and type).
- "Has certified in writing that he/she is familiar with and understands all published state laws and local ordinances relating to explosive materials for the location in which he intends to do business," (consult with your local fire marshal on your desired application and provide the information if necessary).
- "Has submitted the certificate required by section 21 of the Federal Water Pollution Control Act."
- Finger prints need to be provided on ATF's own fingerprint card, FD-258, (the ATF may not accept a card even if provided by an official law enforcement agency).
- Provide two passport style head-shot photographs.

At the time of this publishing, a user license or permit is valid for a period of three years. The license applicant fee is $200 with a $100 renewal fee. A separate license and fee are required for each business premises and for a corporate business entity. The permit application fee is $100 with a $50 renewal fee. A limited permit fee is $75 for a 12-month period.

Each applicant is subject to a background investigation including a personal visit by an agent of the ATF. An ATF agent will also inspect places of business and explosive storage magazines.
They will want to be sure that the magazines are built to the requirements as specified in the ATF Orange Book as well as confirm they are placed at proper distances from occupied dwellings and other magazines.

Manufacturing

A Type 20 **Manufacturer's License** is required for the commercial or business use of manufacturing explosives materials or mixing of ANFO or other binaries.

Partners and Employees

If a company's partners or employees have access to explosive materials, they need to be registered as ***Responsible Persons.***

A "Responsible Person" is defined as an individual who has the power to direct the management and policies of the applicant pertaining to explosive materials. Responsible persons generally include sole proprietors and explosives facility site managers.

In the case of a corporation, association, or similar organization, responsible persons generally include only those corporate directors/officers, and stockholders, who have the power to direct management and policies as they pertain to explosive materials. The official definition is listed at section 555.11.

The ATF will conduct background checks on all responsible persons and employee possessors. Their information including fingerprints and photographs will be required to be on an ***Employee Possessor Questionnaire***, ATF form 5400.28. New employees need to be registered within 30 days of hire.

A **Notification of Clearance** will be issued to the licensee or permit holder, responsible persons and employee possessors, advising whether they have been cleared to possess explosive materials. For more information, see section 555.33.

License/Permit Renewals and Revocations

The ATF should notify license and permit holders of renewal prior to the expiration date. This is to allow sufficient time for a renewal application to be sent in and approved prior to the expiration date.
If a licensee or permittee does not receive a renewal notification, it is their responsibility to ensure that an application is filed prior to the expiration date. For more information, see section 555.46.

A license or permit can be revoked by the ATF if the holder has violated any regulations or has become ineligible to receive explosive materials as outlined in sections 842 (i), 843 (d), 555.71 or 555.74.

An applicant that has been convicted of a criminal charge punishable by imprisonment exceeding one year (a felony), is not eligible to be issued a license or permit.
If an active licensee or permittee is indicted for, or convicted of a felony, the ATF may revoke their license or permit 30 days after the indictment or the date the conviction becomes final.

If the licensee or permittee is subject to being revoked, they can file an application for relief from disabilities within 30 days of the indictment or conviction. For more information, see sections 845 (b) and 555.142.

Black Powder Exemption There is an exception for purchasing black powder. U.S. citizens may purchase up to 50 pounds of commercially manufactured black powder per year for personal, recreational, sporting or cultural use in antique firearms.

This also includes percussion caps, safety and pyrotechnic fuses, quills, quick and slow matches and friction primers. A license is required for anyone importing, manufacturing or dealing in black powder.

Other Exemptions ATF does not regulate small arms ammunition or the non-explosive compounds in binary explosives.

Individual State Licensing Requirements

Approximately half of the United States requires a state blaster's license to operate a blasting company or in some cases, operate as a blaster for another company.
While the federal process is reasonably straight forward, state requirements vary greatly and may have requirements that include a number of hours or years of training and experience that also include the passing of exams. Some states also break up their state license by use such as underground, surface, demolition, or explosive ordnance disposal.

Blasters may be exempt from state licensing requirements if they are involved in non-commercial operations, such as blasting on their own property only. The state's Fire Marshall's Office is a good place to start to determine the state's licensing and legal requirements. The Fire Marshall will also want a record of any storage magazines placed within their jurisdiction.

Canadian Requirements

In Canada, the explosives regulatory agency is **Natural Resources Canada – Explosives Regulatory Division (ERD)**.

Similar to the ATF in the United States, the ERD administers and enforces the *Explosives Act and Regulations*, the body of Federal law that regulates manufacture, use, purchase, and storage of explosives.

Website http://www.nrcan.gc.ca/mms-smm/expl-expl/erd-dre-eng.htm

Transport Canada is the Canadian agency that administers and enforces the *Transport of Dangerous Goods Act and Regulations*, the body of Federal Law that defines how explosives and other hazardous materials are packaged, marked and documented for transport by road, rail, water or air within Canada.

Website http://www.tc.gc.ca/en/menu.htm

See **Appendix B** for additional agency contact information.

ATF Required Record Keeping

License and permit holders must keep records of all activity. This includes acquisitions, dispositions, and storage of explosive materials. Explosive materials must be recorded in their original format of documentation. For example, pounds of ANFO, number of dynamite sticks and feet of safety fuse. For more information, see sections 842(f), 847; 555.107, 555.122-125, and 555.127, Subpart G.

Acquisitions and Sales

License or permit holders purchasing explosive materials can use the seller's invoice and/or a ***Federal Transfer Receipt (FTR)*** sheet to record and document the purchase. The documentation should include the date, manufacture, brand, product, ***Date-Shift Code***, and quantity in pounds, units, feet, etc.

Joe's Blasting Supply, Inc.

1234 Main Street, Sweet Home, Oregon 97555

Cash Sales Receipt

ATF License: 9-OR-445-20-9F-00659

Date: 12-1-09 Invoice No.: 3215-09

Customer Name: OUR COMPANY BLASTING, EUGENE, OR, JOE BLASTER, PRES,

Product / Date-Shift Code	Quantity	Amount	Total
CUSTOMER ATF LICENSE: 9-OR-562-20-9F-00817			
ACME DYNAMITE 60% 09FEØ7S1	50	$2.75	137.50
ROCKBLASTERS #8 CAPS, 12' LEADS 15JAØ9S2	100	$6.00	600.00
LUCKY 7 ANFO BAG, 50 lb 15MAØ8S2	2	$38.50	77.00
SAFETY GLASSES - SURESITE X2	2	$5.00	10.00

PICK UP DATE DECEMBER 1, 2009 Total Amount Due: $ 824.50

Quality powder and blasting supplies since 1949

An example of a Federal Transfer Receipt for purchasing explosive materials from a dealer.

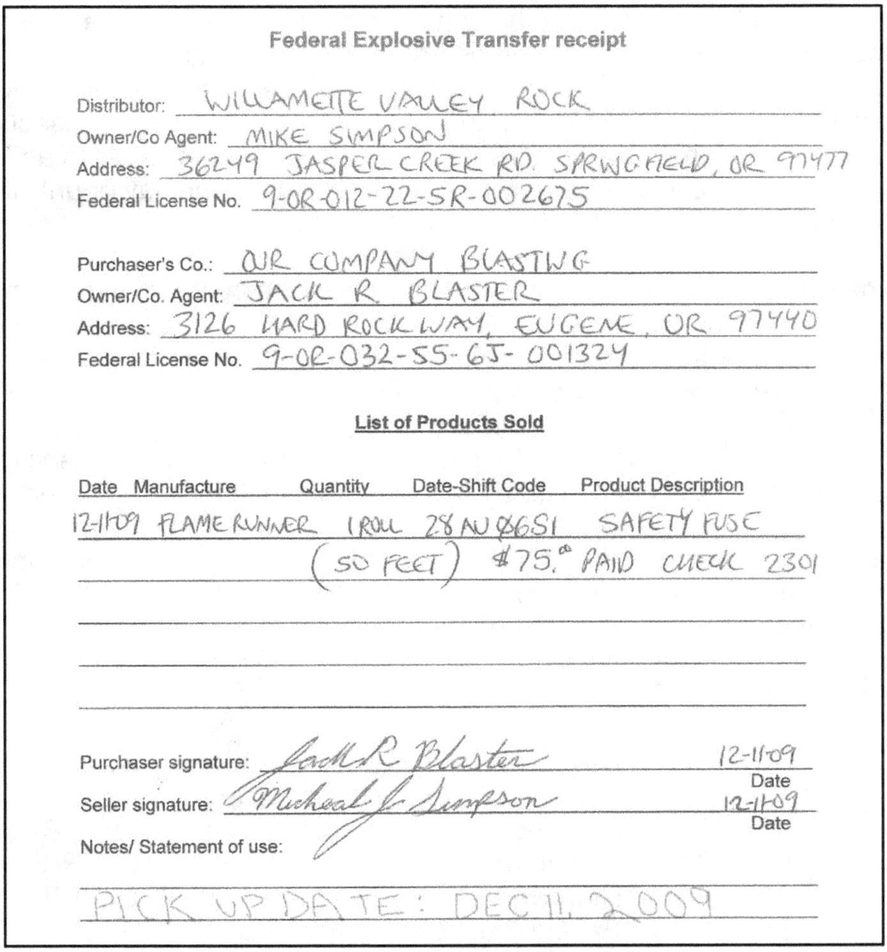

Federal Explosive Transfer receipt

Distributor: WILLAMETTE VALLEY ROCK
Owner/Co Agent: MIKE SIMPSON
Address: 36249 JASPER CREEK RD. SPRINGFIELD, OR 97477
Federal License No. 9-OR-012-22-5R-002675

Purchaser's Co.: OUR COMPANY BLASTING
Owner/Co. Agent: JACK R BLASTER
Address: 3126 HARD ROCK WAY, EUGENE, OR 97440
Federal License No. 9-OR-032-55-6J-001324

List of Products Sold

Date Manufacture Quantity Date-Shift Code Product Description

12-11-09 FLAME RUNNER 1 ROLL 28 AU Ø6S1 SAFETY FUSE
(50 FEET) $75.00 PAID CHECK 2301

Purchaser signature: Jack R Blaster 12-11-09
Date
Seller signature: Michael J. Simpson 12-11-09
Date
Notes/ Statement of use:
PICK UP DATE: DEC 11, 2009

An example of a Federal Transfer Receipt used by one licensee to sell or transfer explosive materials to another.

Magazine Storage

Magazine holders must maintain a record of the magazine's inventory through a ***Daily Summary Transaction Sheet***. This is done by keeping a folder or binder for each magazine, in each magazine or in the business office.

Each type of explosive material that has its own Date-Shift-Code, should have its own records sheet. Each Daily Summary Transaction Sheet includes the manufacturer's name, the explosive type and brand name and the date-shift code. The sheet then lists the total quantity of materials received and removed from the magazine during the day, and the total remaining on hand at the end of the day.

Based upon the ATF Orange book, this information needs to be recorded no later than the close of the next business day.
For more information see section 555.127. The ATF agents will tell you however that it is very important to record the daily summary transaction sheet information in *real time*, meaning to record the transactions as they actually occur instead of waiting until the end of the day or until the next day.

It may seem easier to just remove the materials then at the end of the day, return what was not used, and recording only what was detonated. The problem with this method is that by waiting, there is no record of what was removed from the magazine.

The following is an example of maintaining a daily summary transaction sheet. A company purchased a case of dynamite that will be placed in a high explosive magazine. A new daily summary transaction sheet is started for each product that has its own different Date-Shift-Code and the transactions should be recorded in real time:

ACME brand dynamite, 60% nitro, half pound sticks, date-shift code 09FE07S1

12-01-18	Beginning Balance	50	sticks	By ANO
01-05-18	Removed	25	sticks	By JRB
01-05-18	Retuned	5	sticks	By JRB
01-05-18	Ending Balance	30	sticks	By JRB
02-07-18	Removed	30	sticks	By JRB
02-07-18	Ending Balance	0	sticks	By JRB

Government agencies may be exempt from much of the record keeping required of commercial blasters, it is still important to keep good records and should be part of your agency's SOPs.

The following forms are four examples of magazine daily summary sheets for two different magazines. 'Big Red 001' is for powder and 'Yellow 002' is for blasting caps and safety fuse. Remember a new sheet will be required anytime a material is recorded with its own unique date shift code. Note as in the above example, these forms are filled out in real time as materials are removed and replaced.

The ATF also has a requirement that magazine holders do an annual explosive material inventory. For more information, see section 555.122-125.

DAILY SUMMARY
ATF EXPLOSIVES STORAGE MAGAZINES

Explosive Product: ANFO **1.**5

Date: 12-1-2017 **Magazine:** BIG RED Ø1

Manufacture: LUCKY 7 BRAND

Brand Name: ANFO 7 PRE-MIX 50 lb BAGS

Date/Shift Code - Lot: 15MA17S1

Unit of Issue: Each (Pound) Feet Meters **Size:** 50 lb BAGS
(Circle one)

Beginning Balance	Quantity Out	Quantity In	Ending Balance	Date	Name (Print Clearly)
Ø		100	100	12-1-17	JOE BLASTER
100	100		Ø	1-5-18	JOE BLASTER
Ø		50	50	1-5-18	JOE BLASTER
50	50		Ø	2-7-18	JOE BLASTER

DAILY SUMMARY
ATF EXPLOSIVES STORAGE MAGAZINES

Explosive Product: ELECTRIC BLASTWG CAPS #8 **1.**4

Date: 12-1-2017 **Magazine:** YELLOW Ø2

Manufacture: LUCKY 7 BRAND

Brand Name: ROCK BLASTERS No 8 SIZE

Date/Shift Code - Lot: 15JA17S2

Unit of Issue: (Each) Pound Feet Meters **Size:** #8-CASE OF 100
(Circle one)

Beginning Balance	Quantity Out	Quantity In	Ending Balance	Date	Name (Print Clearly)
Ø		100	100	12-1-17	JOE BLASTER
100	25		75	1-5-18	JOE BLASTER
75		4	79	1-5-18	JOE BLASTER
79	25		54	1-22-18	JOE BLASTER
54		6	60	1-22-18	JOE BLASTER
60	30		30	2-7-18	JOE BLASTER

DAILY SUMMARY
ATF EXPLOSIVES STORAGE MAGAZINES

Explosive Product: DYNAMITE 60% **1.**1

Date: 12-1-2017 **Magazine:** BIG RED Ø1

Manufacture: ACME

Brand Name: NYTRO 60% 1/2 lb STICKS

Date/Shift Code - Lot: 09FE16 S1

Unit of Issue: (Circle one) Each (circled) Pound Feet Meters

Size: 1/2 lb - 100 STICK CASE

Beginning Balance	Quantity Out	Quantity In	Ending Balance	Date	Name (Print Clearly)
Ø		100	100	12-1-17	JOE BLASTER
100	50		50	1-5-18	JOE BLASTER
50		6	56	1-5-18	JOE BLASTER
56	50		6	2-7-18	JOE BLASTER
6	6		Ø	2-10-18	JOE BLASTER

DAILY SUMMARY
ATF EXPLOSIVES STORAGE MAGAZINES

Explosive Product: SAFETY FUSE **1.**4

Date: 12-1-2017 **Magazine:** YELLOW Ø2

Manufacture: ACME

Brand Name: FLAME RUNNER SAFETY FUSE -ORANGE

Date/Shift Code - Lot: 28AU16 S1

Unit of Issue: (Circle one) Each Pound Feet (circled) Meters

Size: 1,000' ROLL

Beginning Balance	Quantity Out	Quantity In	Ending Balance	Date	Name (Print Clearly)
Ø		1,000	1,000	12-1-17	JOE BLASTER
1,000	60		940	1-5-18	JOE BLASTER
940	60		880	1-25-18	JOE BLASTER
880	70		810	2-5-18	JOE BLASTER
		20	830	2-5-18	JOE BLASTER
830	60		770	2-10-18	JOE BLASTER

3. STORAGE AND TRANSPORTATION

Chapter Topics:

- Learn the various types of storage magazines.
- Understand the "Table of Distance."
- Understand how to store various types of materials.
- Understand DOT guidelines for transporting materials.

Understanding proper storage and transportation procedures is a crucial part of any explosives operation. Storage and transportation are also areas that encompass the majority of regulation.

Quotes and section references in this chapter are made from the **ATF Orange Book, publication number 5400.7**, revised June 2012.

Storage Requirements

Permit and license holders needing to establish storage for explosive materials do so under ATF requirements. Storage regulation and magazine requirements are covered in Subpart K, sections 555.201 to 555.217.

Containers used to store explosives in are referred to as magazines. ATF requires all explosive materials are to remain in locked magazines with the following exceptions:

- In the process of manufacture.
- In the process of being used in a blasting operation.
- In the process of being transported to a place of storage or use.

Magazine storage requirements are based upon the classification of the materials. ATF uses the standard three classes:

- High explosives (dynamite, flash powders, and bulk salutes).
- Low explosives (black powder, safety fuses, igniters, igniter cords, fuse lighters, and "display fireworks")
- Blasting agents (ammonium nitrate-fuel oil and certain water gels).

The ATF categorizes magazines as follows:

Type 1 Permanent structure for high explosives

These magazines are permanent dug-in bunker style or free-standing buildings. They are made to be bullet, fire, weather, and theft resistant. They are typically made from masonry, steel or a wooden frame covered in steel. The door is no less than ¼ inch steel with heavy hinges and two locks protected by ¼ inch steel hoods. For more information, see section 555.207.

Type 2 Portable box for high explosives

These magazines are heavy steel boxes that are placed on skids or pads indoors or outdoors. They are built to be a bullet, fire, weather and theft resistant. They are made from a minimum of ¼ inch steel plate lined with 2 inches of hardwood. The door is also ¼ inch steel with heavy hinges and two locks protected by ¼ inch steel hoods. For more information, see section 555.208.

Type 3 Temporary storage box for transport

These are portable magazines known as ***day boxes***. Two are used for transferring explosive materials to a job site; one for high explosives and one for blasting caps. They must be made to be fire, weather and theft resistant. They are made from a minimum of 12-gauge (.1046 inch) steel plate lined with 1/2-inch plywood or Masonite hardboard. The door must overlap by one inch with heavy hinges and a hasp for one padlock. For more information, see section 555.209.

Type 4 Permanent or portable, for low explosives

These magazines are built from metal containers approximately 1/8" thick and are often made from truck trailers and storage containers. They are made to be fire, weather and theft resistant. They are typically made from masonry, steel or a wooden frame covered in steel. The door is secured with two locks protected by ¼ inch steel hoods. For more information, see section 555.210.

Type 5 Delivery truck or trailer for blasting agents

These magazines are bulk delivery trucks or trailers. They are made to be fire, weather, and theft resistant. They are typically made from masonry, steel or a wooden frame covered in steel. The door is secured with two locks protected by ¼ inch steel hoods.

For more information, see section 555.211. For truck and trailer information, see ATF Orange book appendix's A-E.

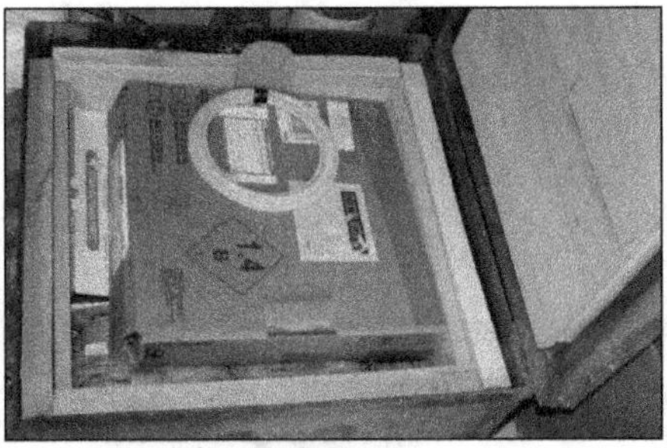

Type 2 magazines for high explosives.
Note the heavy steel boxes are lined with hardwood.

Blaster's Tool and Supply Co.

Type 3 day box *Type 2 indoor magazine*

Table of Distances

This table specifies the minimum distances necessary for positioning magazines and separating them from surrounding structures. This includes the distance required from occupied dwellings, inhabited buildings, roadways and railways. The Table of Distances is covered in sections 555.218 to 555.224.

One of the primary factors is how far a magazine is from an ***Inhabited Building***. This does not include an explosive-based business or manufacturing site, although it would include the nearest residence, school, church, or other business to the magazine property. For example, the licensee's own residence on the property is not an inhabited building, but you closest neighbor's house is.

If they rent out the apartment over the garage to a tenant, that is now an inhabited building because someone lives on your property other than the licensee. For a definition, see section 555.11.

In the following example an ATF permit-license holder wants to place two magazines on his property for his blasting business. He has to review the ***ATF Orange Book Table of Distances (TOD)*** to determine the best location to store both a powder magazine and a cap magazine. The first step is to determine how much materials need to be stored.

He estimates he will probably not store more than 200 pounds of materials and 30 pounds of blasting caps. To be safe and to give him room to expand, he picks great weights of 250 pounds of materials and 50 pounds for blasting caps. After reviewing the Table of Distance chart at 555.218 we see the following:

Pounds Not over	Inhabited Buildings	Public Hwy 3,000 fewer	Separation of Magazines
250	510'	210'	46'
50	300'	120'	28'

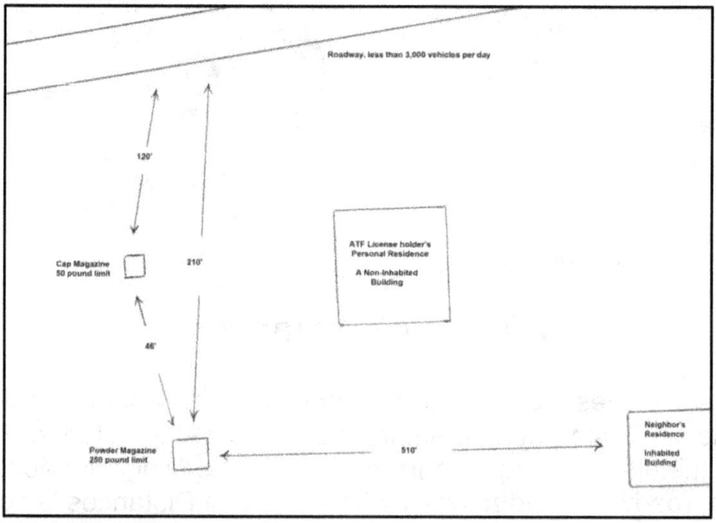

A Table of Distance diagram is created to ensure there is adequate distance for the separation of the two storage magazines, the roadway, and the nearest inhabited building.

From the map below, we can see from these numbers that the main magazine can store up to 250 pounds and needs to be 510 feet from the nearest inhabited building and 210 feet from the public roadway if traffic is less than 3,000 vehicles per day.

It also needs to be 46 feet away from the cap magazine. The blasting cap magazine can store up to 50 pounds and needs to be 300 feet from the nearest inhabited building and 120 feet from the roadway.

Barricading a magazine can reduce the TOD in half. In this case our mags are set back into a hillside with a concrete wall.

A licensee will make a diagram map for the ATF and notify them in writing before you place your magazines in service. Once the ATF is notified of active magazines, they will have up to three years to physically inspect them and confirm that the distances are correct. Note that your local fire marshal or fire authority will also want the magazine storage location information.

Special Storage Considerations

Blasting Agents

A special Table of Distance applies in section 555.220 for ammonium nitrate and other oxidizers stored near boosters and other explosives.

Blasting Caps

Blasting caps, detonators and igniters may be stored with safety fuse, electronic squibs, igniters or igniter cord. Blasting caps must be stored separate from other high and low explosives that include detonation cord.

Blasting caps can be stored in a Type 4 magazine if they are in their original "non-mass detonating" packaging.

Note that if blasting caps are stored loose outside of their original crush-resistant packaging, there hazmat rating can change from 1.4 to 1.1. this change would require a Type 1 or 2 magazine.

Fireworks

Fireworks are defined under two categories; consumer and display as defined in section 555.11.

Consumer Fireworks

Are not subject to ATF storage regulation as classified under UN numbers of UN0336 and UN0337, and contain less than 50 mg or less of salute powder.

Display Fireworks

Are subject to ATF storage regulation as classified under UN numbers of UN0333, UN0334, and UN0335. These fireworks have salutes containing more than 2 grains (130 mg) of explosive materials, aerial shells containing more than 40 grams of pyrotechnic compositions, and other components which together exceed 50 mg of salute powder.

Display fireworks, with the exception of bulk salutes, are considered low explosives and, at a minimum, must be stored in Type 4 magazines. Bulk salutes, aerial shells or finished salute shells are classified as high explosives and must be stored in Type 1 or Type 2 magazines. For more information, see sections 555.202(b), 555.203(d), 555.207, 555.208 and 555.210.

Maintaining Magazines

Inspecting Magazines

Magazines are required to be inspected at least once every seven days. This is important to determine if there has been any unauthorized entry or removal of materials. If a license or permit holder has magazines that are not accessible due to weather or other conditions, they need to be kept empty until they can be inspected regularly again. For more information, see section 555.204.

Magazine Changes or Additions

An ATF representative needs to be notified in writing within three business days prior to any change in existing magazines or the addition of new magazines. This applied to license and permit holders who are acquiring magazines for the first time.

This regulation excludes mobile or portable Type 5 magazines and magazines used for temporary storage (less than 24 hours). For more information, see section 555.63.

State and local authorities having jurisdiction for local regulation and fire safety must also be notified. By telephone the same day storage begins and in writing within 48 hours. See section 555.201(f).

Exemptions to ATF Storage Regulation

Certain explosive materials are exempt from ATF storage regulation. These materials include the following:

- *Up to 50 pounds of black powder, see section 845(5).*
- *External burning pyrotechnic hobby fuses less than 3/32." See sections 845(5).*
- *Small arms ammunition, see section 845(4).*
- *Oxidizers, such as ammonium nitrate unless it stored near boosters and other explosives. If so, a special table of distance applies at section 555.220.*
- *Fireworks that are classified as "Consumer," as defined in section 555.11.*

Magazine Storage Housekeeping

Here are a few points to consider for safe and successful storage:

- Do not smoke within 50 feet of any magazine.
- Do not place explosive materials next to the interior magazine walls to assist with ventilation.
- Store materials so that the contents can be easily counted or inspected.
- Keep containers closed and only open them outside of the magazine with a non-sparking tool.
- Keep magazine interiors clean, dry, and clear of empty containers or debris.
- Remove all magazine contents before conducting any repairs or maintenance.
- Light magazines with battery activated safety lights or electric lights that meet the safety standards of "National Electric Code" NFPA 70-81.
- Post clear signage when required or appropriate. In some circumstances, it may be more secure not to posted signs on magazines.

Transportation Requirements

ATF requires a license or permit to transport explosive materials, however the **United States Department of Transportation and the Department of Homeland Security** has jurisdiction over transportation. This includes any transport by highway, water or railroad both interstate and intrastate. For more information, see section 845(a)(1).

Commercial Truck Drivers

Common contract carriers are not required to obtain an ATF license or permit, but are subject to the Department of Transportation or Department of Homeland Security regulations. While drivers are not required to possess a license or a permit, they are required to provide their identification upon request. For more information, see sections 555.103(b) and 555.105(b).

Commercial drivers are required to have a commercial driver's license (CDL) with a **Hazardous Materials Endorsement**. For more information, contact the **Federal Motor Carrier Safety Administration, (FMCSA)** at telephone (202) 366-6121.

U.S. Department of Transportation

The division that regulated the transportation of hazardous materials is the **Pipeline and Hazardous Materials Safety Administration (PHMSA)**.

U.S. Department of Transportation
Pipeline and Hazardous Materials Safety Administration
East Building, 2nd Floor, 1200 New Jersey Ave., SE
Washington, DC 20590

Website http://www.dot.gov/

Explosives page http://www.phmsa.dot.gov/hazmat/regs/sp-a/approvals/explosives
Telephone 202-366-4433 Fax 202-366-3666
HAZMAT transport information line 800 467-4922

The statutes referenced in this section are from the U. S. Department of Transportation's (DOT), Title 49 Transportation hazardous material codes, hereafter referred to as DOT Title 49, with section number.

A web link to the DOT Title 49 statutes are at:
http://www.access.gpo.gov/nara/cfr/waisidx_99/49cfrv2_99.html

The U.S. DOT claims jurisdiction over the transportation of explosive materials based upon DOT Title 49, section 171.1.
U.S. Department of Transportation officials state that they have jurisdiction over all explosive or hazardous materials in transport if the materials are "in commerce."

This includes additional U.S. DOT regulation for any amount of hazardous material class 1.1 to 1.3 (high explosives) and over 1,000 pounds of 1.4 to 1.6 (low explosives, gun power, blasting caps, fuse and blasting agents).

The DOT recommends employees involved in commercial explosives transport received training as stated in section DOT Title 49, section 172.704.

DOT HazMat Classification Numbers

Explosives are classified has a hazardous material in Class 1.
The ratings go from 1.1 to 1.6 based upon the material's strength and potential hazard.

UN Numbers United Nations numbers are also used by DOT and ATF as a method of identification and classification of products for shipping purposes. For more information, see section 555.11.

Placard Sign Requirements

The DOT states that placard signs are required to be posted on all explosive materials transported with a hazard classification in Table 1, based upon DOT Title 49, section 172.504(a).

Table 1

Explosive Categories	
1.1	Mass explosive hazard
1.2	Non-mass explosive hazard
1.3	Mass fire, minor blast

The DOT states that placard signs are required to be posted on all explosive materials transported with a hazard classification in Table 2, if more than 1,001 pounds, based upon DOT Title 49, section 172.504(c)(1).

Table 2

Explosive Categories	
1.4	Moderate fire, no blast
1.5	Explosive substance, insensitive
1.6	Explosive article, extremely insensitive

For information relating to the commercial shipment of explosive materials, the U.S. Department of Transportation's (DOT), Title 49 Transportation hazardous material codes.

4. EXPLOSIVES CHARACTERISTICS

Chapter Topics:

- How the ATF categorizes explosives.
- How explosive materials are defined and rated by their characteristics.
- How the power and performance of explosives are measured and rated.
- Understanding UN and NA numbers for storage and transportation.

We all know what explosions look like, but did you ever think about how they happen? Chemical compounds are initiated by heat or impact, creating a large volume of gas escaping in a fury of high pressure and temperatures that create a detonation. Based upon the speed of the shock wave, it is either a low explosive ***Deflagration***, (subsonic), or a high explosives ***Detonation***, (supersonic).

There are hundreds of various formulas and compounds of explosive materials, however, most materials consist of elements of carbon, nitrogen, hydrogen, and oxygen. Explosives can consist of a chemically pure compound such as nitroglycerin in dynamite, or a mixture of a catalyst fuel and oxidizer mixture such as ammonium nitrate and fuel oil.

The majority of explosives materials are made up from a mixture of a ***fuel*** that is a sensitizer, and an ***oxidizer*** that provides oxygen to the fuel.

Fuels include:
Aerating Agents
Aluminum Powder
Carbon
RDX (Cyclonite Hexogen)
Smokeless Powder
TNT (trinitrotoluene)

Oxidizers include:
Ammonium Nitrate
Calcium Nitrate
Sodium Nitrate

Explosive Categories

The ATF classifies explosives into three categories: ***Low Explosives***, ***High Explosives*** and ***Blasting Agents***.

High Explosives

These explosives are used in commercial applications such as construction, demolition, mining, and the military.

They have a detonation rate faster than the speed of sound (supersonic), 3,000 to 9,000 meters per second (MPS).
High explosives are also ***cap sensitive***, meaning they will detonate with a number 8 or larger blasting cap.

High explosives fall into one of the following three categories based upon their sensitivity:

Primary Very sensitive to shock, friction, or heat.

Secondary Somewhat insensitive to shock, friction, or heat, although they can still detonate with enough exposure.

Tertiary Blasting agents are insensitive to shock, friction, and heat. These materials are so insensitive, they require a high explosive *booster* to detonate, such as Ammonium Nitrate and Fuel Oil (ANFO).

High explosives detonate faster than the speed of sound.

Low Explosives

Low explosives have a detonation slower than the speed of sound, (subsonic), approximately 100-400 meters per second (MPS). This slower form of detonation is called deflagration. Low explosives can be initiated with a flame, fuse or blasting cap.

These explosives are primarily used as propellant or to push an object, such as a bullet with gun powder or smokeless power. It is also used in flares, fireworks and pyrotechnics.

Low explosives are typically a mixture of a combustible catalyst fuel and oxidant. The oxidant can be a solid, liquid or gas. If the materials are packed into a confined container, they can detonate like a high explosive. This is called ***Deflagration to Detonation Transition (DDT).***

For example, gunpower that is initiated by flame or fuse will deflagrate slower, possibly 100-200 MPS, (much slower than the speed of sound). However, if the same gunpower is compressed and initiated by a greater shockwave, such as by a blasting cap, the deflagration could convert to detonation by reaching supersonic speed, (faster than the speed of sound).

Low explosives like black powder deflagrate or burn.

Blasting Agents

Blasting agents are a binary that is a mix of an oxidizer and a fuel that produces a high-pressure, high explosive shockwave when detonated.

The most common example of a blasting agent is Ammonium Nitrate and Fuel Oil, ANFO.
This is one of the primary materials used in rock blasting and because it is homemade, it is also been used in bomb making. The definition of a blasting agent is that it cannot be initiated by a number 8 blasting cap. It requires a high explosive to boost initiation to create a high explosive detonation.

Explosive Characteristics

Explosives are further categorized on a number of other characteristics as follows in alphabetical order:

Brisance

From the French term to "break," brisance measures the explosive's shattering effect or the material's power to break.

Density

The density of explosive materials is typically measured in terms of weight divided by volume such as grams per cubic centimeters, expressed as **g/cc**. Grams per cubic centimeters are used due to the measurement of water being the baseline of 1.0 g/cc.

Knowing the density of explosives is important to determine whether they will float or sink in water. Materials with a density of less than 1.0 g/cc should float in water just as materials with a density of more than 1.0 g/cc should sink.

Hygroscopicity

Hygroscopicity or the ***Hygroscopic*** level measures the amount of moisture that can be absorbed by an explosive material.
Water has a negative impact on explosives by reducing the strength, sensitivity, and the velocity of detonation.

Power/Performance

The terms refer to the ability of the explosive charge to accomplish its intended use. Explosive energy can be measured through various tests to determine such factors as air blast, velocity, shock, and fragment projection. These tests include placing an explosive charge in a cylinder to determine how much it expands or fragments. Charges are also placed underwater to measure shockwaves and pressure.

Sensitivity

This refers to the ease of detonation through the factors of ***Heat***, ***Friction*** and ***Shock***. Heat is measured by the temperature to which the material ignites. Friction is measured by the weight and pressure of a scraping pendulum required to ignite the material. Shock is measured by a distance a weight is dropped to ignite the material. Knowing the sensitivity of explosive material is important to select the proper formula that will be the most efficient for the application.

Stability

The stability factor determines the materials shelf life. How long an explosive can be safely stored without deterioration or corrosion of the explosive's container. The primary factor that destabilizes explosives is heat. Temperatures exceeding 70° C, 158° F, as well as constant exposure to the sun's ultraviolet rays may cause explosive materials to decompose more rapidly.

Toxicity

Due to their chemical nature, most explosive materials may have some levels of toxicity. There may be a risk of potential exposure, through contact with the skin or through explosive gasses produced. The primary concern is nitroglycerin in dynamite.

Volatility

Refers to the rate in which explosive material vaporizes resulting in a reduction of stability. Excessive volatility affects the chemical composition of the explosive material, causing deterioration that can make handling more dangerous.

Rating the Power of Explosives

There are two rating factors that blasters need to know. The first is the ***RE Factor***. This provides a way to compare the strength of one material over another.

Relative Effectiveness Factor or RE Factor

This measures the power of explosives as compared to TNT by weight. TNT is the baseline with a RE Factor rating of 1.0. This allows engineers to compare how much explosive material is needed when substituting one explosive for another.

For example, if a job requires one pound of TNT, substituting ANFO would require 1.25 pounds, or .8 of a pound of C-4 for approximately the same effect.

To calculate the difference, divide the amount by the RE factor number: 10 lbs ÷ .94 = 10.63 lbs. TNT is RE 1.1 so 10 pounds = 10 pounds. Using dynamite with a RE of .94 requires an additional .63 pounds to make up the difference. Using C-4 at RE 1.34, 10 ÷ 1.34 = the equivalent of 7.46 pounds.

RE Factor ratings for popular explosives:

ANFO	0.80
Black powder	0.55
C-4	1.34
Dynamite	0.94
Erythritol Tetranitrate	1.60
HMX	1.70
Nitroglycerin	1.55
PETN	1.66
RDX	1.60
Semtex	1.66
Tetryl	1.73

The second important rating is the ***Velocity of Detonation (VOD)***.

Velocity of Detonation

The explosive power of materials is measured by their velocity rate based upon ***Meters per Second, (MPS)***, or ***Feet per Second (FPS)***. Just as firearm shooters us a bullet chronograph to measure speed, explosive manufacturers do the same thing. Like in shooting, speed equals power.

The following are Velocity of Detonation ratings for popular explosives based on meters per second:

Ammonium nitrate	5,270
ANFO	4,000
Black powder	400 (Deflagrates)
C-4	8,040
Dynamite, 60% nitro	5,400
Erythritol Tetranitrate	8,100
HMX	9,100
Nitroglycerin	7,700

PETN	8,400
RDX	8,750
Semtex	8,420
Tetryl	7,370
TNT	6,900

A lower VOD causes a heaving and less breakage, a higher VOD causes a shattering or more breakage in a shot. As an example, the slower detonation of ANFO is used to heave rock while the extreme speed of C-4 can cut steel.

Another rating that may be relevant is the ***Figure of Insensitivity (FoI)*** used to measure the sensitivity to detonation of a material.

Figure of Insensitivity or F of I

This is a scale of measurement to rate the possibility of detonation by shock and impact. This is done through a drop test where a sample of explosive material is placed on a steel anvil and a one-kilogram steel weight is dropped on it.

The weight is dropped from a measured height ranging from 10 centimeters to 3 meters. The higher the number the more sensitive the material is. For example, RDX has a rating of 80 while TNT has a rating of 100. Joules is a measurement that is often use for military and nuclear ordinance.

Joules

A measurement of energy that can be used by the number or by ratio to kilograms to measure density. For example, a stick of dynamite contains 2,100,000 joules or 7.5 megajoules/kilogram.

Regulated Explosive Numbers & Classifications

Explosive materials are classified by various groups of numbers issued by the United Nations Organization, (UNO), and the U.S Department of Transportation, (US DOT). These numbers appear on all material labeling and shipping documentation.

UN Numbers

UN numbers are from the United Nations and they are used in the United States as well as internationally. They are a four-digit number to identify explosives, flammables, toxins, and other hazardous materials. UN numbers can include a hazard identifier which groups explosives and other hazardous materials.

UN numbers range from UN 0001 to UN 3500 and are issued by a United Nations committee of experts on the transport of hazardous materials.

The following are some examples of common UN numbers:

- UN 0027 Black powder in granular form
- UN 0029 Detonators, non-electric for blasting
- UN 0033 Bombs with bursting charge
- UN 0042 Boosters without detonator
- UN 0043 Boosters, explosive
- UN 0048 Charges, demolition
- UN 0059 Charges, shaped without detonator
- UN 0065 Cord, detonating, flexible
- UN 0092 Flares, surface
- UN 0093 Flares, aerial
- UN 0101 Fuse, non-detonating
- UN 0105 Fuse, safety
- UN 0121 Igniters
- UN 0143 Dynamite
- UN 0180 Rockets, with bursting charge
- UN 0196 Signals, smoke
- UN 0209 Trinitrotoluene or TNT
- UN 0222 Ammonium nitrate
- UN 0255 Detonators, electric for blasting
- UN 0267 Detonators, non-electric for blasting
- UN 0335 Fireworks, professional (1.3G)
- UN 0336 Fireworks, consumer (1.4G)

NA Numbers

NA numbers are for North America, and are issued and used by the U.S. Department of Transportation. NA numbers are identical to UN numbers except there are some additional NA numbers for substances that do not have UN numbers. They fall into the range of NA 8000 to NA 9999.

Hazard Class and Division   Class 1 Explosives

This rating is the hazardous material, (HAZMAT), designation. Explosive materials fall under the Class 1 rating, varying from 1.1 to 1.6 based upon the material's strength and potential hazard.
A modifying letter typically follows the number to further classify the material. This classification is from the United Nations and is internationally recognized as a way to classify potential hazardous materials with a minimal amount of markings.
The following are the Class 1 designations:

1.1 Mass Explosion Hazard. (Commercial and Military High Explosives)

1.2 Non-mass explosion, fragment-producing. (Display Fireworks)

1.3 Mass fire, minor blast, or fragment hazard. (Display Fireworks)

1.4 Moderate fire, no blast or fragment. (Blasting Caps and Consumer Fireworks)

1.5 Explosive substance, very insensitive with a mass explosion hazard. (Blasting Agent like ANFO)

1.6 Explosive article, extremely insensitive

Modifying Letter Code:

A Primary explosive substance (1.1A)

B An article containing a primary explosive substance and not containing two or more effective protective features. Some articles, such as detonator assemblies for blasting and primers, cap-type, are included. (1.1B, 1.2B, 1.3B professional pyrotechnics,1.4B)

C Propellant explosive substance or other deflagrating explosive substance or article containing such explosive substance. (1.1C, 1.2C, 1.3C, 1.4C)

D Secondary detonating explosive substance or black powder or article containing a secondary detonating explosive substance; in each case without means of initiation and without a propelling charge, or article containing a primary explosive substance and containing two or more effective protective features. (1.1D, 1.2D, 1.4D, 1.5D)

E Article containing a secondary detonating explosive substance without means of initiation, with a propelling charge other than one containing flammable liquid, gel or hypergolic liquid. (1.1E, 1.2E, 1.4E)

F Containing a secondary detonating explosive substance with its means of initiation, with a propelling charge other than one containing flammable liquid, gel or hypergolic liquid or without a propelling charge. (1.1F, 1.2F, 1.3F, 1.4F)

G Pyrotechnic substance or article containing a pyrotechnic substance, or article containing both an explosive substance and an illuminating, incendiary, tear-producing or smoke-producing substance other than a water-activated article or one containing white phosphorus, phosphate or flammable liquid or gel or hypergolic liquid. (1.1G, 1.2G, 1.3G, 1.4G)

H Article containing both an explosive substance and white phosphorus. (1.2H, 1.3H)

J Article containing both an explosive substance and flammable liquid or gel. (1.1J, 1.2J, 1.3J)

K Article containing both an explosive substance and a toxic chemical agent. (1.2K, 1.3K)

L Explosive substance or article containing an explosive substance and presenting a special risk (e.g., due to water-activation or presence of hypergolic liquids, phosphides or pyrophoric substances) needing isolation of each type. (1.1L, 1.2L, 1.3L)

N Articles containing only extremely insensitive detonating substances. (1.6N)

S Substance or article so packed or designed that any hazardous effects arising from accidental functioning are limited to the extent that they do not significantly hinder or prohibit firefighting or other emergency response efforts in the immediate vicinity of the package. (1.4S)

Date Shift Code

In 1971, manufactures in membership with the ***Institute of the Makers of Explosives (IME)***, implemented a new product identification system for manufactured and packaged explosive products that is similar to a serial number for each batch of materials made on a shift.

The Date Shift Code is based upon the date and shift of manufacture along with the plant location. This code is stamped on each package or individual unit of each product made during a shift at each plant.

For example, you will see it on each stick of dynamite and on the box of blasting caps or spool of det cord.

Here is an example: **14AP08J1**

This product was made on the 8th of April, 2014, location J, on day or first shift as follows:

Day	Month	Year	Location	Shift or Machine
2 digit	2 digits	2 digits	1 digit	1 digit
14	**AP**	**14**	**J**	**1**

5. BINARIES AND BLASTING AGENTS

Chapter Topics:

- Learn about blasting agents.
- Understand how explosive boosters are used.
- Learn about binary explosives.
- Understanding Ammonium Nitrate and Fuel Oil.

Binaries and blasting agents are important to understand for both the study of commercial and homemade explosives. Commercial blasters use them because they are inexpensive and safer to store, transport and use. They are also used in homemade explosives due to the ease to obtain the individual 'non-explosive' ingredients.

Blasting Agents

Blasting agents are materials that by themselves are not considered explosive, but explosive agents that are a combination of fuel and oxidizer. The fuel is a sensitizer and the oxidizer provides oxygen to the fuel. What makes blasting agents unique is that even after they are mixed together, they would typically remain insensitive so they will not detonate with a number 8 or smaller blasting cap. This makes blasting agents ***Non-Cap Sensitive***. From our own testing we have confirmed that three number 8 caps will set off a one-pound quantity of ANFO.

The primary examples of blasting agents are ***Ammonium Nitrate and Fuel Oil (ANFO)***, non-cap sensitive ***Emulsions, Water Gels,*** and **Slurries**. Because blasting agents are non-cap sensitive, they require a high explosive to initiate them known as a ***Booster*** or ***Primer***.

The U.S. Government defines a blasting agent as follows:

> "Blasting agent - any material or mixture, consisting of a fuel and oxidizer, intended for blasting, not otherwise classified as an explosive and in which none of the ingredients are classified as an explosive,
> provided that the finished product, as mixed and packaged for use or shipment, cannot be detonated by means of a No. 8 test blasting cap when unconfined."

Booster and Primer Explosives

A booster is a high explosives with enough power and velocity to ensure the reliable detonation of a blasting agent.

In the blasting sequence, a blasting cap ignites the booster that detonates the main blasting agent charge.

Dynamite sticks and slurry sticks can be used as a booster, although booster sticks made for this purpose use a much higher velocity material such as RDX or a RDX/TNT blend. They are often referred to as 'cast' because the molten explosive material is poured into a cardboard tube before cooling into a hard crystal.

The terms *booster* and *primer* are often used interchangeably. Technically a primer is a booster already capped with a blasting cap and ready to place in a borehole.

Austin Powder Company cast boosters

Binary Explosives

A Binary is an explosive that is made up from two typically non-explosive materials. This is done by adding a catalyst fuel to a main oxidizer base.

The Tannerite M-2 Nitro-Stick demolition charge binary.

Binary explosives may or may not be blasting agents, it depends if the final mixture is cap sensitive. If the final mixture is cap sensitive, it becomes a 1.1 high explosive. The advantage is safety and convenience as the blaster does not mix the two materials until needed.

Note that the ATF considers mixing a binary for commercial use, even in a kit form, is considered manufacturing that requires a ATF Type 20 Manufacturing license over a permit.

Tannerite exploding rifle targets are a binary designed to detonate with a high-velocity rifle bullet.

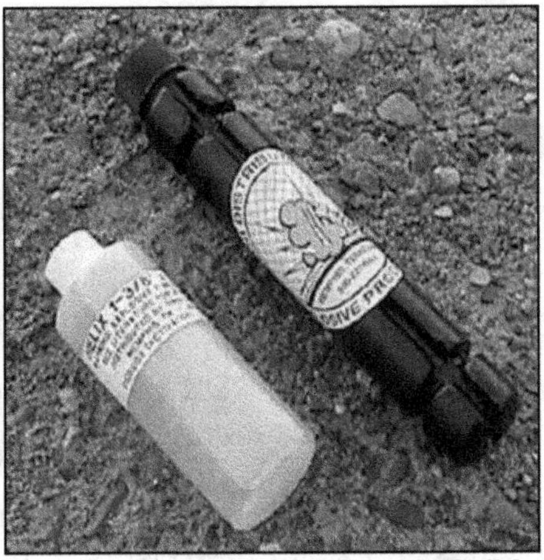

Omni Explosives HELIX is a liquid binary that is cap sensitive.

Ammonium Nitrate and Fuel Oil (ANFO)

ANFO is very stable and insensitive, as it requires a high explosive booster to detonate. Its low VOD, approximately 4,000 meters per second, provide a heaving effect that is ideal for moving earth for rock quarry work.

ANFO is a blasting agent that is mixed at ammonium nitrate (94%) and fuel oil (6%) by weight. Explosives grade ammonium nitrate is 99% pure in its white pellet form known as *prills*. The fuel oil is typically No. 2 fuel oil or diesel fuel. Two U.S. quarts to 50 pounds of ammonium nitrate will provide an approximate 6% fuel oil mixture.

With a RE Factor of .80, it is the least powerful explosives option but the strength of its detonation can be increased. To do so, it is important to understand that ANFO takes on the characteristics of the high explosive booster used to detonate it.

Ammonium nitrate pellets are known as prills.

For example, if dynamite is used, the ANFO charge will explode closer to the velocity of dynamite (5,400 MPS). This is why commercial blasters will use an RDX cast booster to considerably increase the power of the detonation.

Ammonium nitrate is hygroscopic, meaning it is very sensitive to moisture and water. Exposure to moisture and water will greatly reduce its effectiveness.

Ammonium nitrate is sold as a fertilizer, although the agricultural grade prills are coated and do not mix well with oil to make homemade ANFO. Agriculture grade ammonium nitrate is also now controlled and the transfer of larger quantities is now registered.

6. COMMERCIAL EXPLOSIVES

Chapter Topics:

- A preliminary list of some of the most common commercial explosive materials and possible precursors.
- A brief description of each material that may include its use, make up, characteristics and history.

There are hundreds of chemical formulas for explosive materials. In fact, the ATF Orange Book includes approximately 234 as listed in our **Appendix A**. The following list of explosive materials is primarily the most common in use for commercial applications that blasters can purchase off the shelf.

Ammonium Nitrate and Fuel Oil (ANFO)

A Blasting Agent consisting of ammonium nitrate and fuel oil and by far the most common used explosive for industrial mining and quarrying operations.

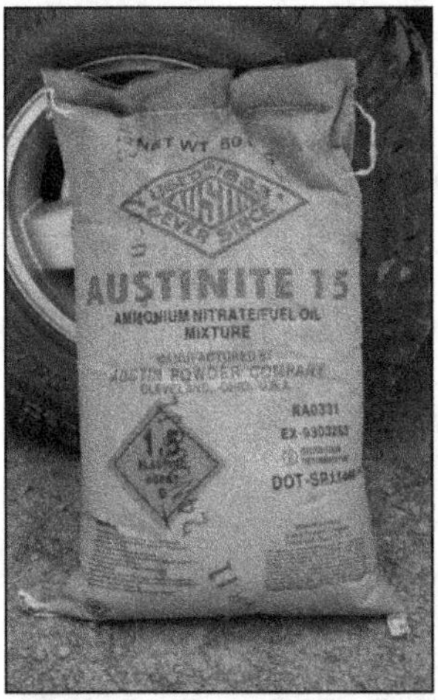

Ammonium Nitrate and Fuel Oil is one of the most common commercial explosive compounds.

It is a blasting agent because it requires a high explosive booster to detonate.

It comes in the form of small white pellets known as *prills.*

In can be purchased in pre-mixed bags or mixed on site for large blasting operations.

It is a binary explosive meaning it requires the mixture of two non-explosive compounds, ammonium nitrate (94%) and fuel oil (6%) by weight. ANFO is very stable and insensitive, as it requires a high explosive booster to detonate.

Primary use:	Breaking rock and moving earth
VOD Meters per second:	4,000
RE Factor:	0.80
Water Resistance:	Poor

Black Powder, Gunpowder & Smokeless Powder

These names are used interchangeably for the oldest known explosive and invented by the Chinese in the 9th Century. While black powder is also called gun powder, modern firearms use a different mix called smokeless powder. U.S Citizens can purchase up to 50 pounds per year for sporting purposes without an ATF license.

Black Powder is a low explosive and a mix of Potassium Nitrate (75%), Charcoal (15%) and Sulfur (10%) by weight. Some black powder is coated with graphite to reduce the chance of a static electricity charge. The burn rate of black powder is based upon its coarseness. For example, the coarsest grade is Fg, FFg for medium, FFFg for fine, and FFFFg for extra fine.

The smaller the file or cannon bore, the finer the powder used. Black powder can remain stable for years as long as there is no exposure to moisture, inspiring the term "keep our powder dry."
Black powder is typically used in applications where deflagration is needed over high shock detonation.

This makes the powder ideal for signal flares, fireworks, rescue line launchers and rockets. Black powder is a low explosive so not typically used for blasting rock. Due to its low brisance, or shattering power, it is often used for blasting monumental rock such as marble and granite.

Primary use:	Ammunition, fuse
VOD Meters per second:	400 - deflagrates
RE Factor:	0.55
Water Resistance:	Poor

Smokeless Powder is powerful, cleaner burning and less hydroscopic. It is composed of a mixture of nitrocellulose from the development of guncotton and the other is nitroglycerine.

Phil Schreier, Senior Curator at the National Firearms Museum, NRA Blog

Smoky Black Powder burning vs. cleaner Smokeless Powder, a huge advantage on early battlefields to conceal rifleman.

Composition 4 or C-4 Plastic Explosive

C-4 is a U.S. Military explosive that is occasionally used for civilian demolitions due to its excellent ability to cut steel.

C-4 is RDX (96%) with oil (4%) by weight, plasticized to be pliable and off white in color. All plastic explosives manufactured within the U.S. includes a chemical *'Taggant'* so its use can be traced in any unlawful activity.

It handles like putty and remains pliable in temperatures ranging from –70 to 170 degrees Fahrenheit.

It is also non-hygroscopic so it is ideal to use in wet environments or even underwater. Its pliable form is ideal for pressing into metal structure or forming into shaped charges.

C-4 is also very insensitive due to its use in a battlefield environment. It is made to withstand fire and bullet strikes without detonation. This added element of safety also means that sometimes, one Number 8 blasting cap will not detonate it. We suggest to double cap it or boost it will a line of det cord.

Primary use:	Demolition, Cutting, Breaching
VOD Meters per second:	8,077
RE Factor:	1.34
Water Resistance:	Excellent

C-4 formed into a shaped charge with the help of a funnel.

*C-4 formed into a linear shaped charge.
Due to its insensitivity, the charge is boosted
with det cord to ensure detonation.*

Detonating Cord or Det Cord

This high explosive fuse that is made from plastic or wax enclosed PETN. It explodes so quickly, four miles of the fuse will only take one second to detonate. It is so powerful, that about eight inches equals a blasting cap. It is waterproof and extremely versatile for using at a trunk line fuse or connecting and synchronizing multiple explosive charges.

Det cord is used in both commercial and military blasting. It is sized based upon grains per foot.

For example, commercial det cord it typically used in 25 or 50 grains per foot and is brightly colored such as green or orange.

Military det cord is increases to 100, up to 400 grains per foot for additional cutting power and is typically olive drab in color. Note that det cord looks very similar to paracord in sizes and colors. Security officers need to understand that det cord could be braded into bracelets and other objects typically made from paracord.

When using det cord, it is also useful to understand the ***Rule of 7000***. 7,000 grains equal one pound. For example, to determine the net explosive weight of 200 feet of 25 grain det cord: 200 x 25 = 5,000 then divide 5,000 into 7,000. 5,000 ÷ 7,000 = .714 pounds.

Primary use:	Initiating by exploding fuse
VOD Meters per second:	6,100 to 7,000
RE Factor:	N/A
Water Resistance:	Excellent

25 grain Autin Powder Company using the name A-Cord

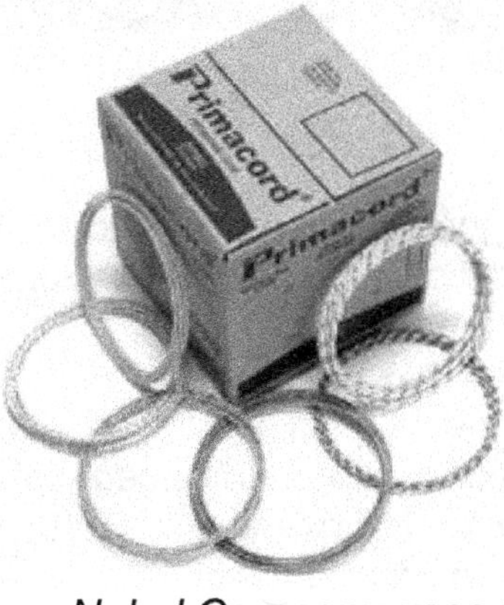

Varous sizes of Dyno Nobel Company uses the name Primacord

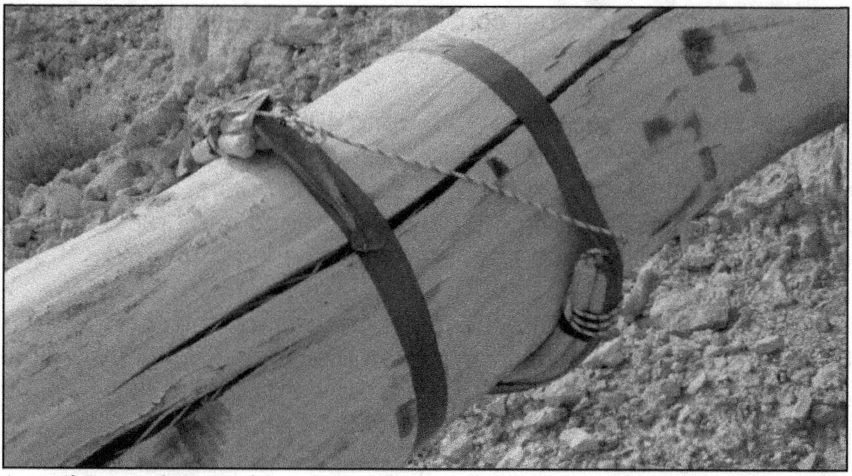

Detonation or det cord is an exploding fuse that is set off with a basting cap and is ideal to initiate multiple explosive charges.

Det Cord is so powerful, 8" is the equivalent to a blasting cap.

Dynamite

A nitroglycerin-based high explosive invented by Alfred Nobel in 1864 and was used as a more powerful and safer replacement to black powder in mining operations.

Dynamite has not changed much since it was invented. Nobel found a way to stabilize nitroglycerin with diatomaceous earth, a chalky absorbent stone used in cat litter, which made the potentially volatile nitroglycerin much safer to handle.

Modern dynamite uses sawdust to stabilize the nitroglycerin oil.

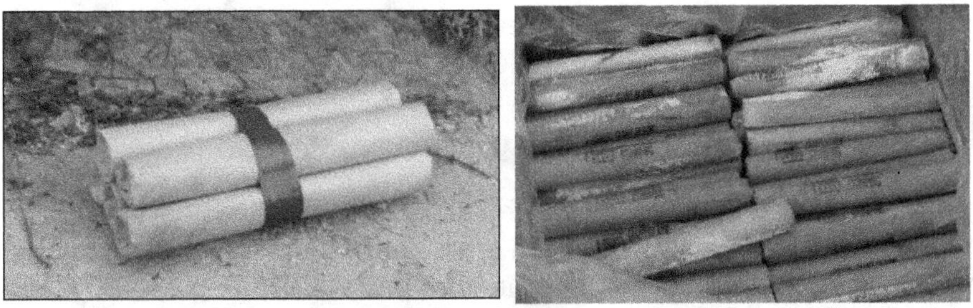

Dynamite sticks typically wrapped in wax paper. Dynamite comes in various sizes and percentages of nitroglycerin. A common size is a half-pound stick at 60% nitroglycerin.

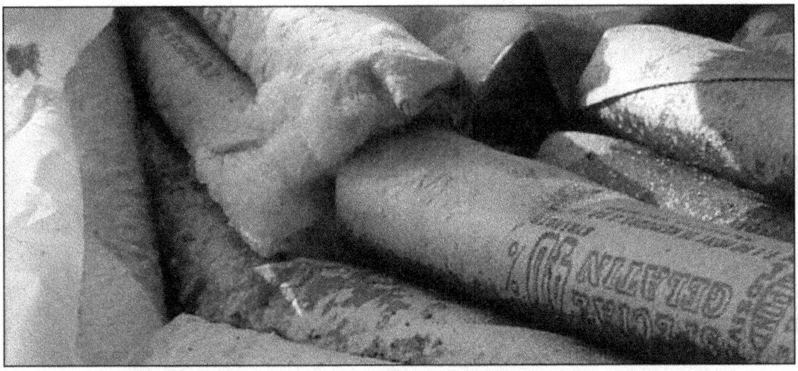

When dynamite crystallizes or leaks nitroglycerin oil, use extreme caution as it is an indicator that it has become highly unstable and should be disposed of.

The term stick of dynamite is used very generically, however, dynamite comes in various sizes and strengths. It is rated as a percentage of is Nitroglycerin content, ranging from 40 to 80%. A common size typically used is a half-pound stick rated at 60%, 1.25" x 8" in size.

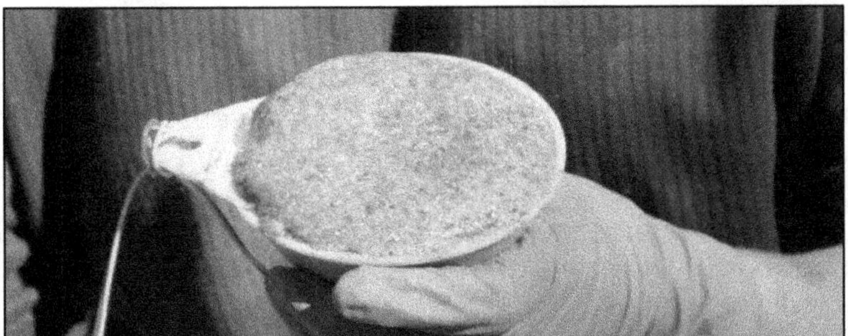

Dynamite cut open and pressed into a funnel for a shaped charge. The wet material is nitroglycerin stabilized by sawdust.

Dynamite is still used because it is powerful and inexpensive at about $4 per stick. It does have its cons which have resulted in it being replaced by more stable and modern explosive products. Nitroglycerin is toxic and should never be handled without rubber gloves. Contact through skin or inhaling the fumes can cause illness and a very severe nitro headache.

Dynamite also has a short shelf life, especially in extreme hot and cold environments. Within a year it will start to breakdown, getting mushy and oily as the nitro leaks out of the wax paper wrapping. As it gets older, it will start to form white crystals on the outside of the packaging. It will work in this condition, but it is just much nicer to handle fresher material, so buy only as much as you are going to use within a year. Its shelf life can be extended by turning the sticks in the case.

Use extreme caution with old dynamite in its crystalized condition. It is often disposed of by carefully burning with diesel fuel. We disposed of a case of dynamite from 1983. It looked rather ominous, but after 33 years, there was no more nitro left in the sticks to explode.

Primary use:	General Blasting, Demolition
VOD MPS at 60% nitro:	5,400
RE Factor:	0.92
Water Resistance:	Fair

Emulsion, Slurries and Gels Sticks

These semi-liquid high explosives are made from oxidizers dissolved in water, oil chemical mixture typically based from Ammonium Nitrate, Methyl Ammonium Nitrate, Sodium Nitrate and/or Calcium Nitrate with Aluminum fuels to make the material cap sensitive and water resistant.

Based upon if they are blasting cap sensitive, these can be classified as a high explosives (cap sensitive) or a blasting agent (non-cap sensitive).

Slurries come in all lengths and diameters and come in plastic-wrapped tubes that look and feel a bit like cookie dough. Slurry gel explosives have nearly replaced nitroglycerine dynamite because they are less toxic, safer to manufacture and have a much longer shelf life.

Registered name brands include; *Boostrite, Dyno Split C Emutrench, Emulex. Iremete, Powermite* and *Irecoal Tovex, Tovan, Dynogel, Slurran* and *Seismogel.*

Primary use:	Rock Quarry Blasting
VOD Meters per second:	5,000
RE Factor:	n/a
Water Resistance:	Good

Tovex Water Gel Sticks

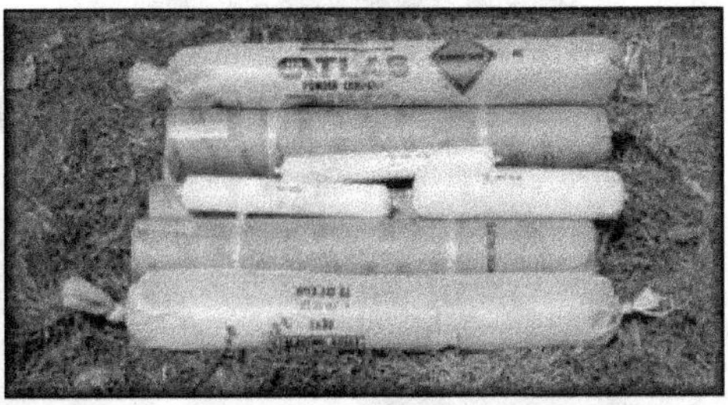

Atlas Sticks

Austin Powder Slurry sticks

Dyno Nobel AP Stick

Slurries made a great and safer alternative to dynamite.

PETN or Pentaerythritol

A very powerful high explosive typically used as a booster. It is used in blasting caps, det cord and land mines. It is also the active ingredient in the plastic explosive *Semtex*.

Primary use:	Boosters, Det Cord, Blasting Caps
VOD Meters per second:	8,300
RE Factor:	1.66
Water Resistance:	Excellent

PETN is powerful enough for Blasting Caps and Det Cord

Its natural form is white powder or crystals.

RDX or Cyclotrimethylenetrinitramine

RDX is one of the most powerful high explosive available with a VOD of 8,750 MPS.

It is a yellow-brown crystal solid that can be used in a pure form, blended with other explosives. Its high speed velocity of detonation makes it the ideal ingredient in many boosters, blasting caps and plastic explosives such as C-4. RDX was developed by the *British Research Department* for military use and named after its "Formula X." RDX also stands for *Royal Defense Explosive*.

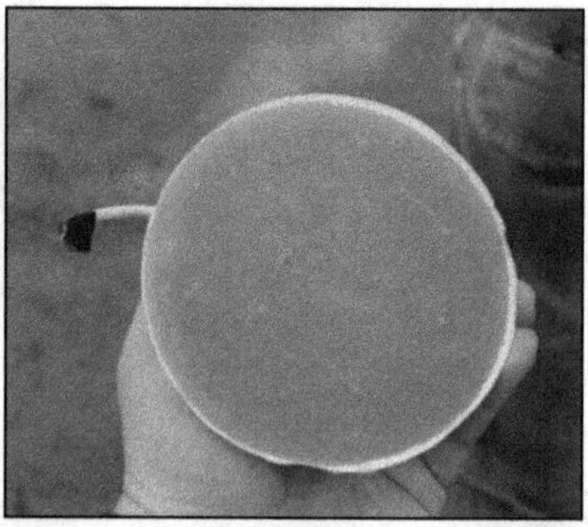

RDX is one of the more powerful explosives due to its high velocity and high brisance. Its high energy makes it ideal for shaped charges and boosters.

RDX yellow-brown crystals.

Primary use:	Boosters, Blasting Caps
VOD Meters per second:	8,750
RE Factor:	1.60
Water Resistance:	Excellent

7. MILITARY EXPLOSIVES

Chapter Topics:

- A preliminary list of some of the most common military explosive materials and their precursors.
- A brief description of each material that may include its use, make up, characteristics and history.

Amatol

A high explosive with good brisance, it is a mixture of TNT and ammonium nitrate mixed in either 20/80 or 50/50 ratios that provides a yellow-brown crystal. This is a low-cost explosive that was used in military ordinance throughout WWI and WWII various countries. The following characteristics are based upon an TNT (20%), ammonium nitrate (80%). Add 20% aluminum powder and you have ***Minol***.

Primary use:	Military
VOD Meters per second:	4,900
RE Factor:	1.17
Water Resistance:	Poor

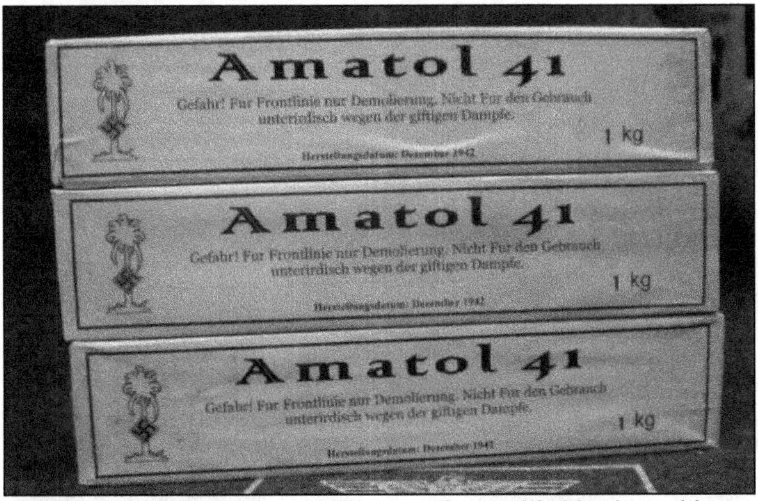

German Amatol from WWII complete with Nazi markings.

Baratol

Baratol is a composition of barium nitrate and TNT from the WWII era. TNT is 25-33% of the mixture with 1% wax as a binder.

Composition A

Composition A is a wax-coated, granular explosive used in U.S. land mines and rockets. It is a mixture of RDX (91%) and Plasticizing Wax (9%).

Primary use:	Military
VOD Meters per second:	8,230
RE Factor:	1.40
Water Resistance:	Excellent

Composition B, also known as Cyclotol

A high explosive that is a mix of RDX (59.5%), TNT (39.5%) and wax (1%) by weight. It is primarily used to fill military ordinance like in land mines and hand grenades. Remember making "sticky bombs" in *Saving Private Ryan*?

Primary use:	Military
VOD Meters per second:	7,620
RE Factor:	1.20
Water Resistance:	Excellent

Composition B used as a block or in a land mine.

Composition C-3

Composition C-3 was developed to obtain a putty-like consistency for molding shaped charges but it has now been replaced by C-4.

Composition C-3 is RDX (77%), Tetryl (3%), TNT (4%), NC (1%), MNT, Mononitrotoluol (5%), and DNT (Dinitrotoluol) (10%) and Tetryl (3%), and is light brown in color.

Primary use:	Military
VOD Meters per second:	7,925
RE Factor:	1.25
Water Resistance:	Excellent

Composition 4 or C-4 Plastic Explosive

C-4 is a U.S. Military explosive that's high velocity makes it ideal for demolitions due to is excellent ability to cut steel. Plastics have a long history of military use dating back to WWII being used by *British Special Operations* and the *French Resistance*. Plastics are also the explosive of choice by most major terrorist groups due its versatility and power.

C-4 is RDX (91%) Polyisobutylene (2.1%), Motor Oil (5.3%), Ethylhexyl Sebacate (2%) by weight, plasticized to be pliable and off white in color. All plastic explosives manufactured within the U.S. include a chemical *'Taggant'* so its use can be traced in any unlawful activity.

It handles like putty and remains pliable in temperatures ranging from –70° to 170° degrees Fahrenheit. It is also non-hygroscopic so it is ideal to use in wet environments or even underwater. Its pliable form is ideal for pressing into metal structure or forming into shaped charges.

C-4 is also very insensitive due to its use in a battlefield environment. It is made to withstand fire and bullet strikes without detonation.
This added element of safety also means that sometimes, one number 8 blasting cap will not detonate it. We suggest to double cap it or boost it will a line of det cord.

Primary use:	Demolition, cutting, breaching
VOD Meters per second:	8,077
RE Factor:	1.34
Water Resistance:	Excellent

Some other examples of plastic explosives include:

C A-3	RDX (91%) petroleum wax (9%), tan in color
C A-4	RDX (97%) petroleum wax (3%), tan in color
C-2	RDX (80%) explosive oil plasticizer (20%), brown
C-3	RDX (73%) explosive oil plasticizer (23%), yellow
M-112	C-4 in U.S. Military 1.25 pound demolition blocks
M-186	C-4 in U.S. Military roll shaped into a flat strip on a 50' spool.

U.S. Air Force

U.S. Military M112 1-¼ pound bars of C4.

Plastic Explosives used around the world:

Material	Country
C-4 (Composition 4)	United States
Demex, Rowanex, PE 4	Great Britain
PE 4, Plastrite (Formex P 1)	France
PWM, Netrolit	Poland
Spreng Körper DM 12	Germany
PP – 01 (C 4)	Yugoslavia
Chemex (C 4), Tvarex 4 A	Slovakia
Knauerit	Austria
Sprängdeg m/46	Sweden
Semtex	Europe, Asia, Middle East

Detonating Cord or Det Cord

This high explosive fuse that is made from plastic or wax enclosed PETN. It explodes so quickly, four miles of the fuse will only take one second to detonate. It is so powerful, that about eight inches equals a blasting cap. It is waterproof and extremely versatile for using at a trunk line fuse or connecting and synchronizing multiple explosive charges.

Det cord is used in both commercial and military blasting. It is sized based upon grains per foot.

For example, commercial det cord it typically used in 25 or 50 grains per foot and is brightly colored such as green or orange.

Military det cord is increases to 100, up to 400 grains per foot for additional cutting power and is typically olive drab in color. Note that det cord looks very similar to paracord in sizes and colors. Security officers need to understand that det cord could be braded into bracelets and other objects typically made from paracord.

When using det cord, it is also useful to understand the ***Rule of 7000***. 7,000 grains equal one pound. For example, to determine the net explosive weight of 200 feet of 25 grain det cord: 200 x 25 = 5,000 then divide 5,000 into 7,000. 5,000 ÷ 7,000 = .714 pounds.

Primary use:	Initiating by exploding fuse
VOD Meters per second:	6,100 to 7,000
RE Factor:	N/A
Water Resistance:	Excellent

The white center of det cord is the very high explosive PETN.

Heavy 100 grain per foot plus military det cord is ideal for priming explosives. This wrapping technique is known as whipping.

Detasheet

Detasheet is a plastic sheet explosive containing PETN with Nitrocellulose and a binder made by *DuPont*. It is manufactured in thin flexible sheets with a rubbery texture, and is red in color for commercial, or olive drab for military. In use, it is typically cut to shape for precision engineering charges.

The explosives strength in sheet is measured in grams per square inch referred to as C-1 through C-8. The number indicating the number of grams of net explosive weight per square inch of sheet.

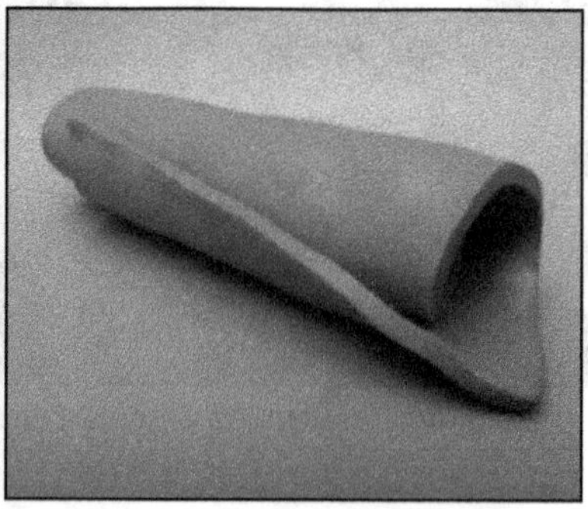

Detasheet by DuPont, OD for military or red for civilian use.

Dynamite – U.S. Military

Military dynamite contains no nitroglycerin, but is it made to equal the power of 60% nitroglycerin commercial dynamite.

It is made up from RDX (75%), TNT (15%), SAE 10 engine oil and Polyisobutylene (5%) and Cornstarch (5%). It is an oily granular substance that is yellow-white to tan in color.
This combination is closer to Comp B instead of traditional dynamite, but this mixture is more stable and safer to store and handle than commercial dynamite. It is also relatively insensitive to friction, drop impact, and rifle bullet impact.

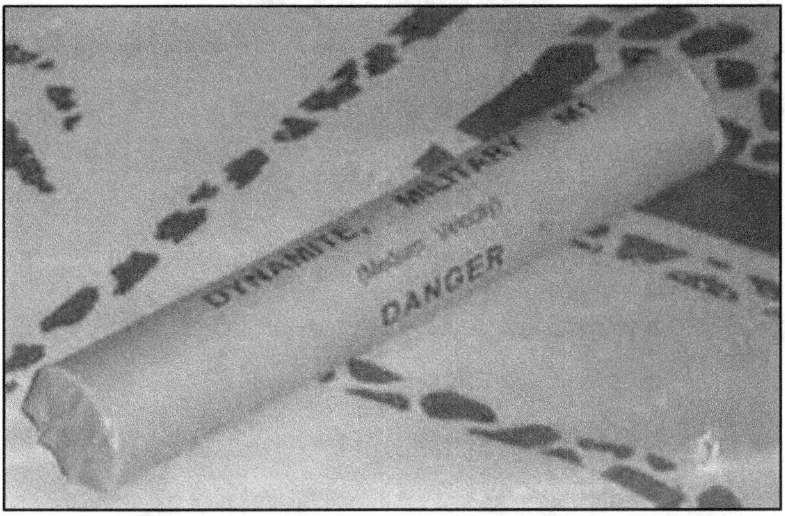

U.S. Military dynamite comes in OD or yellow packaging.

There are three variations based upon the size:

M1	**8" X 1.25"**
M2	**8" X 1.50"**
M3	**12" X 1.50"**

Primary use:	Military
VOD Meters per second:	6,096
RE Factor:	0.98
Water Resistance:	Good

HMX or Octogen

A powerful and insensitive nitroamine-based high explosive. Similar to the explosive RDX, it can be used in a pure form, blended or as a plastic.

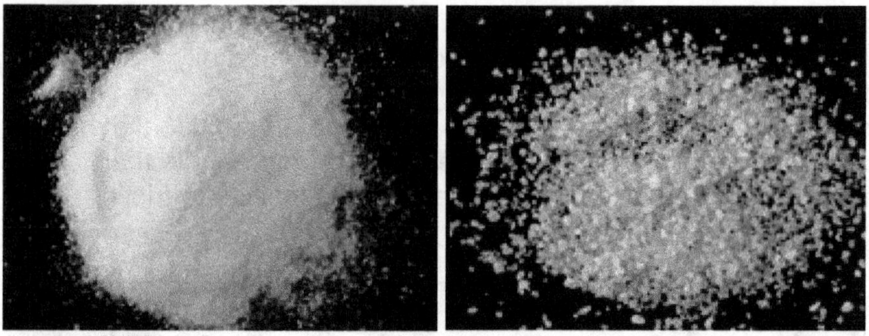

HMX or Octogen is a white crystal in its natural form.

Octal or Cyclotot

A high explosive blend of HMX and TNT. TNT (70-75%) and TNT (25-30%).

PE 4

A RDX (88%) based plastic explosive manufactured by the U.K. *Mondial Defense Systems*. It is used by the France and British military and is white in color.

PE 4 plastic stick used by the France and British Military.

Primary use:	Military
VOD Meters per Second	7,500
RE Factor:	1.18
Water Resistance:	Excellent

Pentolite

A high explosive mixture of PETN (50%) and TNT (50%) by weight. It was primarily used for WWII military ordinance.

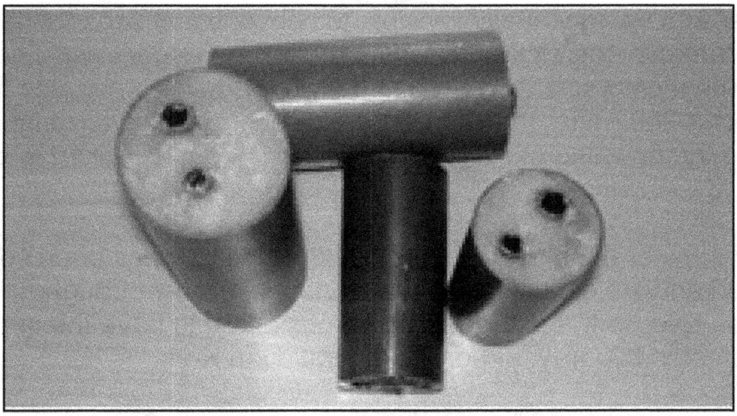

Primary use:	Booster and bursting charges
VOD Meters per second:	7,400
RE Factor:	1.26
Water Resistance:	Excellent

Semtex

A plastic explosive containing a mixture of RDX and PETN in different combinations that include; **Semtex 1A**, **Semtex H**, **Semtex P2**, and manufactured after 1987, is known as **Semtex 10**. It comes in colors ranging from red, to orange and brown, and is pliable and waterproof like C-4, only slightly less powerful. It does stay pliable under a greater range of temperatures, -40° C to +60° C.

It was invented by a Czechoslovakia chemist in 1950, and has been manufactured by *Explosia a.s.* in Czechoslovakia, since 1964.

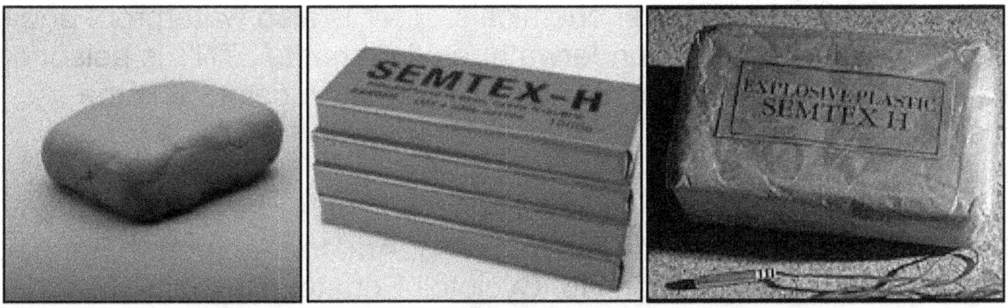

Semtex plastic explosive in various forms.

It has been sold in great quantities throughout Europe, Asia, and the Middle East including tons of product to the most dangerous groups and countries around the world. These countries include the North Vietnamese Army, IRA, Iran, Iraq, Yemen, Syria and North Korea. Col. Muammar el-Qaddafi, the president of the Libyan Arab Republic received over 700 tons alone.

Its power and being virtually invisible to conventional security devices made it the easy top pick to terrorist groups. A Taggant was finally added with a color change to red and orange. Sales were also finally restricted in 2002 after the Semtex was used in various terrorist attacks including the downing of *Pan Am Flight 103*, and the Lockerbie bombing in 1988.

Semtex is by far the most dangerous explosive that has been sold, smuggled and stolen all around the world, especially throughout the 80's and 90's. Even with the taggant, it is considered to have the capacity to be undetected by x-ray, airport scanners, even K-9s.

Model	VOD MPS	Color	Format
1A	7,200	Red	Brick
H	7,400	Yellow	Brick
10	7,300	Black	Sheet

TNT or Trinitrotoluene

A high explosive compound named 2-4-6 trinitrotoluene. Yellow insensitive crystals that can be melted at 80° and cast without detonation. Invented by German chemist Joseph Wilbrand in 1863, it is often confused with dynamite, although there is no similarity, nor do they share the same ingredients. TNT is one of the most commonly used explosives for commercial and military applications because it is very insensitive to shock and friction.

TNT is one of the most stable explosives as it can be safely melted, poured and mixed with other chemicals. TNT is also waterproof and is ideal for working in wet or underwater environments. TNT is poisonous and will cause skin irritation, turning skin yellow in color. It is the baseline in the RE factor.

While TNT can be purchased in it's pure form, it is blended with many other explosives that include the following: Amatol, Ammonal, Baratol, Composition B, Composition H6, Cyclotol, Ednatol, Hexanite, Minol, Octol, Pentolite, Picratol, Tetrytol, Torpex and Tritonal.

Primary use:	Demolition
VOD Meters per second:	6,900
RE Factor:	1.00
Water Resistance:	Excellent

Half-pound cans of TNT. The hole on the Top of the can is for inserting a blasting cap.

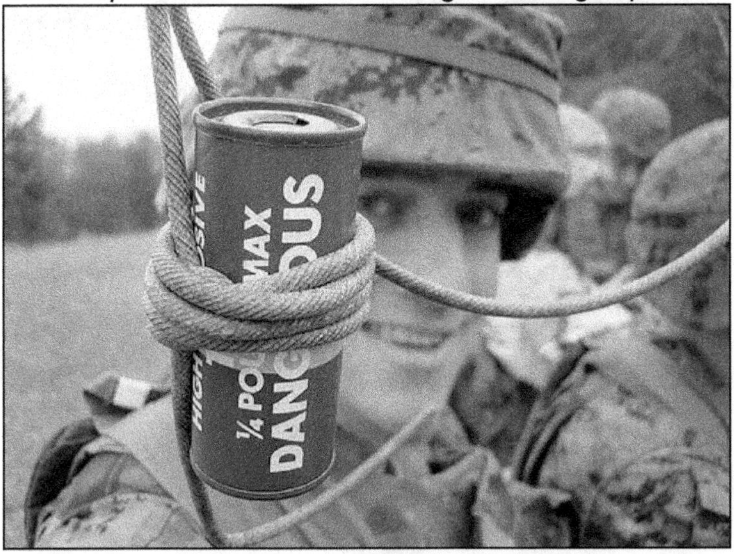

Quarter pound TNT can primed with heavy military det cord.

8. HOMEMADE EXPLOSIVES

Chapter Topics:

- A preliminary list of some of the most common homemade explosive materials and precursors.
- A brief description of each material that may include its use, make up, characteristics and history.

Homemade Binaries

Many homemade explosives are binary, meaning the mixture of two or more chemicals that consist of an Oxidizer and a Fuel.

Oxidizers	**Fuels**
Ammonium Nitrate	Aluminum Powder
Hydrogen Peroxide	Gasoline
Potassium Chlorate	Nitro Methane
	Petroleum Fuels
	Sugar

Precursors to single or binary explosives include:

Acetone
Alcohol
Aluminum Powder
Ammonium Nitrate
Potassium Perchlorate
Chlorine
Glycol
Hexamine
Heavy Acid
Hydrogen Peroxide (High Percentage)
Propane
Sugar
Triacetone Triperoxide (TATP)
Urea Nitrate

Acetone

Acetone is a common household and industrial solvent.
It is available in every hardware store and it is inexpensive and can be purchased in large quantities.

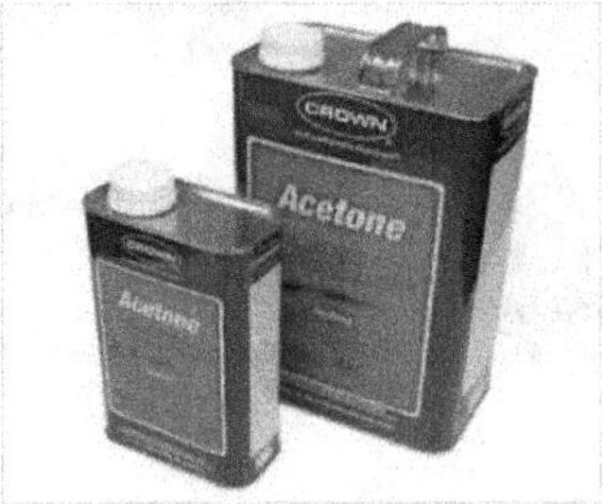

It is one the primary ingredients in Acetone Peroxide.

Acetone Peroxide or Triacetone, Triperoxide, Peroxyacetone, TATP and TCAP

A highly unstable white crystal organic peroxide high explosive. It is cheap and easy to manufacture and extremely sensitive to heat, friction and shock. Acetone Peroxide is unique because it will explode underwater and it does not contain nitrogen.

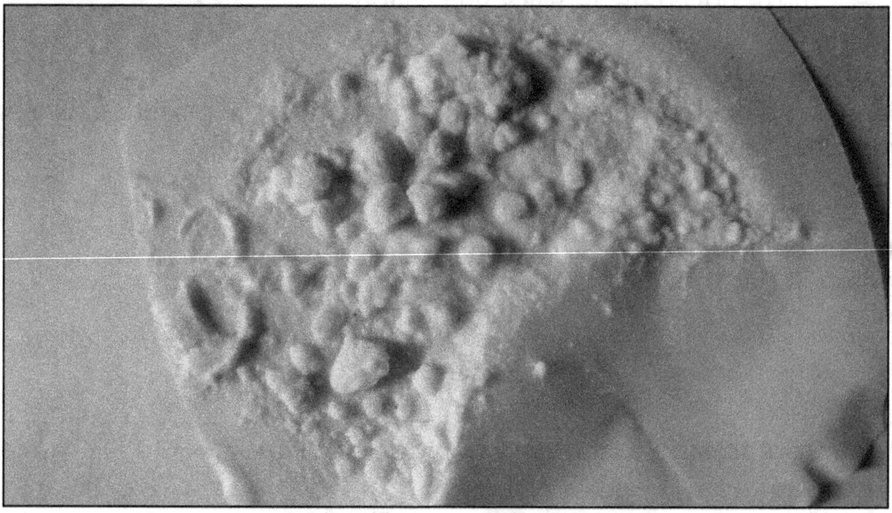

Crystallized Acetone Peroxide looks like drugs.

It is made up from: Acetone, Hydrogen Peroxide and Muriatic Acid. This explosive was used in numerous airline terrorist plots including the attempted bombing of an *American Airlines* plane by Richard Reid, "*the shoe bomber.*"

Richard Reed attempted to bring down an American Airlines flight with these shoes. Being nitrate free, TAAP is harder to detect.

The lack of nitrogen (Nitrates) makes the substance difficult to detect, making it a popular explosive choice among terrorist groups. This is because bomb sniffing dogs, equipment and chemical tests are designed to detect nitrates.

Ammonal

An explosive made from Ammonium Nitrate, Trinitrotoluene and Aluminum Powder. The substance flairs when openly burned or explodes when incased or contained.

Ammonium Nitrate and Fuel Oil (ANFO)

ANFO has been used as an IED since 1970, when radical student protesters learned that fertilizer can be made into an explosive in a booklet entitled, "Pothole Blasting for Wildlife."
Since then, it has been used by various terroristic groups like the IRA and two major attacks with the United States, the World Trade Center in 1993 and Oklahoma City bombing in 1995.

Ammonium nitrate pellets are known as prills.

Ammonium Nitrate is sold as fertilizer all over the world. It is now regulated in larger quantities. Agricultural ammonium nitrate is also now different from explosives grade ammonium nitrate through a special coating on the prills. The coating on the agricultural material helps prevent the oil from absorbing into the prills, degrading the detonation potential for ANFO.

Ammonium nitrate fertilizer can be soaked with diesel fuel or stove oil at 6%, but will probably not fully detonate as powerfully as commercial grade ANFO. The other challenge criminals have on a homemade level, is finding a high explosive to boost it.

Nitrate can be distilled from urine, human or animal, see ***Urea***. Males have higher concentrate of nitrates than female. Cows and horses have a higher content of nitrates then from human urine. It can also be distilled from hardwood ashes from oak, maple.

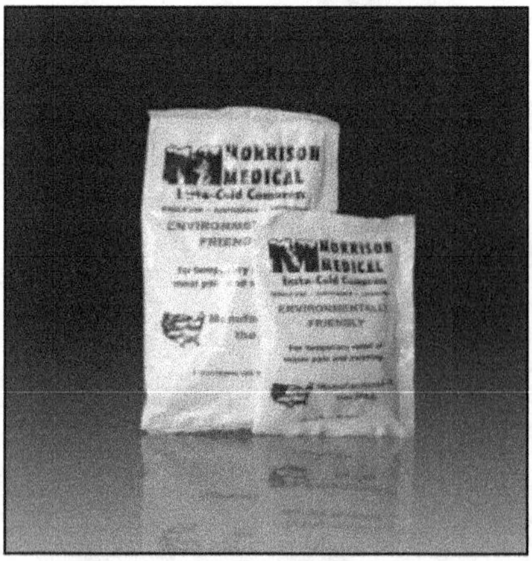

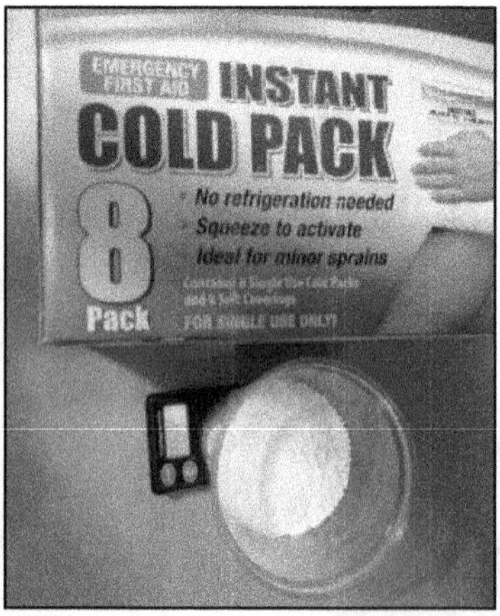

Ammonuim Nitrate is also removed from cold packs.

Armstrong's Mixture

Armstrong's Mixture is made from Red Phosphorus, a fuel from match striker pads and road flares and Potassium Chlorate, an oxidizer made from crushed match heads.

Armstrong's Mixture made from match heads and striker pads.

It is extremely sensitive to shock, heat and friction but the stability can be increased by substituting sulfur for most of the Phosphorus. It is lot of work to make for such a minimal blast, but still a common HME. The mixture can be turned to into a paste and painted on objects to explode on impact.

Black Powder or **Gunpowder**

Black Powder can be homemade through a mix of Potassium Nitrate (75%), Charcoal (15%) and Sulfur (10%) by weight. In the United States however, a citizen can purchase up to 50 lbs per year for sporting purposes.

U.S citizens can purchase 50 pounds of black powder annually.

Black powder is a low explosive, but it does explode if contained. That's way it is used in pipe bombs and now pressure cookers, like at the 2013 Boston Marathon Bombing.

Gun powders will take on the detonation velocity of a detonator used to it initiate it. For example, a flame from a fuse it will take longer to build pressure to shatter a container resulting in a lower order explosion.

Citric or Heavy Acid

Citric acid is used for making the explosive, HMTD because stronger acids tend to reduce yields.

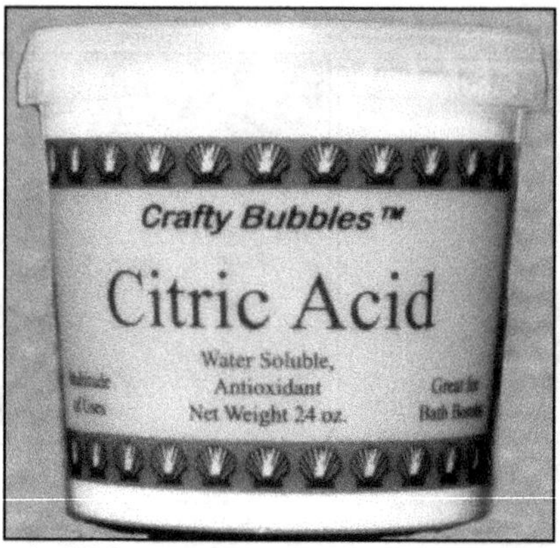

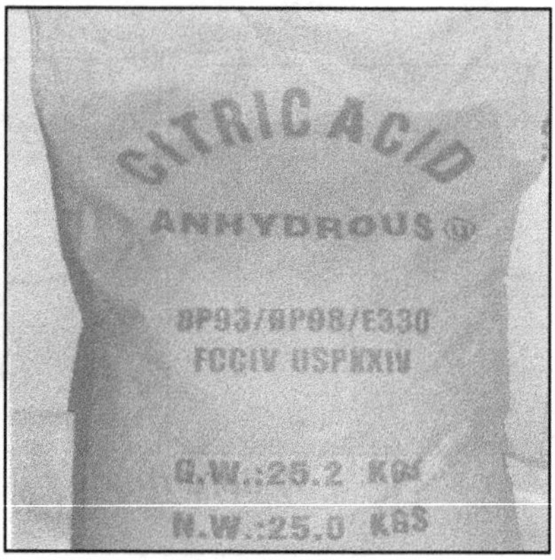

Citric Acid is easily purchased as it is used in foods, drinks, making soap and preventing discoloration in canning foods.

Flash Powder

Flash Powder is made up from Potassium Perchlorate (70%) and Aluminum Flake Powder (30%).

It is powerful and sensitive to shock, sparks, static and friction. Flash Powder will explode in a loose pile in a quantity of 30 or more grams, while Black Powder deflagrates. The finer the aluminum powder, 2-3 micron, the best being dark flake aluminum, 600 mesh size due to less surface area.

Flash Powder from Potassium Perchlorate mixed with Aluminum Flake Powder

It is used in pyrotechnics such as M-80 firecrackers and aerial salutes.

The important thing to know about Flash Powder is that it is cheap and easy to make and it can detonate strongly enough to possibly boost blasting agents.

Glycerin – Glycerol and Ethylene Glycol

Glycerin can be used to make nitroglycerin and when dripped onto KMnO4, Potassium Permanganate. Ethylene Glycol it is a moderate explosion hazard when exposed to flame. Ethylene Glycol is an odorless liquid able to be mixed completely with water and many organic liquids.

Sources include anti-freeze and veterinary products.

HMTD Hexamethylene Triperoxide Diamine
TATP Triacetone-Triperoxide

HMTD and TATP are made through the reaction of an aqueous solution of Hydrogen Peroxide and Hexamine in the presence of Citric Acid or Dilute Sulfuric Acid as a catalyst.

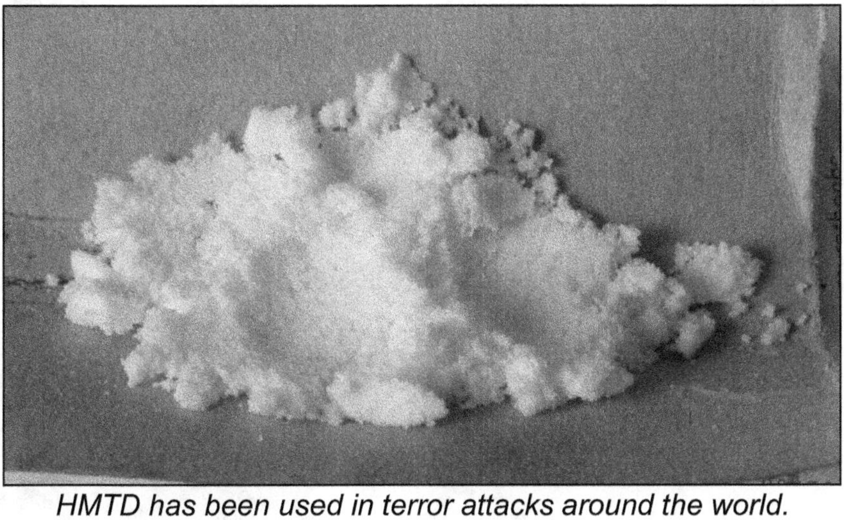

HMTD has been used in terror attacks around the world.

HMTD is unstable and detonates upon shock, friction, and heat. It has been used as a primary explosive in mining applications, but it has long been replaced by more stable products due to its poor thermal and chemical stability.

Despite being unstable and extremely dangerous to manufacture, it is a common homemade explosive that has been used in suicide bombings and terrorist plots and attacks around the world.
In the United States, this includes the Los Angeles International Airport Millennium attack plots in 2000.

Hexamine

A white, crystalline, water-soluble powder, Hexamine is used in making explosives, such as HMTD, HDN and RDX.
It can be found in the form of heating tablets at camp stores or at chemical supply companies.

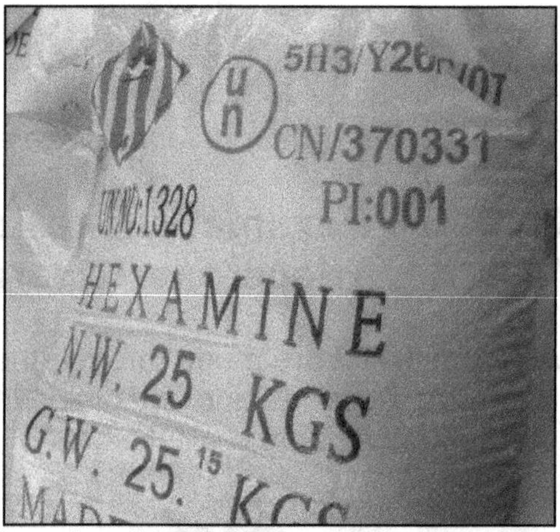

Hexamine is available from heating tablets or in bulk.

Hydrochloric Acid – HCl known as Muriatic Acid

HCl is used to make Acetone Peroxide and MEKP and making Hydrogen Gas when aluminum is added. HCl is easily available as it has many uses such at cleaning metal, a disinfectant, pool chemical or toilet bowl cleaner.

HCl is easily purchased as a cleaner or for a pool treatment.

Hydrogen Peroxide

It can be purchased at any pharmacy in a 3% solution, which will work for Acetone Peroxide, but greatly reduce yields.
3% can be boiled down for a greater strength, 10-20%.
Can be purchased at industrial strength levels, such as pool supply stores, of 27 to 35%.

Consumer use Hydrogen Peroxide is only 3%, it can be as high as 35% as a pool treatment chemical.

MEK Methyl, Ethyl Ketone

It is used to make Methyl Ethyl Ketone Peroxide (MEKP), an explosive close to Acetone Peroxide, but in a liquid form.

Methyl Ethyl Ketone can be easily purchased as a solvent.

Mercury Fulminate

An explosive that is extremely sensitive to friction, heat and shock. It was discovered by Edward Howard in 1980 and was used in early caps and rifle flints.

It is made by dissolving Mercury in Nitric Acid and adding Ethanol to create a white or off-white powder. Silver Fulminate is similar, but so sensitive, it can explode by its own weight.

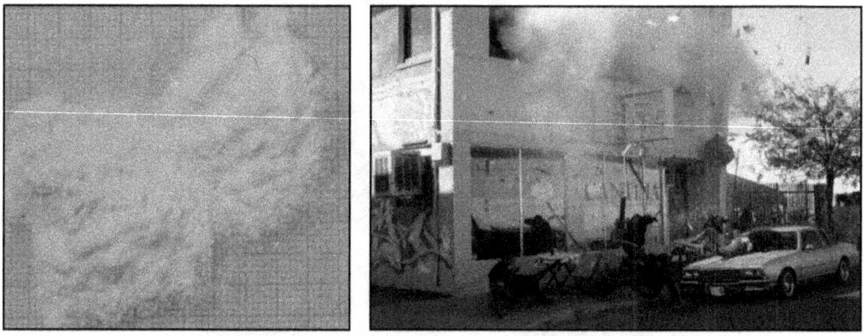

Mercury Fulminate may have been made more popular by being featured in an episode of AMC's Breaking Bad.

Sulfuric Acid

Sulfuric acid can be used to make many different explosives including Acetone Peroxide, TNT and Nitroglycerin. It is very corrosive, will cause severe burns from contact to any body tissue.

It can be purchased as drain opener or from car batteries.

Nitroglycerin

Being the active ingredient in dynamite, nitroglycerin is extremely powerful and volatile. It can be made with: red nitric acid, of 98% pure, sulfuric acid (99%H_2SO_4) and glycerin.

Nitroglycerin oil

PETN Pentaerythritol Tetranitrate

PETN is a very powerful explosive that is use in blasting caps, det cord and mixed with other materials like RDX for Semtex plastic. It can be homemade with: Nitric Acid, Pentaerythritol, Lye and Acetone.

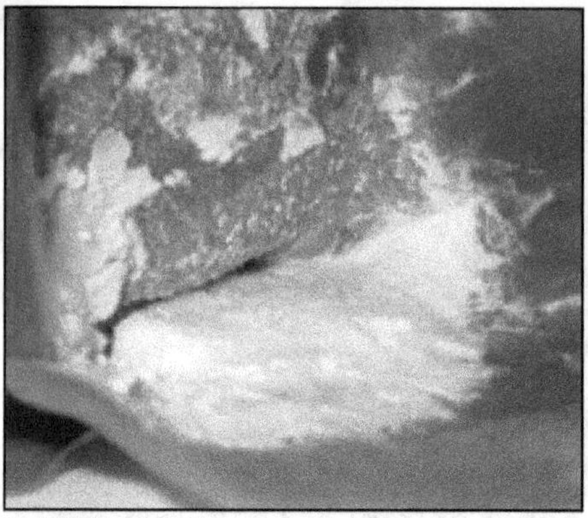

PETN's white powder crystals.

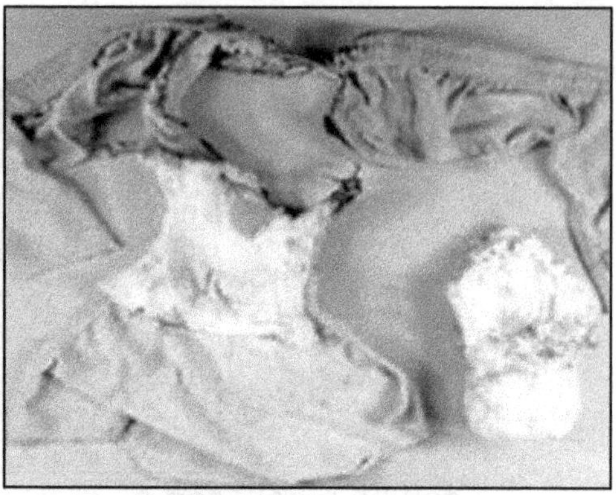

The 2009 Underwear Bomber used PETN.

Plastic Explosives or **Plastiques**

With its incredible speed, brisance and versatility, plastic explosives were designed for demolitions. The have also become the top choice for terrorists around the world using plastiques for attacks for decades. Thirteen ounces of Semtex brought down Flight 103, killing 270 over Lockerbie, Scotland in 1988. Other high profile uses include at attack on the *U.S.S. Cole* and the *Khobar Towers* military housing complex in Saudi Arabia.

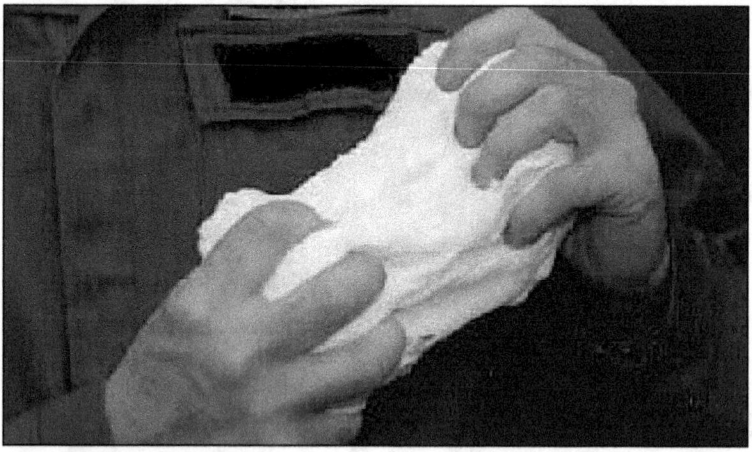

Homemade C-4

A C-4 looking plastic can be made using two basic ingredients: Potassium Chlorate for the oxidizer and petroleum jelly for the fuel.

Homemade Semtex

Semtex can also be made, but its recipe requires the actual high explosive ingredients: RDX, PETN and for the fuel, motor oil, petroleum jelly or vegetable oil.

Thermite

Thermite is a burning reaction to a metal powder, a Fuel and Metal Oxide. When ignited by a strong heat source, thermite undergoes an exothermic reduction-oxidation reaction. This is not a detonation but an extreme burn hot enough to melt through metal. The mixture burns as a liquid due to the high temperatures reached, up to 2,500° C or 4,500° F with Iron(III) Oxide.

Fuels include Aluminum, Magnesium, Titanium, Zinc, Silicon, and Boron. Oxidizers include Iron(III) Oxide, Iron(II,III) Oxide, Boron(III) Oxide, Silicon(IV) Oxide, Chromium(III) Oxide, Manganese(IV) Oxide, Copper(II) Oxide, and Lead(II,IV) Oxide.

Thermite can burn through about anything at 4,500° F and can be easily purchased online.

Thermite was first discovered in 1893 and patented in 1895 by German chemist Hans Goldschmidt. He discovered it can be used for welding which it is still used today for welding railroad tracks together, even underwater welding. It is also used for industrial metal refining and demolitions. The military used thermite charges to quickly destroy by melting and burning anything from artillery pieces to computer servers.

Thermite requires an extremely high heat source to ignite. A fuse or blasting cap will not burn hot enough. Sparklers, a torch or ideally a magnesium ribbon is used. It contains its own supply of oxygen and does not require any external source of air. Once burning, thermite is difficult extinguish. Spraying water can spread jets of molten metal.

As the TV series *Myth Busters* confirmed, putting it on ice will cause it to explode.

The U.S. military uses *Thermate-TH3* is a mixture of thermite and pyrotechnic additives that make it ideal for demolitions such as melting metal weapons and components. The public can order thermite kits on-line. We found an eight-pound kit for $38.

Urea Nitrate

A fertilizer based high explosive made from dried urine, Urea, mixed with Nitric Acid. With a VOD of 3,400 to 4,700 MPS, its power is similar to ANFO, but unlike Ammonium Nitrate, Urea Nitrate is blasting cap sensitive.

It can be purchased from chemical supply companies and is sold as a fertilizer and to de-ice aircraft. It can be homemade with enough urine from animals or humans. Urea Nitrate is very popular with terrorists primarily in the Middle East.

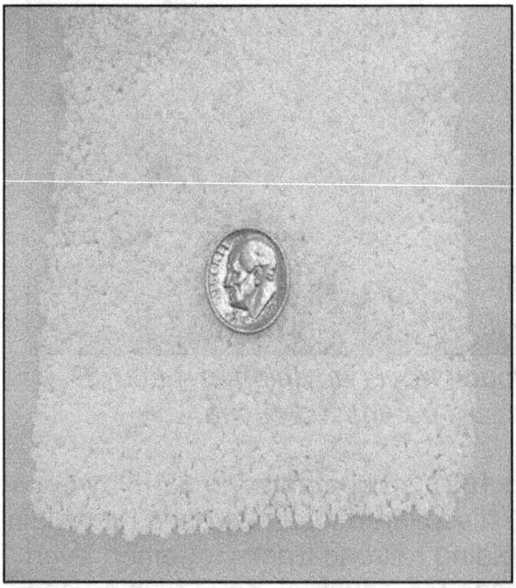

Urea Nitrate is similar to ANFO but it is blasting cap sensitive.

9. BLASTING CAPS/ DETONATORS AND FUSES

Chapter Topics:

- Understanding Electric, Fuse and Nonel blasting caps.
- Learn to handle blasting caps safely.
- Understanding pyrotechnic fuses.

Most explosive materials are intentionally made insensitive to only detonate with the use of a blasting cap. This chapter will show what blasting cap options are available and how they are initiated. Then we will review the various types of fuses are available.

Blasting Caps - Detonators

Blasting caps are a quarter-inch metal cylinder filled with high explosives (usually PETN) used to detonate a primary explosive charge. The terms; ***Blasting Cap***, ***Detonator*** and ***Initiator*** are used interchangeably.

Blasting caps come in four styles:

Electric *Initiated with an electric charge through wires*

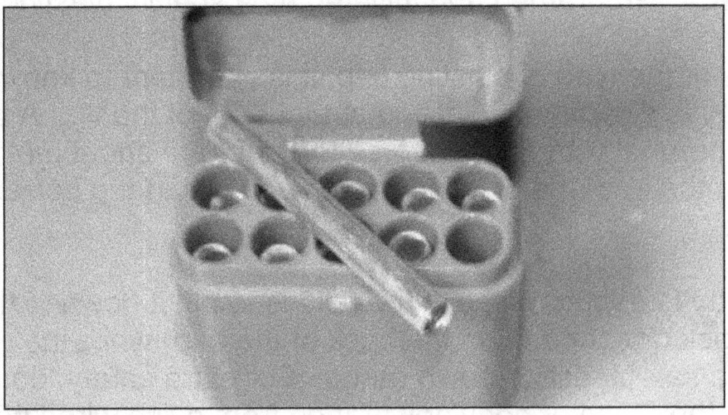

Fuse Cap *Initiated by a burning Safety Fuse*

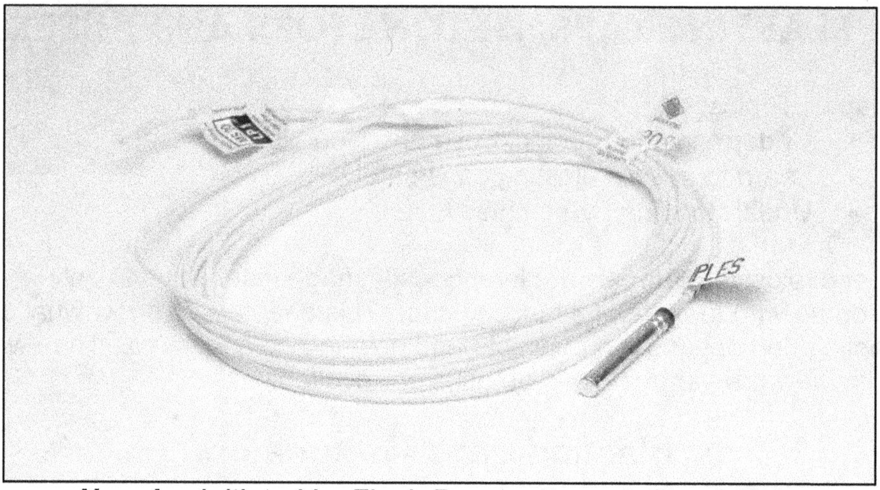

Nonel *Initiated by Flash Powder through Shock Tube*

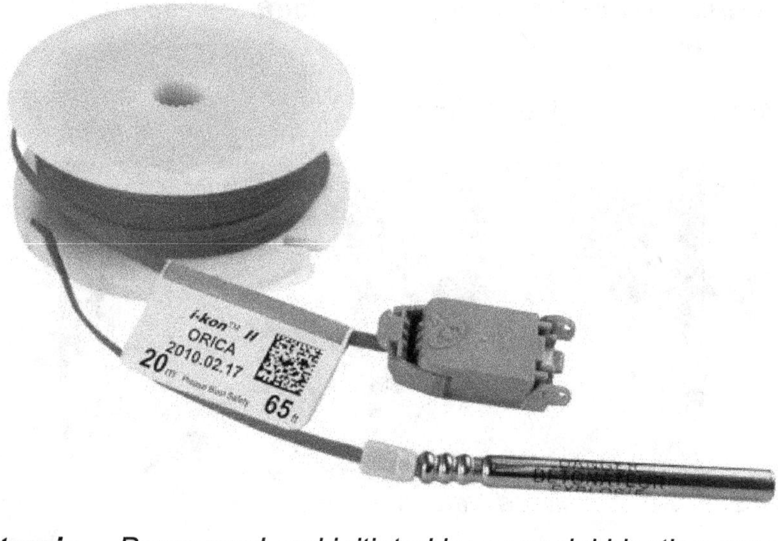

Electronic *Programed and initiated by a special blasting computer*

Regardless of the type of blasting cap, it is important to know that the cap's energy is directional, blasting straight out of the tip. A blasting cap will throw shrapnel with enough force to penetrate sheet metal. For safety, treat the end of a blasting cap as you would the barrel of a loaded gun.

The best way to secure a cap in the field is to pin it down to the ground (setting a rock or sandbag on the back of the cap) while the cap is pointing in a safe direction down range. For extra safety, do not let anyone put their face or body downrange from a live wired blasting cap.

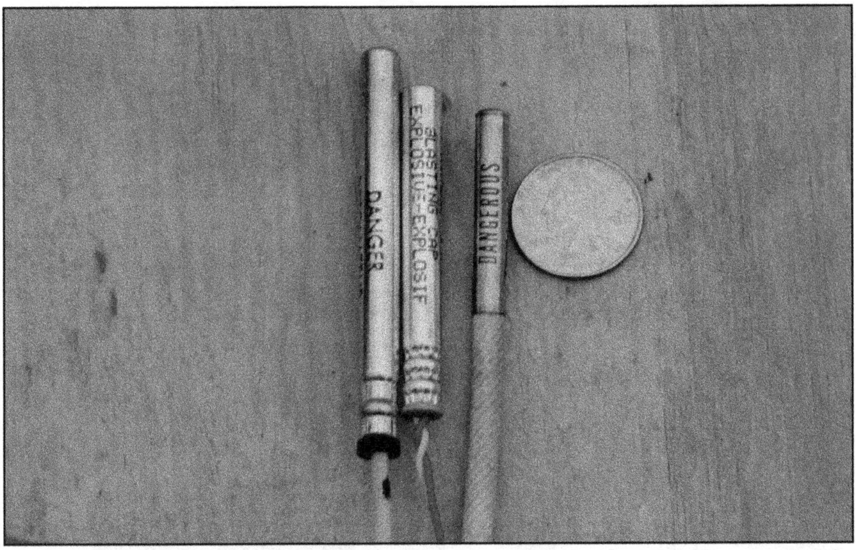

Blasting caps are rated by numbered sized based upon the grain count.
Left to right; 10 grain nonel, 8 grain electric, 6 grain fuse cap

Blasting caps are powerful enough to penetrate steel.
For safety, always point the end of a blasting
cap as you would the barrel of a loaded gun.

Blasting Cap Summary Diagram

Pyrotechnic Fuse Type Blasting Cap

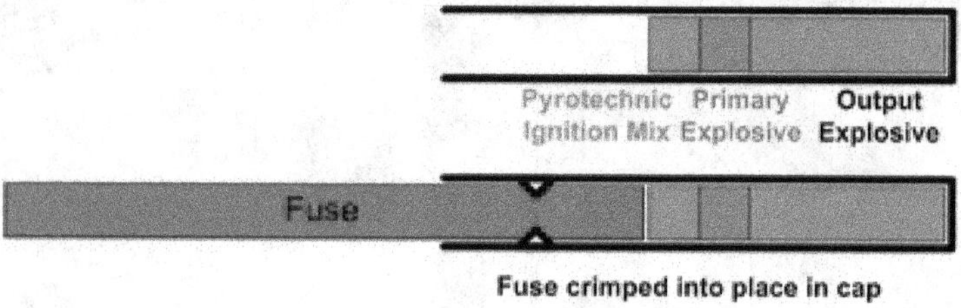

Solid Pack Electric Type Blasting Cap

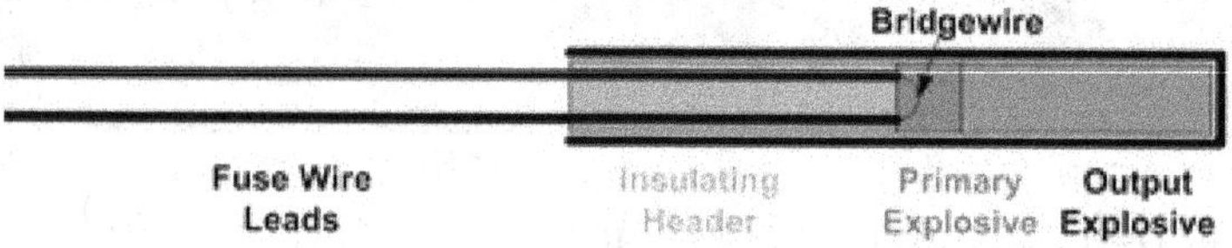

Match or Fusehead Electric Type Blasting Cap

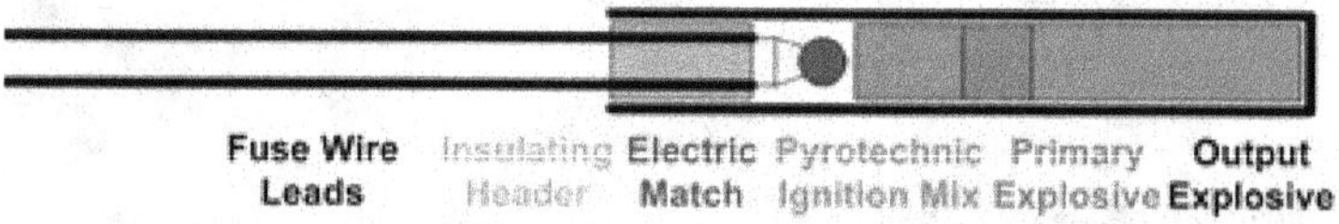

Exploding Bridgewire Type Blasting Cap

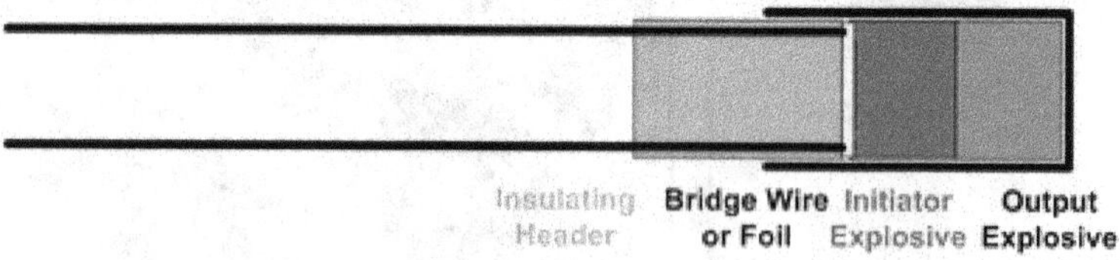

Slapper Type Blasting Cap

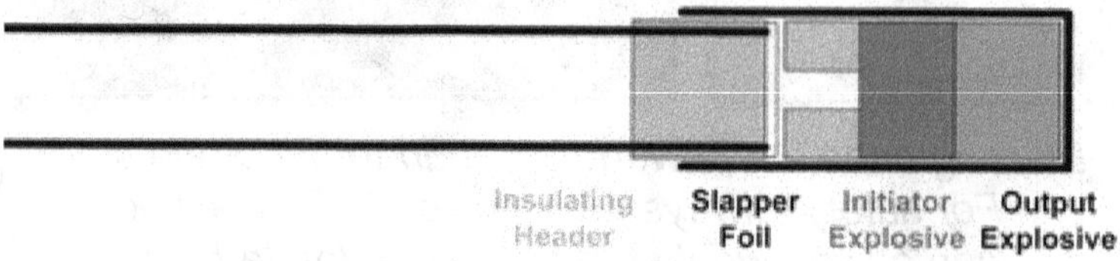

Electric Blasting Caps

Electric caps detonate with an electrical charge of 1.5 amps or more delivered by a battery powered ***Blasting Machine***.

Electric caps have leg wires in various lengths, the most common being 12 to 16 feet. These wires are connected to a reel of wire that is then connected to a blasting machine. When an electrical charge reaches the cap, an element, (the bridge wire) ignites the firing train that initiates the high explosive charge at the end of the cap.

Modern electric caps also contain a filter system that makes them less sensitive to static, lightning, radio transmissions and other forms of stray electrical current. We would not use electric caps in a thunderstorm, but we are also not aware of any modern caps going off due to stray electric current.

Electric caps may detonate instantaneously or have a delay feature. There are tags on each cap with a number indicating the amont of any millisecond delay. If there is no delay the take will show **0** MS. If the cap is delayed, the tag indicates the amount in milliseconds, such as 25 MS.

Electric caps are simple and reliable.

Pyrotechnic Fuse Blasting Cap

Pyrotechnic Fuse caps are crimped onto a ***Safety Fuse***. The cap is a metal cylinder with a hollow end for the fuse to slide into.

The hollow end of the cap is then crimped using a special pair of pliers to secure the fuse into the cap. Fuse caps are the oldest and simplest systems.

Military Detonators are designed to be used with insensitive explosives. They have a load of about 13.5 grains in the main charge, compared to typical commercial detonators that have about 7.0 grains in the main charge.

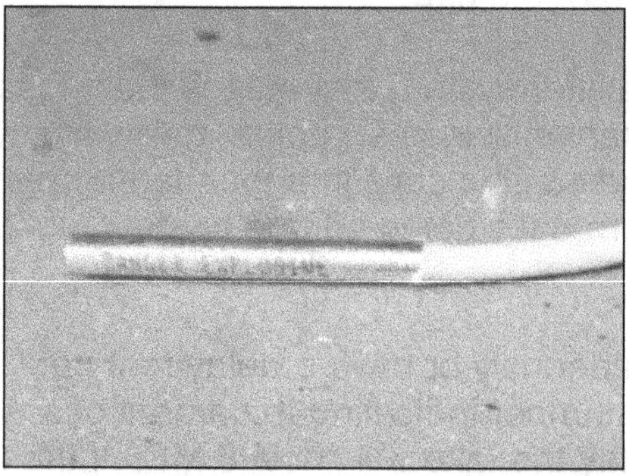

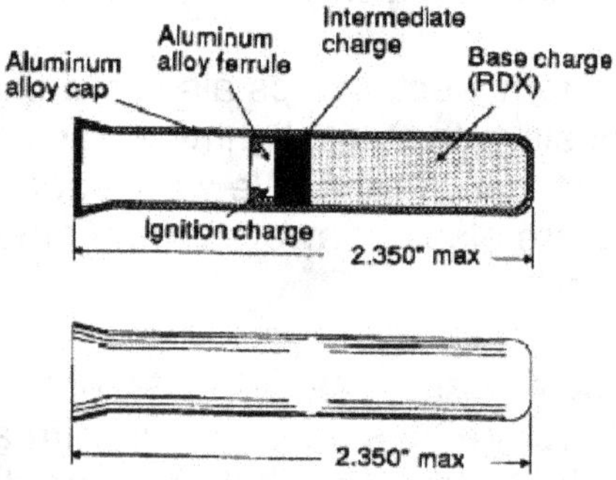

Number 10 pyro fuse cap crimped to safety fuse.

Nonel Blasting Caps

The Nonel cap system stands for "Non-Electric." The Nonel system is durable, reliable, and versatile, as it is used in most commercial blasting applications as well as by law enforcement agencies for door breaching and EOD work.

Nonel caps are initiated by a flash powder type pyrotechnic material that is HMX and Aluminum Powder in a 90% to 10% mix. One pound of this mixture is used per 70,000 feet of tubing provides only .1/100th of a grain per foot that provides a low energy shock wave that keeps the plastic tubing intact with a VOD of 2,000 meters per second.

Nonel caps come in three different styles:

Single or In-Hole delay

A single cap with a length of shock tubing. These can initiate instantly or be set to various millisecond delays used in rock and quarry blasting. These caps may have numbered tags on them that indicate their delay. For example; **0** is instant, **1** is 25 millisecond, **2** is 50 millisecond, **3** is 75 millisecond and so on.

These single caps can be initiated through a roll of shock tube, known as Lead Line or Truck Line, or their shock tube tail can be tied to a line of det cord.

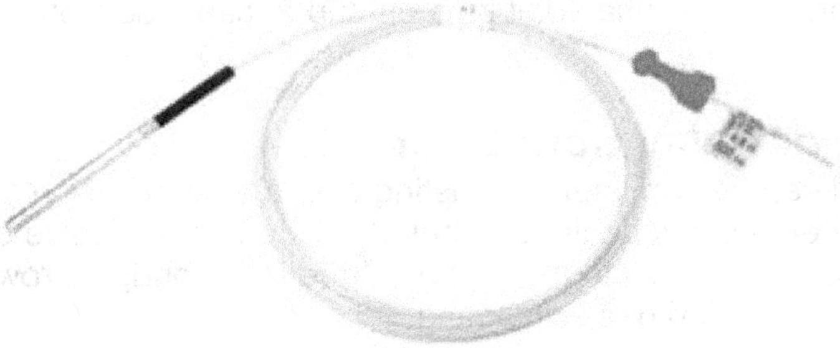

A Nonel In-Hole cap. The clip on the opposite end of the blasting cap is used to clip to a line of det cord. The tag indicates its timed delay.

Dual Delay

These Nonel caps have a blasting cap on each end of a length of shock tube. One cap is designed to cap into an explosive charge. The opposite end cap is mounted into a connector block that snaps into the next Nonel line the shot. This style is used to daisy chain up to hundreds of caps together for rock quarry blasting. These caps easily allow multiple charges to be connected in a durable and reliable way without complex wiring.

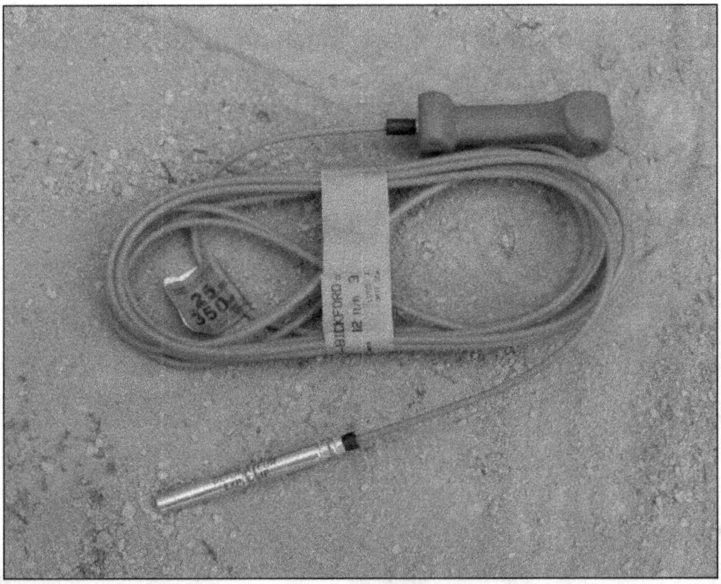

The Nonel Dual Delay cap has a connector block with an internal blasting cap on the opposite end of the primary blasting cap. This block connects the next cap in the sequence.

This dual delay cap system is an ideal way to easily hook up any multi-shot charge without complex wiring. A single blasting cap attached to the first cap in the sequence and initiate as many caps as needed. Once the first cap is initiated, it sets off cap 2, cap 2 sets off cap 3 and so on.

Surface or Relay Connector

This Nonel cap has an internal blasting cap in a connector block used to clip into other shock tube lines. They do not prime explosive charges, but are used to connect to other shock tube lines, bridging rows of shots together for rock and quarry blasting.

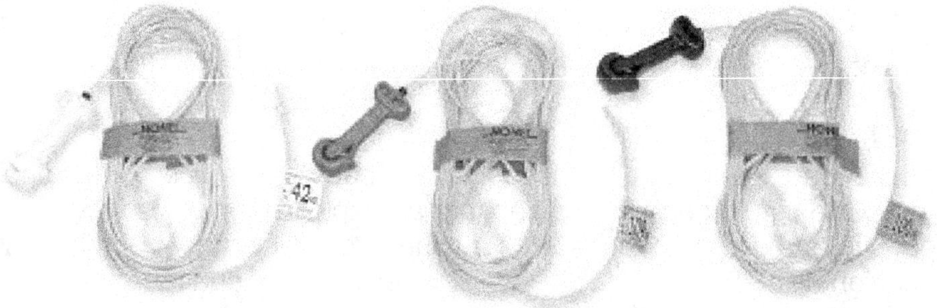

Surface or Relay Nonel caps used to connect rows of other Nonel caps.

Pyrotechnic or Burning Fuses

The first fuse is believed to be made in China in the 10th century. It was gunpowder rolled in paper and 1,000 years later, the technology has not changed much. The following are the modern variations of fuses:

Black Match

Used in fireworks, it is a cotton string coated with a dried slurry of black powder and glue.

Detaline Cord by *DuPont*

Detaline is a low energy detonation cord that only contains 1.4 grains of powder per foot. While a form of det cord, it is so insensitive a number 8 blasting cap may not ignite, nor can it be reliably tied into knots. *Detaline* is sold in kits that include a green arrow shaped plastic igniter with special millisecond delay connectors.

Flying fish or Bumblebees

A special fuse used in the manufacturing of fireworks. Similar to Visco, except it contains metallic spark effects causing the fuse to jump, sparkle and report.

Igniter Cord

A very consistent and dependable wire wrapped fuse. As the fuse burns, the burning metal wire wrap constantly preheats the next section of fuse to help ensure it remains lit, typically burning 12 seconds per foot.

Igniter Safety Fuse Electric (ISFE)

Used as an electric starter to ignite a burning fuse. Often used in large and complex firework displays.

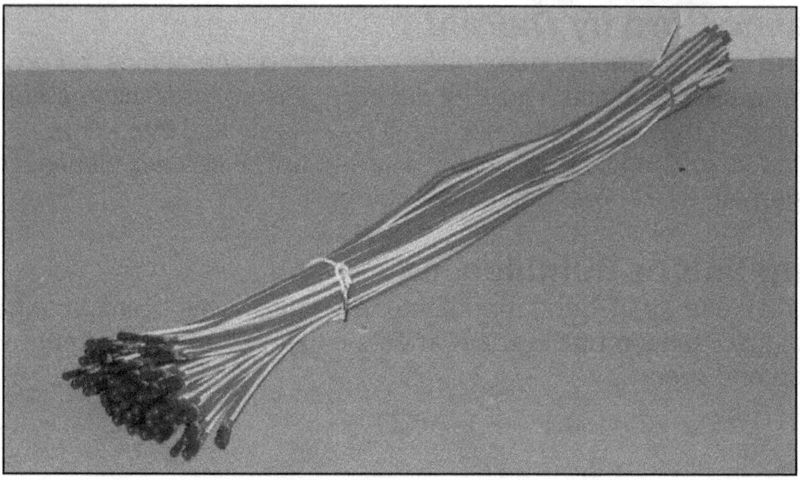

Igniter Safety Fuse Electric (ISFE)

Safety Fuse

A waterproof internally burning fuse used for commercial and military applications. It has a black powder core wrapped in tar and fabric or a plastic sheathing. When burning, is discolors or melts the exterior as the fuse burns inside out.

The fuse is designed to be waterproof, but the ends are hydroscopic, so they should be cut off to freshen up the fuse before use.

The diameter is under a quarter inch, and just the right size to slide into a non-electric fuse blasting cap. Safety fuse is rated based upon seconds per foot. The timing ranges from 40 to 60 seconds per foot. The rating will be in the specifications, but it is a good idea to cut off a yard or meter and time it for yourself.

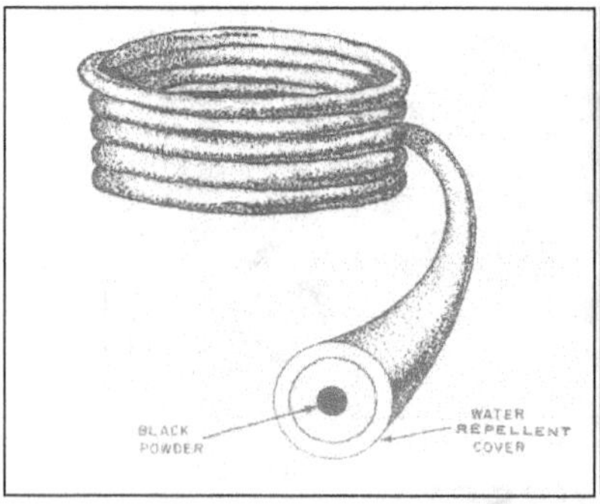

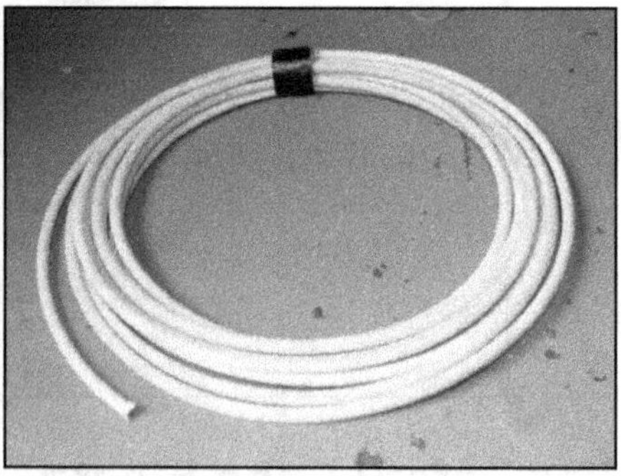

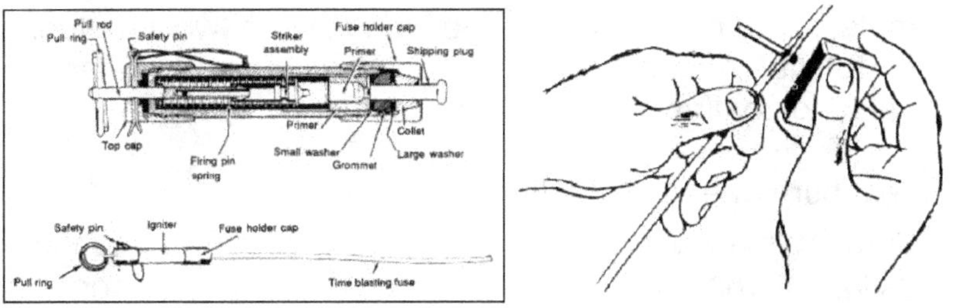

U.S. Army

Safety fuse is designed to ignite with a Pull Fuse Igniter. This diagram is of the U.S. Military's M-60 igniter, although civilian igniters are similar. The fuse will also ignite with a torch or a match is split down the middle to expose the black powder.

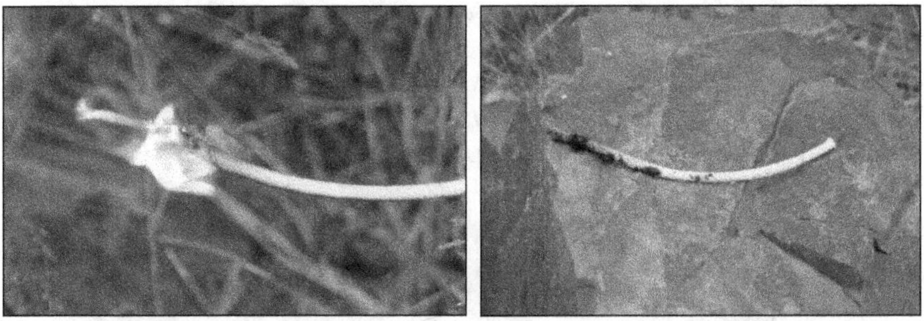

Safety fuse lit with a torch. The end flairs until it burns internally and discolors or melts the exterior cover.

Safety fuse can be lit with a torch if it is cut open to expose in the inner powder, but is designed to be used with a Pull Fuse Igniter. This is a disposable device that uses a primer cap with enough energy to start the fuse. U.S. Military's M-60 is reusable by reloading it with primer caps.

Safety or Time Fuse Timing

Most safety fuse is rated to burn about 40-50 seconds per foot. The trick to using safety fuse is to know the correct length to use. We recommend cutting 2-3 feet of fuse and testing it with a stopwatch. Next, determine the time you need to walk back to the safety zone. Now add 25 to 50% more time depending on the application. Ask yourself, if someone trips and injures themselves walking to the safe zone, do you have enough time on the burning fuse to help them to safety?

Determining the length of fuse needed is referred to as the ***Safe Separation Time, SST***. To determine the SST, estimate the time it takes to safely walk to a safe zone, then add 50% more time.

For example, it you can make it to the safe zone in two minutes, one more for a total of three minutes of fuse. Now to be exact, test burn one meter of fuse to confirm its burn time. Here is an example:

- Test burn one meter of time fuse = 2 mins
- Convert to seconds 120 seconds
- Divide by 100 centimeters 120 / 100 = 1.2 centimeters per second
- Safe separation time = 3 minutes which is 180 seconds
- Divide 180 seconds by 1.2 meters = 150 Centimeters
- 1.50 meters of safety fuse needed for a 3 Minute SST

Shock Tube

A 3 mm hollow plastic tubing filled with a HMX and Aluminum Powder that provides a low energy shock wave that keeps the plastic tubing intact with a VOD of 2,000 meters per second.

Slow Match

Provides a durable, slow burning glowing tip used to light other devices such as matchlock guns or cannons. Made from cotton or hemp rope saturated with an oxidizer such as potassium nitrate.

Quick Match or Piped Match

An extremely fast burning black powder fuse that can burn hundreds of feet per second. Used in professional fireworks displays to ignite multiple devices simultaneously.

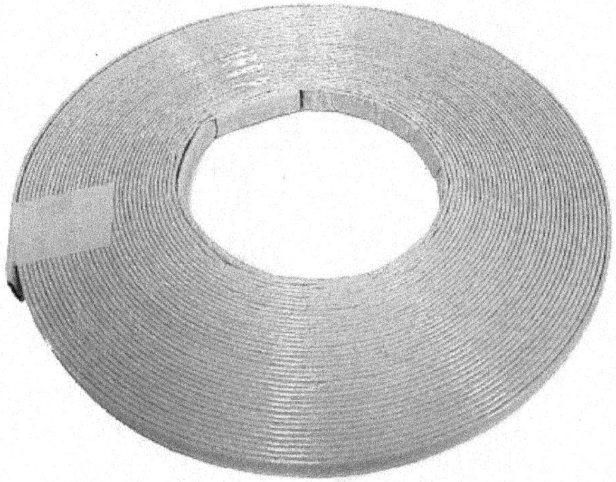

Quick Match or Piped Match fuse.

Visco Fuse or Cannon Fuse

A black powder core, paper wrapper-based fuse coated in wax or lacquer to increase water resistance and durability. They burn at a uniform rate with an easy-to-see external flame. Higher quality Visco fuses can burn underwater. The fuse is made with specific burn times, the most common is 36 seconds per foot.

Visco fuse burning. Burns hot and reliable, often used in pyrotechnics and fireworks.

10. PREPARING EXPLOSIVE CHARGES

Chapter Topics:

- Understand how to cap explosive charges with blasting caps and det cord.
- Understand various types of explosive trains.
- Learn the firing sequence of each train.
- How to set up multiple charge explosive trains.
- How to select the correct initiation system.

Now you have a better understanding of explosives and blasting caps, we are going to start off by learning how caps are applied to explosives charges. Then we will review the fire sequence of different explosive trains. Finally, we will cover how to rig multiple explosive charges with electric and Nonel systems. From the push of a button to the explosion at the end, here is a start to finish look on how it is done.

Capping Explosives

Blasting caps need to be properly attached into explosives so their energy will shoot through the explosive charge, ensuring a complete detonation. The following are correct methods of attaching blasting caps to commonly used explosives.

Cast Booster Sticks

RDX cast booster sticks, TNT blocks and other cast material explosives are made with cap wells already in them. RDX sticks have a hole through the stick and a second hole on one end that is the cap well. Run the blasting cap through the hole, then into the cap well.

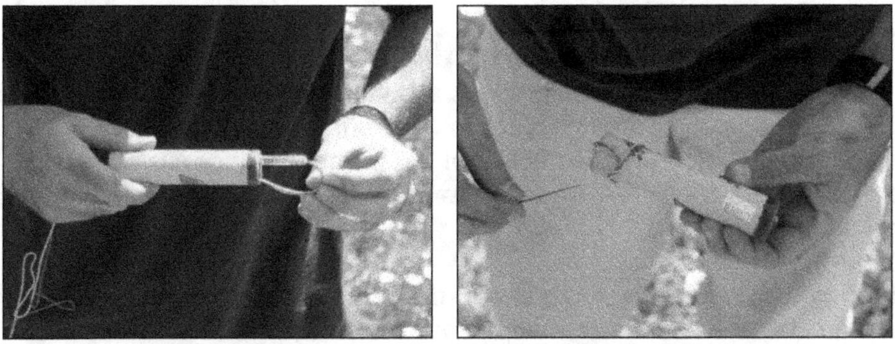

Electric blasting cap inserted through a RDX booster stick and into the cap well, then secured with a half-hitch knot.

Finish it off with a half hitch knot around the stick with the blasting cap wire. The combination of running the cap through the stick and tying it off makes for a very secure connection.

Det Cord

Because det cord is both a high explosive and a fuse, it is very versatile and powerful to prime explosive materials. Det cord is blasting cap sensitive. To prime det cord, tape a blasting cap into a loop with the cap pointing towards the charge.

To prime det cord, tape a blasting cap into a loop with the cap pointing toward the charge.

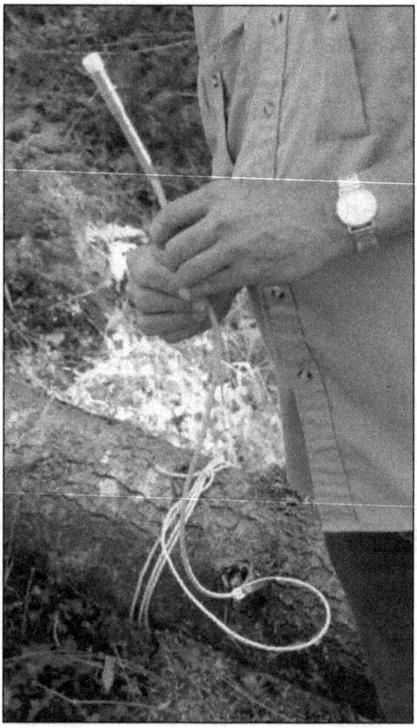

Dynamite and Emulsion Sticks

Dynamite and other emulsion sticks are initiated by a blasting cap or det cord. To prime dynamite with a cap, end punch the stick with a non-sparking probe, ideally the handle of M2 crimpers. Insert the cap and secure the electric wires, shock tube or safety fuse with a half hitch knot and secure with tape.

To prime with det cord, run a line of det cord up the stick, then wrap the cord around the stick with multiple loops overlaying the previous cord laid down. Run the cord through the final loop to tie tie off, then secure with tape. This method is called ***Whipping***.

Det cord is highly explosive, enough to prime other explosives without a blasting cap.

Note that the cap is taped into a loop of det cord facing toward the charge.

This form of priming sticks with multiple wraps is called Whipping

Plastics

C-4 and other plastics are initiated by a blasting cap or det cord. To cap plastic with a cap, slide the cap between layers or punch the block with a non-sparking probe, ideally the handle of M2 crimpers. Insert the cap and secure by pressing the material around the cap.

To cap with det cord, mold plastic material around enlarged knots of cord and secure by pressing the material into the knots and cord.

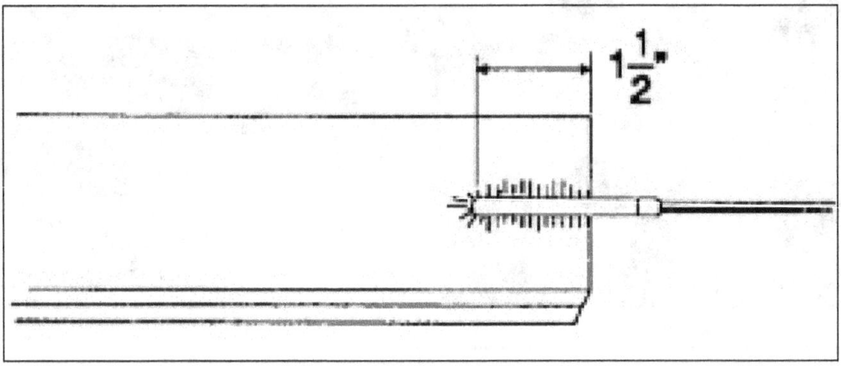

Capping a plastic explosive block with a blasting cap. U.S. Army

Det cord tied into a concentrated Uli knot that is ideal for priming C-4.

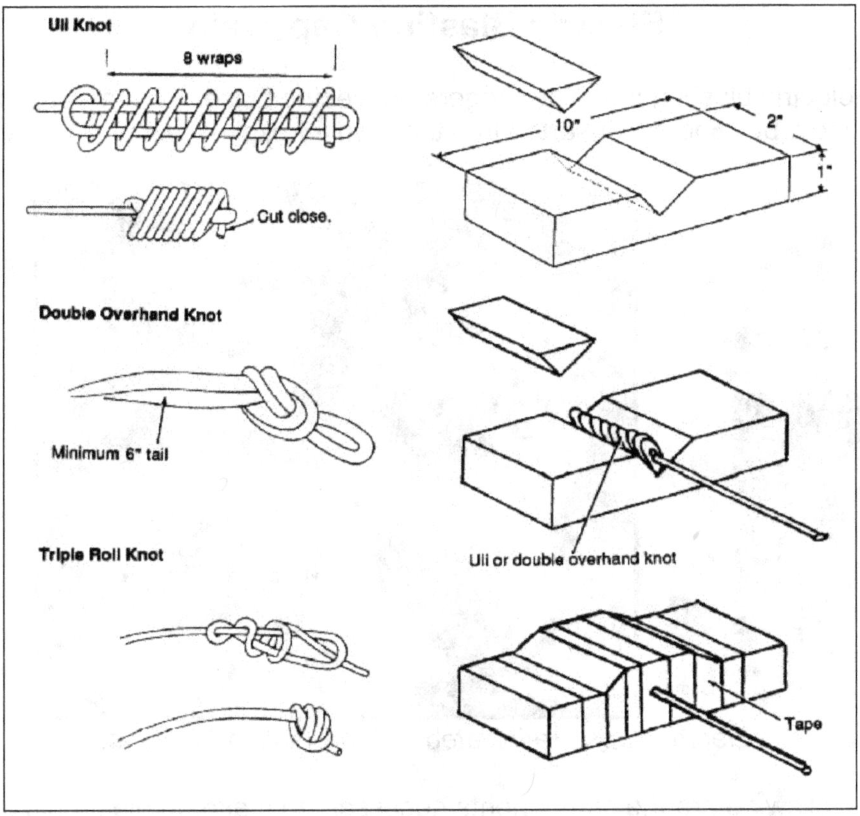

Capping plastic explosive blocks with det cord. U.S. Army

Explosive Trains

The steps or sequence to detonate a primary explosive charge is called an ***Explosive Train***. Trains consist of the following:

A way to initiate the system
Blasting Machine or Pull Fuse Igniter or Shock Tube Initiator.

A transfer method
Wires or Burning Fuse or Shock Tube.

Blasting Cap
Electric or Fuse or Nonel.

Primary Explosive Charge
ANFO and Booster or Sticks, or Det Cord or a Combination

The following are examples of three different explosive trains:

Electric Blasting Cap Train

An electric blasting machine triggers an electric pulse down a spool of wire to a blasting cap inserted into the primary explosive.

Electric caps are initiated with a Blasting Machine.

The following are the components necessary to make up electronic and pyrotechnic trains:

Electric Blasting Machine

An electronic generator that triggers a pulse of energy to initiate a blasting cap. Original styles generate energy with a plunger and magneto, while modern blasting machines use a 9-volt battery.

Electrical Wire

The blasting machine is connected to a spool of ***Lead wire*** that runs to the blasting cap. Most blasters use 14 to 16-gauge thick wire wound on reels for lengths up to 500 feet. 20-gauge wire can be used for shorter distances. ***Leg*** or ***Bus wire*** is an expendable wire, used in series or parallel circuits that connect the electric blasting caps.

Blasting wire can be solid or strand. A break in the solid wire can be very difficult to find. Strand works great, but the end wires often need to be cut and freshened up. We have attached alligator clips to the end of the main spool for quicker and neater connections to the blasting cap wires. Reels of wire can be easily checked for conductivity with a multi-meter.

Electric Blasting Firing Sequence

Electric blasting caps require a pulse of electricity to detonate. This type of electric train requires a blasting machine to deliver the electrical charge through the ***Firing Line*** spool of wire to the ***Leg Wire*** blasting cap wires. The following is the correct set of procedures to wire up the train safely:

1. Considering the location of the blast to determine the safest covered area to initiate the charge.

2. Run the wire from the explosive charge location to the blaster's firing position in the in the safe zone.

3. While spooling the wire, let it run between your thumb and fingers to inspect it for any kinks, loops or breaks.

4. Be sure that the blasting wire on the spool is long enough to initiate the charge from a safe distance and that each end of the bare wire leads is connected or shunted, (shorted out), to help insure there is not stray electricity in the line.

5. Shunt (short out), the ends of the blasting wire on the spool end. Connect a blasting cap to the blasting side of the line. Twist the bare wire ends together and secure the two wires together with a loose knot.

   Connecting the blasting cap first is a safety precaution so that in the unlikely event there is any electricity in the line, only the blasting cap goes off and not the explosive charge. Note the blasting machine is secured with the Blaster-in-Charge and does not get attached to the line until that last step.

6. Cover the bare wire ends twisted together with the plastic sleeve cover supplied with the basting cap, then secure all of the leads together by tying them in a loose knot.

7. Attach the blasting cap to the explosive charge.

8. Once clear of the blast zone, if necessary, for multiple shot charges, test the circuit with an approved blasting multi-meter or galvanometer.

9. Secure the blast zone which includes blocking off all access points and notifying local personnel and residents of the pending blast.

10. Once the blast zone is clear and charge is ready to fire, only then does the Blaster-in-Charge test and then attach the blasting machine to the firing wire.

11. Once the charge is fired, the Blaster-in-Charge immediately disconnects and secures the blasting machine and shunts the bare wire ends.

12. Remove the spent blasting cap wires and ensure each end of the spool's bare wire ends are shunted.

Step 3, 4, 10 and 11, shunt, short out, the bare wire ends of the blasting wire spool.

Step 4, connect wires and secure by tying in a loose knot.

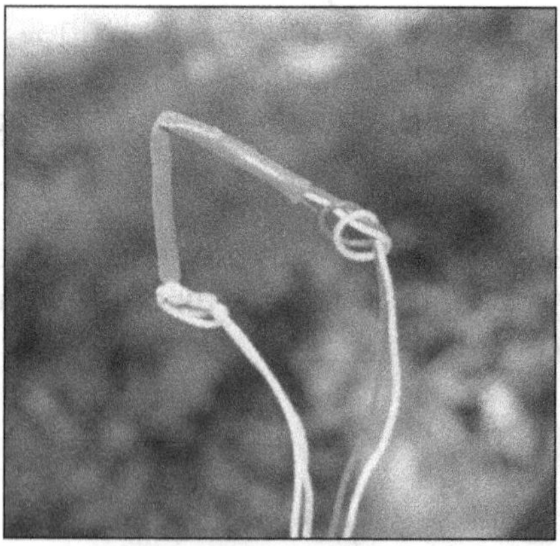

Step 5, Cover the bare wire ends twisted together with the the plastic sleeve, tie all four wires together in a lose knot.

Step 9, the Blaster-in-Charge connects the machine only when ready to detonate.

Advantages:

- Instant detonation with a simple push of a button.
- Blaster can control exact time of detonation.
- Electronic caps are reliable. No misfires yet.
- If there is a misfire, wires can be easily checked.

Disadvantages:

- Requires a blasting machine with good batteries.
- Requires a reel of wire.
- Wire or connections can break or short.
- Greater initial expense to purchase blasting machine and wire spool.
- If a misfire occurs, a 30-minute wait time should be completed before checking on the system.
- There are times when carrying a spool of wire is too heavy or not practical.
- There are shots so large, that you need to be physically farther away when what a spool of wire can provide.

Pyrotechnic Fuse Cap Train

A pull igniter starts a safety fuse that leads to a pyrotechnic fuse blasting cap that is inserted into the primary explosive.

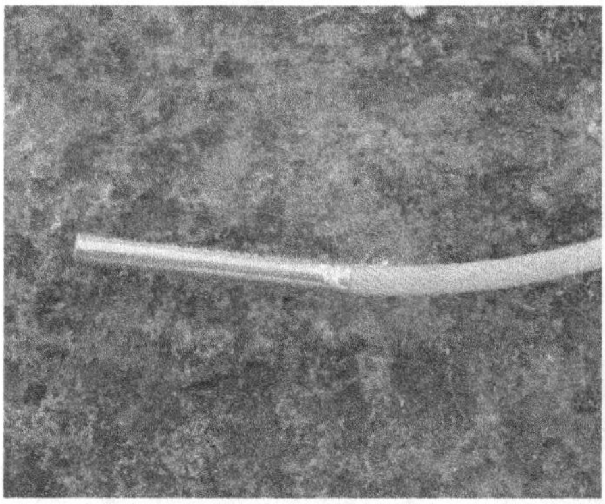

Safety fuse with a crimped pyro-fuse cap on one end and a pull fuse igniter on the other end.

Pyrotechnic Fuse Blasting Cap Firing Sequence

Pyrotechnic blasting caps require a burning fuse to detonate.

This type of pyrotechnic train requires a blasting cap to be properly attached to a fuse. The following is the correct set of procedures to attach a cap safely:

1. Determine the safest location for the Blaster-in-Charge to take cover from the charge.

2. Based on the location from the blast zone, determine how much time you will need to safely get there without running (walk with a purpose).

3. Based upon the fuse's burn time per foot or meter, cut a length of fuse that will give you adequate time plus a little extra. Due to possible damage from exposure to moisture, do not use the first or last six inches of fuse.

4. If you are not sure of the fuse's burn time, measure and light a three-foot section of the fuse to time it.

5. Attach the blasting cap to a fresh and squarely cut end of fuse. Do so by holding the fuse up and sliding it into the cap firmly. If the fuse does not touch the cap's internal charge, it could result in a misfire.

6. Place only approved crimpers on the cap, setting the jaws 1/8" to no more than ¼" from the open fuse end. Place the crimpers on the cap while maintaining pressure of the fuse pressing firming into the cap.

7. Continue to crimp the cap while pointing the end of the cap in a safe direction down range.

8. Inspect the crimp on the cap to ensure the fuse is secured tightly.

9. Attach the pull igniter to the safety fuse. Do so by taking a fresh and squarely cut end of fuse and sliding into the igniter's opening. The inside of the igniter is barbed, so once the fuse is in, it will not pull out. Do not remove the safety pin until ready to ignite.

10. Cap the explosive charge.

11. Secure the blast zone which includes blocking off all access points and notifying local personnel and residents of the pending blast.

12. When ready to detonate the charge, hold the fuse igniter with one hand and remove the safety pin with the other. Give the end of the igniter a good hard pull. The fuse should start to smoke and discolor to verify it has been lit.

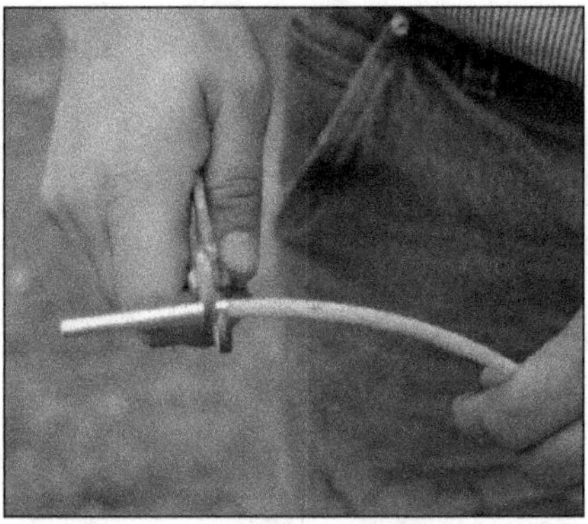

Step 6, set crimpers on the cap, then complete the crimp behind your back.

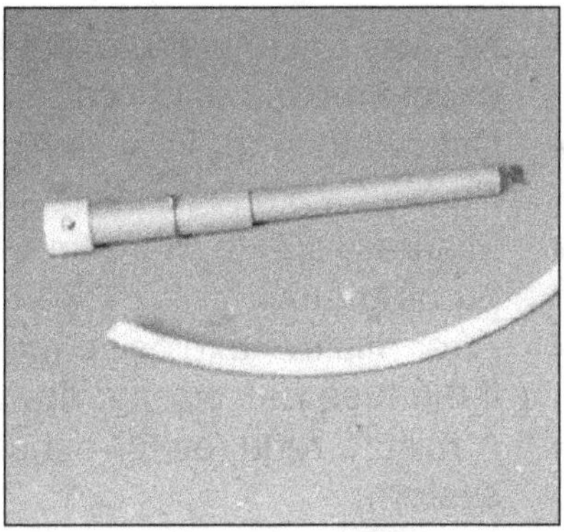

Step 10, attach the pull igniter by pushing a freshly cut end of the safety fuse into its barbed opening.

Failing to crimp the cap onto a pyrotechnic fuse properly can result in serious injury. Just the edge of the fuse end of the cap should be crimped onto the pyrotechnic fuse. Only use special non-ferrous, non-sparking metal crimping pliers.

The crimper seals the cap on the safety fuse in a ring to help make the connection water resistant. Crimping the cap too close to the explosive material inside could result in detonation. Never crimp a cap with your teeth or anywhere near your face!

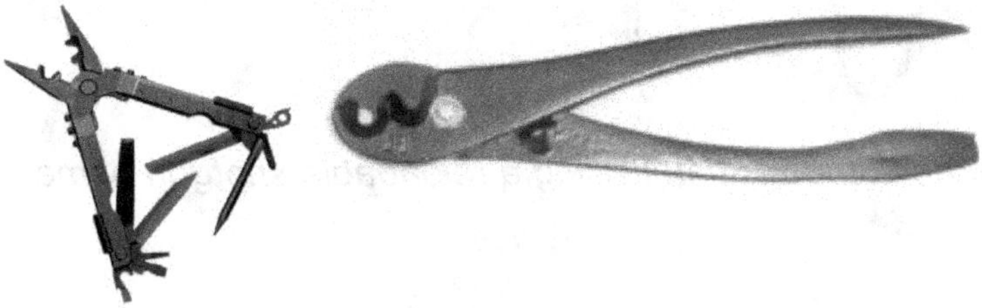

Pyrotechnic blasting caps should be crimped with special non-sparking pliers. Note both types of tools include fuse cutters and a punch to insert caps into soft explosives like dynamite or C-4. Gerber multi-tool (left), military M2 style (right).

Advantages:

- Simple and reliable.
- Ideal for working underground.
- Ideal for large charges when you need to be further away.
- No batteries, electronics, wires, or wire connections to fail.
- Inexpensive to use.

Disadvantages:

- No way to know the exact time of detonation, so best used when exact time is not critical.
- Difficult to stop once ignited and burning.
- Safety fuse can be difficult to tell if it is burning.
- Misfires require more time to clear due to unknown status of burning fuse.
- After misfire, explosive materials can be more difficult to recover if the fuse has burned down into blasting hole.
- A misfire requires 60-minute wait time before approaching system.

Nonel Blasting Cap Train

Nonel caps can be initiated with a shock tube Initiator using a shotgun primer or the shock tube can be tied to a det cord truck line. We will cover the truck line system later in this chapter for multiple charges. At this point we will focus on shooting a single cap.

A Nonel shock tube initiator using a reloadable shotgun primer.

This initiator is a primer cap "Mushroom stopper"

This blasting machine uses a 9v battery

Nonel Blasting Cap Firing Sequence

1. Determine the safest location for the Blaster-in-Charge to take cover from the charge.

2. Based on the location from the blast zone, spool out as much shock tube as necessary to get the BIC to the safety zone.

3. Attach to a Nonel blasting cap to the spool of shock tube using a shock tube connector tube.

4. Cap the explosive charge.

5. Secure the blast zone which includes blocking off all access points and notifying local personnel and residents of the pending blast.

6. When ready to detonate the charge, attach the shock tube initiator device and remove the safety pin or feature to shoot the charge.

Advantages

- Blaster can control the exact time of detonation.
- No need to carry a heavy spool of wire.
- After blast, shock tube can be left behind (tactical ops).
- Caps are not affected by two-way radio signals or static electricity.

Disadvantages

- Single Nonel initiator using 209 primer caps are slow to reload.
- Shock tube requires splicing together with tube connectors.
- It can be difficult to tell if shock tube is spent or not.
- After blast, hundreds to thousands of feet of spent shock tube to dispose of.

Multi Explosive Charge Trains

Blasting applications requiring multiple charges can be set up in a number of different ways. Here are examples for electric, non-electric and pyrotechnic trains.

Electric

Electric multi-charge systems can be wired in one of four formats; ***Common Series Circuit, Parallel Circuit, Leapfrog Series Circuit*** and ***Series Parallel Circuit***. The series circuit is the most common and simple to use. It is a single loop or path for current to flow through where the leg wires of blasting caps are connected end to end.

A wire from the first cap and from the last cap in the series is connected to the firing line wire leading to the blasting machine. Parallel and series-parallel circuits are much more complex and are not recommended due to a high probability of misfire as the initial blast can pull the wires from the following ordnance wired in the line.

A ***Galvanometer*** is a special explosives multi-meter is used to check the circuit first to ensure there are no shorts or breaks in the wiring system or blasting caps. The meter uses limiting resisters and a very low voltage, silver chloride battery that will not detonate blasting caps.

To test for a short circuit using a galvanometer, leaving the end firing wires open and touch one end to the terminal on the galvanometer. If there is no short, the pointer will remain stationary, if there is a short the pointer will move across the dial. When testing for a broken wire in the firing system, connect the two end firing wires together and touch the terminal on the galvanometer. If the pointer moves across the dial the circuit is good, if the pointer fails to move there is a break in the system.

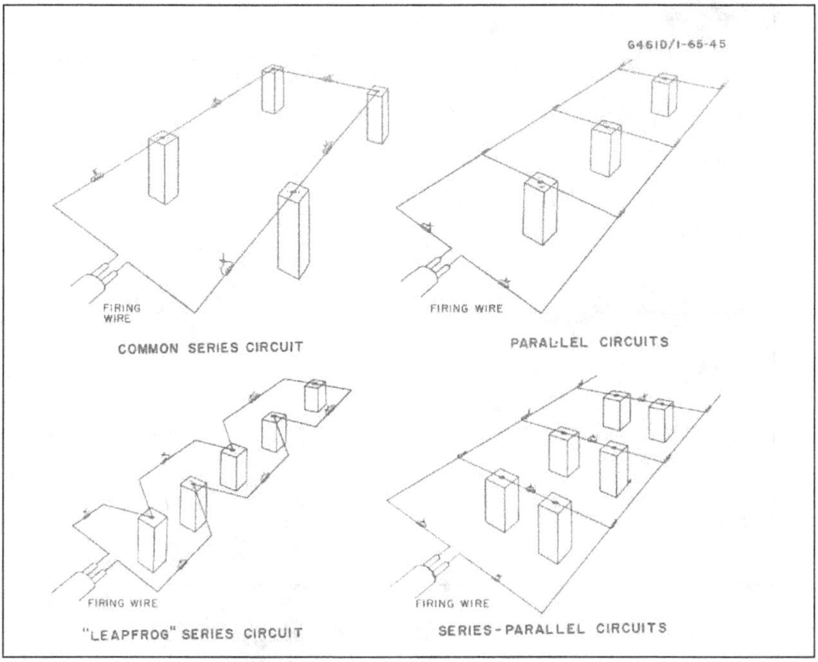

U.S. Air Force

Four methods electronic multi charge systems can be wired.

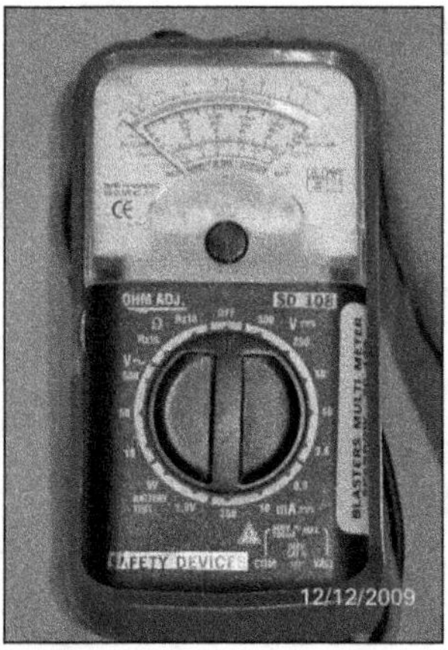

Use a galvanometer, a special blaster's multi-meter for testing firing circuits for shorts or breaks.

The galvanometer provides only enough amperage to test the circuit, but not enough to accidentally fire the blasting cap.

It should be noted that clip together Nonel caps have replaced the need for complex wiring and have made these multi-cap electric circuits obsolete. Clipping together Nonel caps allows the blaster to shoot as many charges as needed in a much more reliable system.

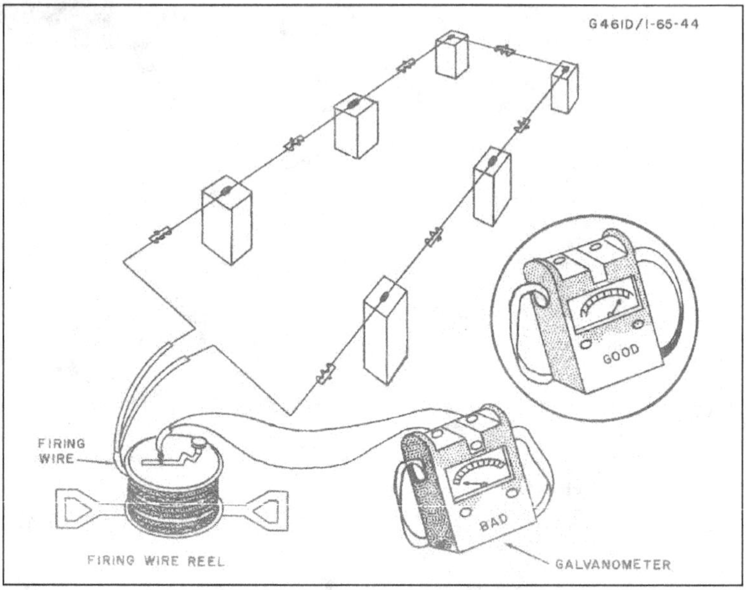

U.S. Air Force

A galvanometer is a low voltage meter to test the electronic firing circuit.

Ohm's Law

Most blasting caps are designed to detonate with a minimum firing circuit of 0.25 amps. When using a blasting Multi-Meter, it is helpful to understand Ohm's Law:

$$I = \frac{V}{R}$$

V = Voltage express in volts
I = Current expressed in amperes
R = Resistance expressed in ohms

For example, if a blasting circuit has 120 volts and resistance of 24 ohms, the current will be 5 amps. 120 ÷ 24 = 5

$$I = \frac{V}{R} = \frac{120 \text{ volts}}{24 \text{ ohms}} = 5 \text{ amperes}$$

Nonel

The Nonel "Non-Electric" cap system was designed to be a reliable, durable, and easy way to connect hundreds of caps together in a sequence used in rock and quarry blasting.

The **Single or In-Hole delay** caps can be initiated individually or clipped on a line of det cord to set off as many as needed.

Det cord trunk line with Nonel branch lines

The **Dual Delay** caps have a blasting cap on each end of a length of shock tube. The initial cap is designed to prime into an explosive charge. The opposite end cap is mounted into a connector block that snaps into the next Nonel line the shot. This style is used to daisy chain up to hundreds of caps together for rock quarry blasting. These caps easily allow multiple charges to be connected in a durable and reliable way without complex wiring.

Shot number one is initiated through a single blasting cap attached to the first cap in the sequence. Once the first cap is initiated, it sets off cap 2, cap 2 sets off cap 3 and so on.

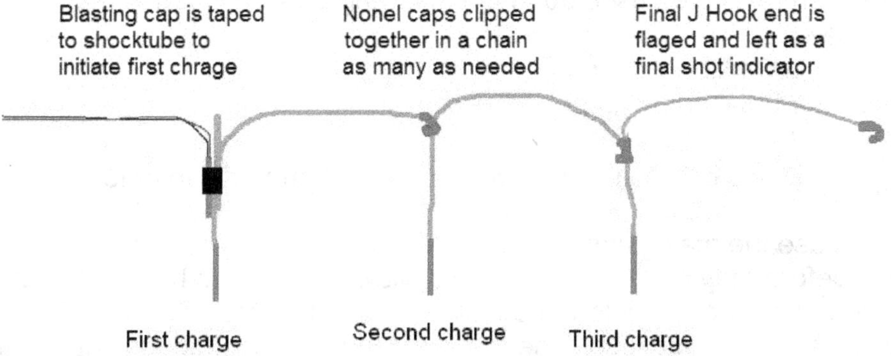

Nonel Dual Delay blasting cap sequence.

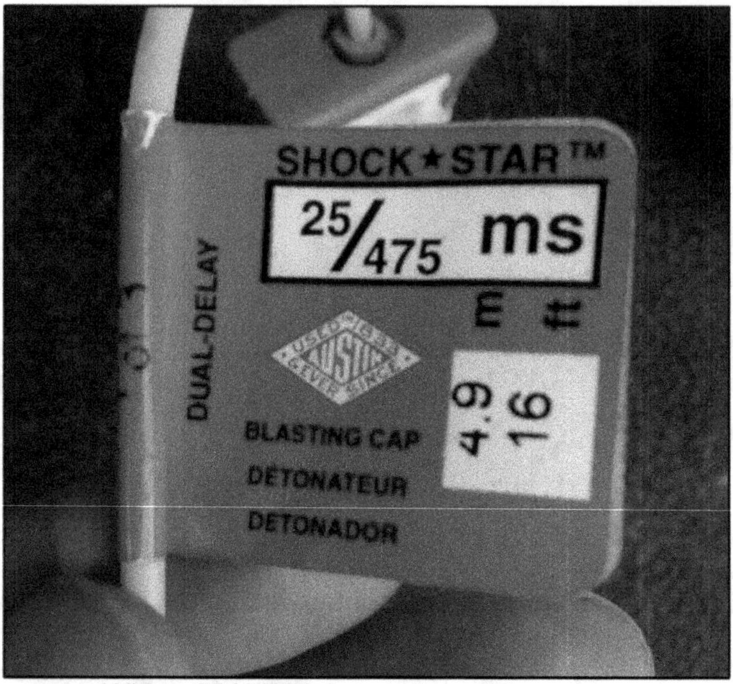

With a 25/475 delay system, 19 caps are initiated before the first detonation.

Dual Delay Nonel caps have a unique delay system in place that helps prevent the lines from being cut off from current blasts. Each cap has a separate delay allowing many caps to be burning in the ground before the firsts charge explodes.

Here is an example based upon the following delay sequence tag, 25/475 MS.

- 1,000 MS = 1 second
- 25/475 Combination
- 475 ÷ 25=19
- 19 caps can be initiated before the first ground cap detonates

In this case the main caps have a 25 MS delay, but there is a 475 MS delay before they are detonated. This allows 19 caps to be initiated and burning underground before the first charge detonates. This helps prevent a misfire because if the first blast throws rock or debris and cuts the shock tube on the surface, it will not matter because the first 19 caps in the sequence are already burning and ready to explode.

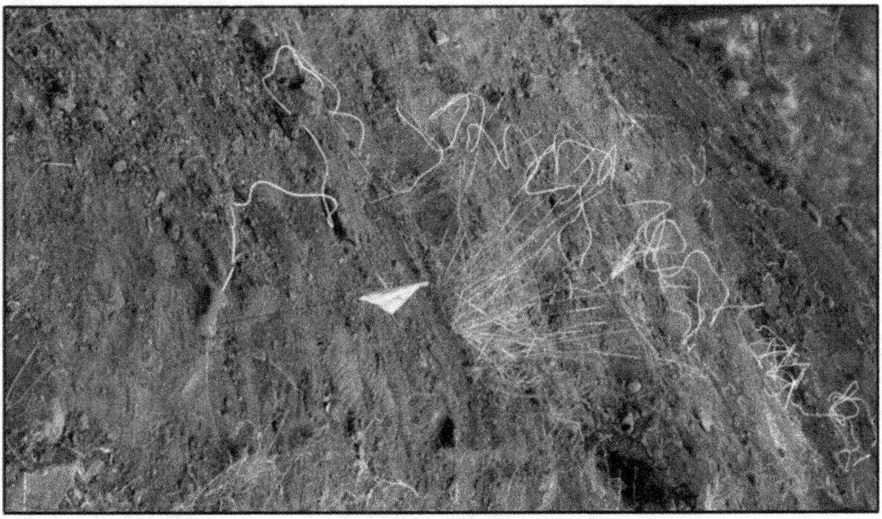

Row of Nonel capped shots ready to go complete with last connection block flagged to help confirm that the entire sequence has fired.

After the shot, the shock tube is a tangled mess. The Blaster in Charge must carefully examine through the debris to find all the blown connector blocks. As a public safety officer, you may be called to investigate "explosive tubes coming out of the ground."

After a shot, all the connector blocks should be blown open. If not, it is an indication of a cuff off and live materials did not explode.

Despite the unique dual delay system, Nonel caps can still misfire. In fact, from our experience, they do all the time. They can still be a cut off or possibly a defective cap. After blasting long enough, you will find unfired connector blocks and shock tube coming out of the ground where buried ordnance has not detonated. If you find shock tube and not sure if it has been spent, cut off the section and blow through it into the palm of your hand. If the shock tube has not been fired, a puff of gray powder will come out.

Live Nonel cap charges can be shot again by attaching a new blasting cap to the protruding shock tube to blast it again. This will typically solve the problem. While the Nonel system is not perfect, it works well and is far more reliable than using multiple electric caps.

Det Cord

Det cord is ideal for connecting and priming multiple charges that will all detonate instantly. Det cord is sold by ***Grains per Inch***. The smallest typically being 25 grains per inch meaning a half a foot is equal to a blasting cap. Stick power should receive a few wraps. Uli knots can be tied in for an extra concentration of powder to be folded into C-4.

Multiple charges can be primed with a line of det cord, then if possible, connect the two free ends for redundancy. Creating this loop allows the charges to be initiated from each direction. Attach a blasting cap into the line pointing the end of the cap down the det cord line pointing to the closest charge.

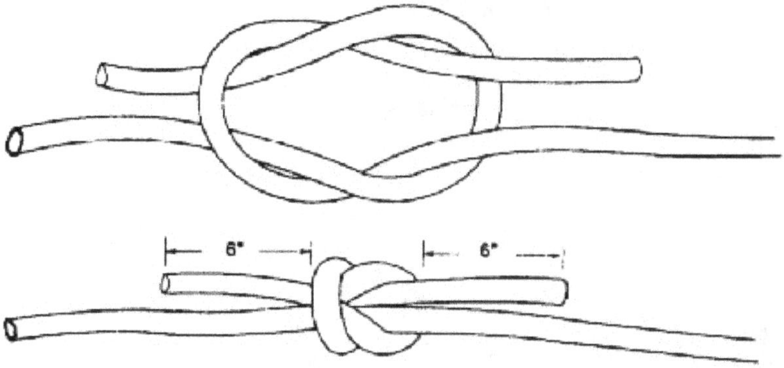

Connecting Det Cord with a square knot U.S. Army

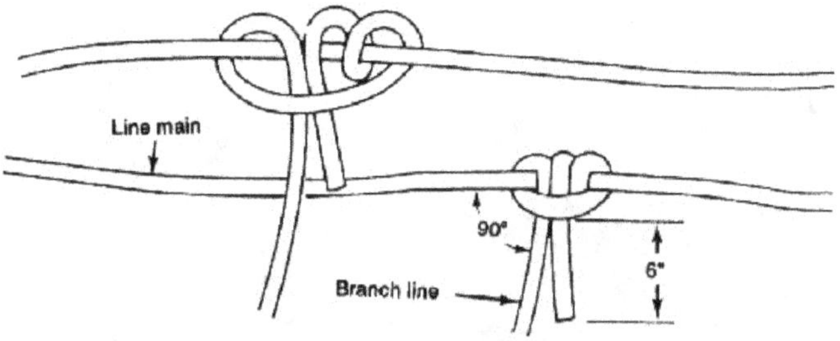

Connecting Det Cord with a girth hitch knot U.S. Army

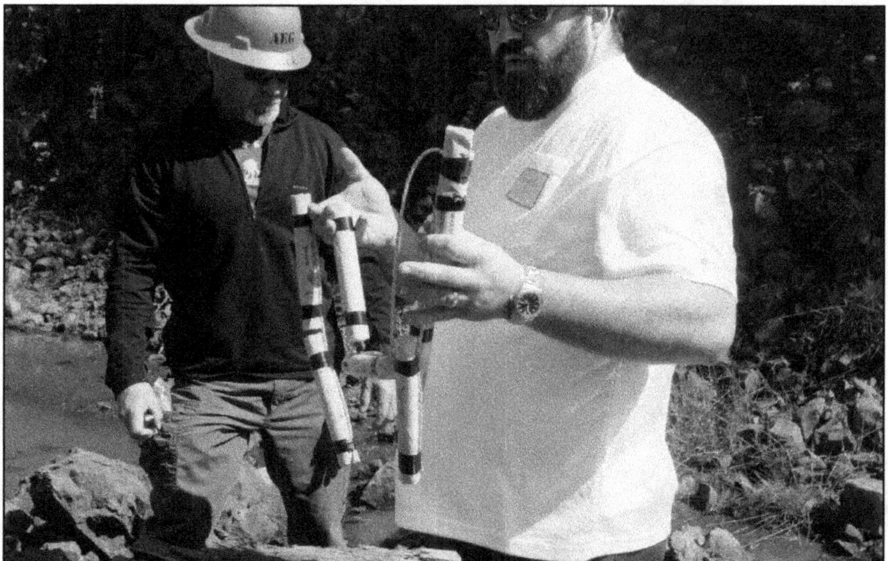

Kasse makes a Hasty Charge out of det cord and dynamite to be used to for cutting a fallen log in half.

11. SPECIAL BLASTING TECHNIQUES

Chapter Topics:

- Understand how explosives energy flows and how it can be directed.
- Learn how shape charges are made and used.
- Understand how tamping increases efficiency.

The raw power of explosives is nothing short of awesome. Not only can you see it, but you can feel is through your body, and as said by a colleague, it is a life changing experience to be anywhere near a charge detonating. But there is a big difference between the crash of lightning across the sky and harnessing that power to provide electricity. Think of explosives the same way.

Explosives like electricity or water, follows the path of least resistance. Even a large explosive charge on the surface will shake the ground and throw a large plume of smoke into the air, but without direction, its energy is just shot into the sky. Explosives are a tool, used for good and bad, but to be efficient, the amazing energy must be directed.

Controlling Explosive Energy

If explosives energy follows the path of least resistance, how then is the power directed? In the following examples, see how a pound of explosive materials reacts to various conditions. The results are substantially different as follows:

Example A: Materials on the boulder only slightly crack the top.

Example B: The Shaped Charge breaks the rock into pieces.

Example C. The tamped Shaped Charge pulverizes the rock to gravel.

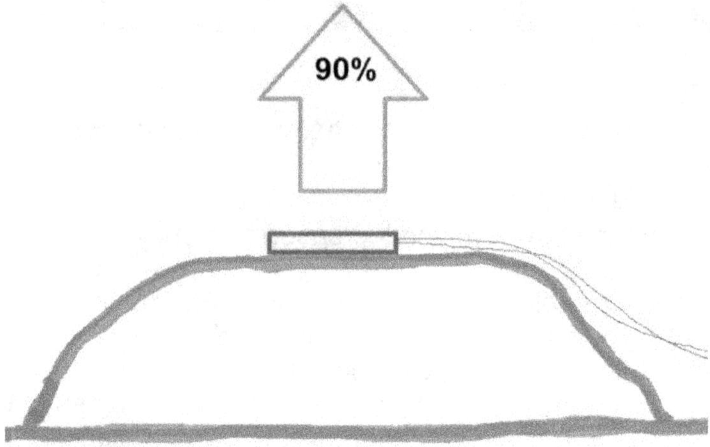

A) With the charge placed upon a rock, it is estimated that approximately 90% of the explosive energy blows into the air.

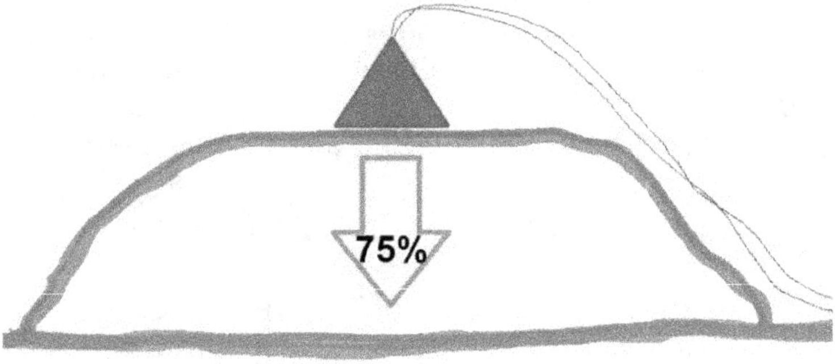

B) The same amount of material and forming it into a coned shaped charge directed approximately 75% down into the rock.

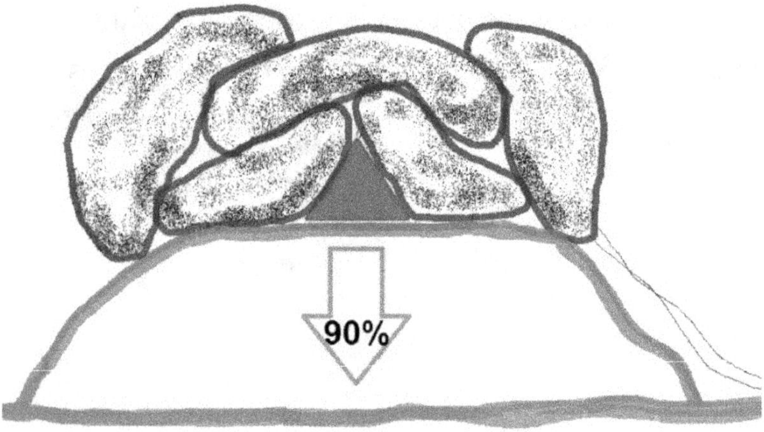

C) Now taking the same shaped charge and covering it with sandbags increases the efficiency further by an estimated 15%.

Shaped Charges

Simply shaping the explosive material into a cone, (and inverted 'V') multiplies the explosive power as it focuses the energy downward while covering more surface area. This shape directs the blast down which provides a very powerful cutting and penetrating jet blast force. This extra focus of explosive power is ideal for fragmenting boulders or cutting structures and steel for demolition.

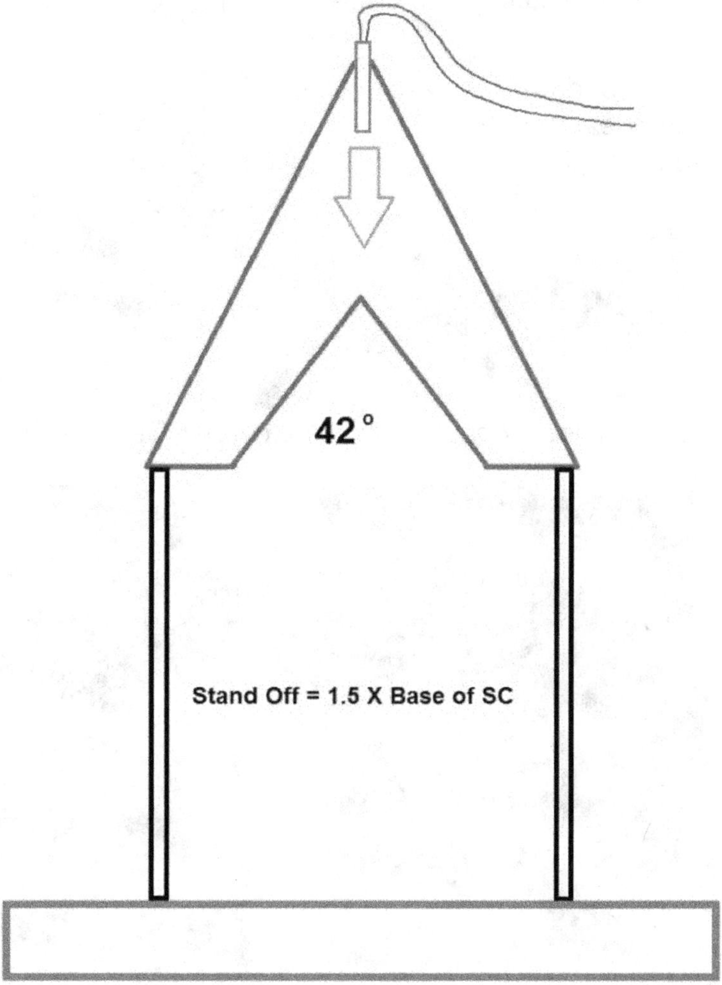

The shape charges 'cone' multiplies the force of the explosive material as it directs the energy of the blast downward. Note the blasting cap initiates the explosive energy and is placed pointing down, top dead center.

Shaped charges can be a ***Single Cone*** or elongated to a ***Linear Shaped Charge***. Linear shaped charges, (LSC) are cone-shaped charges in varying lengths. The top of the cone is contained by a metal cover to encase and confine the explosive material.

Shaped charges are made from the highest velocity explosives such as RDX, C-4, HMX or PETN that have a velocity over 7,000 to 8,000 MPS. When the explosive material is detonated, the cone is compressed into a jet blasting downward at a velocity of 7 to 14 kilometers per second providing substantial cutting and breaking power.

Linear shaped charges are ideal for breaching and cutting steel plate.

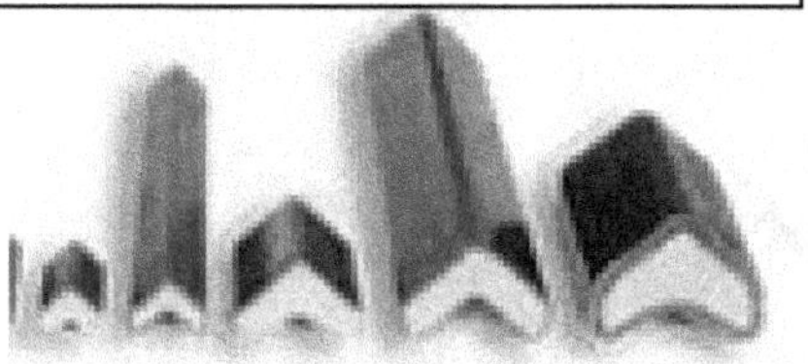

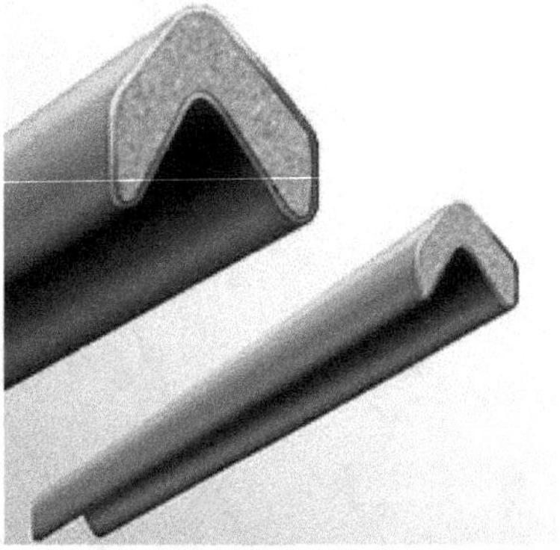

Pre-made linear shape charges are copper filled with RDX.

Austin Power Co.'s Rock Crusher is a simple paper cone filled with RDX but it's boulder shattering power is amazing.

Shape charges can be purchased or made. Commercial shape charges such as *Austin Powder's Rock Crushers* are made from a paper cone filled with RDX with a det cord fuse. A lower cost option is to use sticks of slurry, dynamite or plastic explosives pressed into a plastic funnel. The funnel's spout makes a perfect blasting cap well. Material can also be pressed around the outside of a funnel, or bottle.

Having an internal center cone of approximately 42° further increases the effectiveness of the charge. Shaped charges with this modification are a ***Cavity Shaped Charge***. Standing off the charge from the target allows room for the jet to form. The formula for determining the correct standoff is 1.5 times the width of the cone. This distance allows for a laser point to form for its greatest penetration potential.

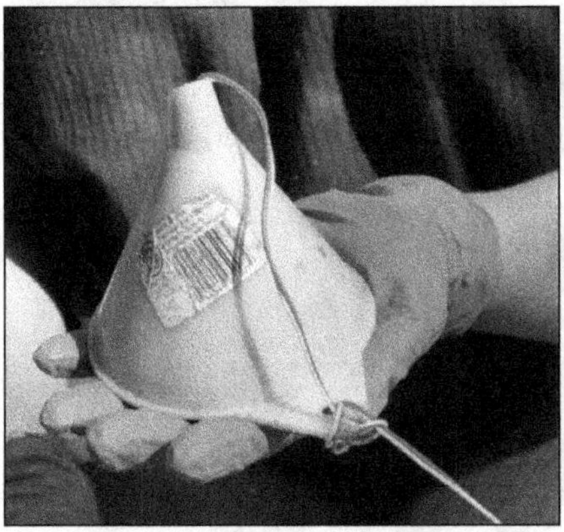

A shape charge is made with a plastic funnel and unwrapped sticks of dynamite. The funnel's spout makes an ideal basting cap well.

While dynamite funnel-shaped charges work great on boulders, dynamite does not have the velocity to cut steel very well. As an example, a one-pound dynamite at 60% nitroglycerin barely placed a dent in a ¼ inch plate of steel. Compare this with a 1.5 pound shaped charge of C-4 that cut through a ¾ inch steel plate with laser precision.

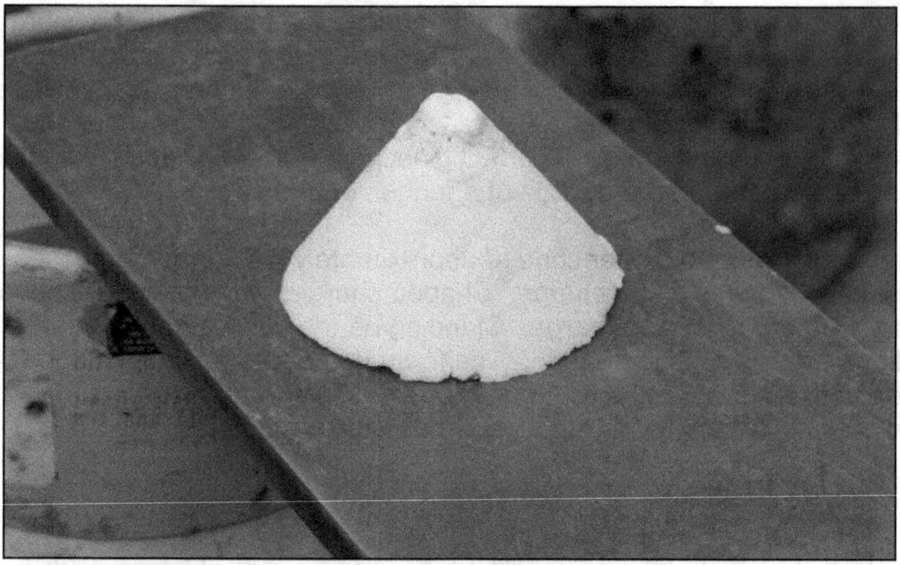

1.5 pounds of C-4 shaped with a funnel on ¾" steel plate.

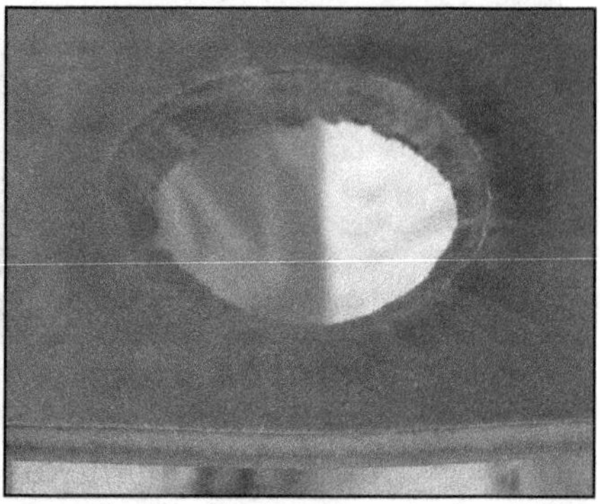

Dynamite vs. C-4 for cutting steel is no contest. C-4 can cut steel like a torch while dynamite's lower velocity places a dent.

One pound of C-4 formed into a linear-shaped charge ripped through a ¼ inch steel plate 18 inches long. Half the amount would have been more than enough.

Tamping Explosive Charges

When using explosives, its critical to understand that explosives follow the path of least resistance. Explosive charges uncovered or without tamping, simply blast their energy into the air. The idea is to direct the blast energy into the target. Shaped charges do just that, but there are other measures that assist with this process.

Commercial blasters tamp and stem their charges meaning they backfill their boreholes with dirt or pack mud and dirt on top or next to charges to help increase the efficiency. One of the easiest ways to do this is to use sandbags to stack on top of, or next to charges.

Water also makes an excellent tamping material because it does not expand. That is why water filled containers are used as **Water Impulse Charges** for breaching or demolitions.

US Military manual image showing the use of sandbags to tamp or direct the energy of explosive charges.

12. SAFETY AND SECURITY

Chapter Topics:

- Understand the roll and responsibilities of the Blaster-in-Charge.
- Learn to prevent accidents and reduce liabilities.
- Understand how to secure explosive materials and operations.

The explosives business can be dangerous, but it beats the slow death of spending your career in a boring profession or stuck in an office cubicle. Statistically, it is not the most dangerous job, but injuries from explosives are more likely to be very serious or fatal compared to other industrial accidents.

The security of our explosive materials is also crucial. When we accept this career, we assume a great deal of responsibility to not allow explosives to fall into the wrong hands, whether it be children, criminals or terrorists. Understanding explosive safety and security may not only prevent you and others from serious injury, it will also help ensure your success in the blasting profession on a long term basis.

Blasting Safety

When it comes to safety, prevention is everything. The best way to prevent an accident is being organized and to use and follow a blasting plan. The following are procedures to organize a blasting operation:

Blaster-in-Charge (BIC)

The senior blast manager with the experience necessary to take responsibility for a blast operation is the Blaster-in-Charge. The BIC makes the final decisions on:

- Blast and security zone location and size.
- When to detonate each blast.
- How to deal with a misfire.
- When the blasting zone is all clear.
- Keeping a journal to record each blast known as a ***Shot Report***.

Blast Emergency Plan

The Blaster-in-Charge coordinates with the blasting crew to develop a tangible plan based upon the circumstances and the environment. The blast emergency plan can be subject to change based on blast conditions and includes the following:

- Identify location of first-aid kits and identify first-aid providers
- A plan for emergency medical evacuation
- Emergency response telephone numbers

Blasting Signals

Industry standard signals have been developed to effectively notify the blast crew of the status of the blasting operation. While these signals would not be practical for tactical operations, they do add an important measure of safety for testing for range work.

• One long whistle	Three minutes to blast
• Two short whistles	One minute to blast
• Three long whistles	Blast zone all clear

A marine air horn works great, as they are very loud and inexpensive to pick up at any sporting goods store.

For tactical operations, it is important that all officers to agree of what the signals are for being ready and knowing when the charge will be fired. What we have seen is a countdown that can be done with fingers in silence if sound is an issue: ***Five, Four, Three, Two, One –Fire in the Hole!*** (Firing device triggered).

Blast Area Security

One of the best ways to reduce the potential accidents or liability is to secure the blast area.

- Blaster-in-Charge determines the size of the blast area.
- Secure the blast area with guards, signs, any means necessary.
- No extra non-essential personnel or visitors.
- Secure extra explosive materials from blast zone.
- When the area is confirmed clear, the blaster in charge connects the initiator or blasting machine for the shot.
- The Blaster-in-Charge provides an audible warning by voice, bull horn or whistle. Usually a Five to One countdown and “Fire in the hole.”
- Blasting personnel should face the blast to watch for flying debris.

- Immediately following the blast, the Blaster-in-Charge disconnects and secures the initiator or blasting machine.
- After the blast, the Blaster-in-Charge examines the area for possible hazards and unexploded materials before giving the 'All Clear."

Risk Management

While planning any shot, you must consider over-pressure and the possibility of flying debris to help determine the possible worst-case scenario. Consider how someone could become hurt or what property could be damaged? Explosives are unforgiving and if a blast team breaks safety protocol and leaves the door open for an accident, sooner or later it will happen. Think about what could happen, and then take whatever steps necessary to help ensure that it does not.

Blast Mats, Screens and Damage Prevention

Commercial blasters must concern themselves with flyrock, the debris that flies further than what the blasters expected. Almost every blast has some type of flying debris. There is no harm in using extra caution and this should be considered when blasting for training, EOD, or field work. Barriers and mats can prevent flyrock damage and reduce noise, dust, and air blast. Barriers can be anything, tarps, plywood, anything to get between the blast and what you want to protect.

After years of blasting, we think the main thing is to make sure everyone is on the same page, they know what and when the blasting is going to happen and keep extra people, vehicles or anything else that could be damaged or injured out of the way.

Explosives Security

Theft or Loss of Explosive Materials

If there is any loss or theft of explosive materials, the ATF wants to know immediately. They also request that the State Police are also notified. The ATF form 5400.5, "Report of Theft or Loss – Explosive Materials." Form 5400.

U.S. Bomb Data Center
Bureau of Alcohol, Tobacco, Firearms and Explosives
99 New York Avenue, NE, Washington, DC 20226
Telephone: 800-461-8841 (Monday-Friday 8:00 AM– 5:00 PM Eastern Time) or 800 461-8841 or 888-283-2662 (after hours and weekends).
www.atf.gov

Securing Explosive Materials

We need to understand the fact that criminals and terrorists would love to have our explosives. Just because they belong to a law enforcement or public safety agency, does not mean they cannot get stolen.

Agencies get gear stolen all the time and we know of at least one federal agency that had hundreds of pounds of materials taken. You must watch over explosive materials like you would your own service weapons.

Security Measure Checklist

- Be aware of out-of-place or repeat sightings of vehicles or individuals, especially individuals or vehicles at gates, perimeter or access roads.
- Be aware of unauthorized individuals in or around secured areas.
- Be aware of vehicles that carry explosives being followed.
- Preparing and implementing a security plan or program. Re-evaluate existing programs to ensure safeguards are in place in the event of an emergency situation.
- Limit public disclosure of information on quantities and locations of explosives in storage except for those who need to know, such as public safety authorities.
- Establish a predetermined action plan for implementation of increased security measures brought on by a declaration of threat level higher than "Yellow" or "Elevated" by Department of Homeland Security, (DHS).
- Control official documents and information. Prevent documents such as licenses, permits, route plans, shipping schedules, and other authorizations from reaching unauthorized individuals.
- Conduct regular inventories more often than once per year to ensure that there have been no theft or loss of explosive materials.
- Limit access to magazines to essential personnel only.
- Secure magazine sites with fences, floodlights, alarms, and security cameras.
- Keep magazines secure and check them regularly for evidence of tamper or theft. The ATF requires them to be inspected every seven days.
- Training your staff to recognize suspicious behavior.

13. EXPLOSIVE ORDINANCE DISPOSAL - EOD

Chapter Topics:

- A list of the many applications for use of explosives.
- Specific examples of common commercial applications.
- Understand the rules of thumb and formulas used to determine the amount of explosive materials necessary.

U.S. Military EOD

EOD is a U.S. Military term for the proud profession of eliminating ordinance with includes: aging munitions, enemy munitions, land mines and improvised explosive devices (IED's).

Summit Entertainment, LLC

The 2008 movie, The Hurt Locker featured and made popular the dangerous work of EOD professionals.

EOD the safe way. Why risk a Bomb Tech, when you can send in a robot with a ***PAN Disrupter****. A 12 gauge cannon that can shoot water or a sabot to disrupt an IED or bomb*

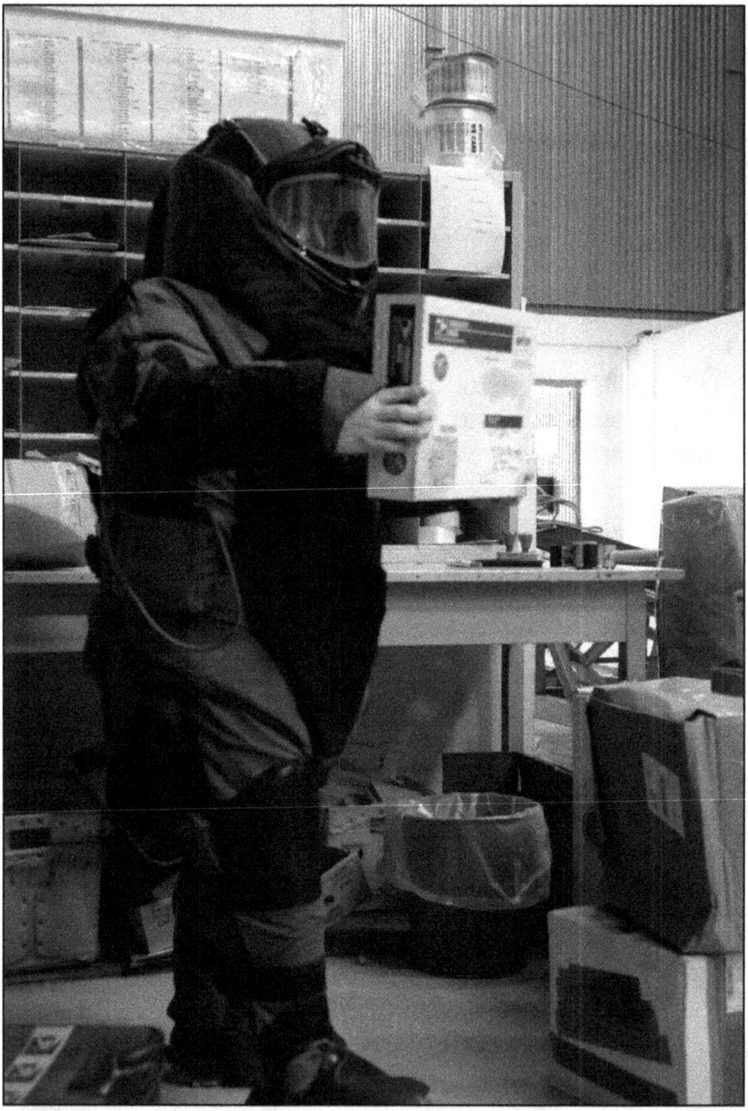

The California National Guard conducts training exercises in their EOD bomb suit. In this case, the tech investigates a suspicious package at a USPS mail center.

All four U.S. branches of the military have EOD technicians who are all trained at the Navy School Explosive Ordnance Disposal, known as NAVSXOLEOD. The Navy EOD program is more specialized as they also are trained to disarm explosives that are underwater or airborne.

These professionals have been in high demand through the current theaters of operation in both Iraq and Afghanistan.

Much of their effort is dealing with roadside IED's and vehicle based IED's that have taken more lives and caused more injuries than about any other form of combat.

New procedures and equipment are constantly being developed to more efficiently and safely remove explosive hazards. This is not only from the battlefield but in the age or terrorism, civilian roadways and buildings. Civilian law enforcement agencies are learning and adapting procedures hard-learned in the world's toughest battlefields.

Civilian EOD-UXO Contractors

Civilian contractors use the term ***UXO***, for **U**n-e**X**ploded **O**rdnance removal. UXO technicians start off as Tech I's after graduating from a UXO tech program and can work their way up to Tech II and supervisory Tech III positions based upon their number of years of experience.

UXO techs are often hired by agencies such as the U.S. Army Corps of Engineers' at U.S or international job sites. The United States has 3,500 munitions response sites alone that include all 50 states. Techs are paid well and receive additional compensation on top of an hourly base rate for travel, food, and lodging.

Techs search historical bombing ranges and land mine sites using grid patterns with metal detectors, then marking potential ordnance locations with survey style GPS. Once a target is confirmed, it is either ***Blown in Place (BIP)***, or removed to be destroyed in a ***Safe Detonation Area (SDA)***.

UXO specialist, Steve Cassidy from www.globally-employable.com finds a WWII era Japanese bomb in Papua New Guina. He and other civilian UXO techs work around the world to clean up bomb sites and historical battle fields.

Considerations for EOD Techs

There are so many variations of explosives, bombs, IEDs and terrorists, that it would be difficult to have a Standard Operating Procedure for every possible scenario. What EOD techs have instead are ***Render Safe Procedures (RSPs)***.

RSPs are guidelines for the safest and most effective way to disarm and dispose of explosive material based upon what is known of the situation at hand. Obtaining the best possible intelligence available is critical to help the Tech determine the full scope of the situation and what to do next.

One of the other considerations is what are the tools available to address that threat. Larger agencies will have bigger budgets and more resources to possibly have robots with on-board water disrupters, Radio Frequency Jammers or other high-tech devices. Or, it may be a matter of a brave soul suiting up to have a look to determine how to best to safely disable and disarm an IED or ordnance with not much more that wire cutters and nerves of steel.

One of the factors the tech has to determine is what is the explosive yield of the charge? Can it be disarmed, disrupted or detonated? If the ordnance is to be detonated, will it be a High Order Detonation (its full explosive power), or Low Order Detonation (limited power due to manipulation or malfunction).

If the Tech decides to detonate the ordnance, the next choice is can it be **Blown in Place (BIP)**? Or can it be moved to another, safer location to be destroyed in a **Safe Detonation Area (SDA)**? Lots of difficult decisions that affect life or death. EOD techs would not have it any other way.

Considerations for EOD Techs

[illegible]

[illegible]

[illegible]

[illegible]

[illegible]

14. HOMEMADE EXPLOSIVE LABS

In this chapter:

- Understand that explosives labs looks like drug labs
- Confirming precursors confirms a lab
- Understand other signs of a possible lab

Homemade labs looks like drug labs. They use much of the same equipment to produce much of the same looking the same-looking white to brown powders and crystals. The point is, if you find a lab, don't immediately assume it is for drugs. Take a closer look to confirm if the lab is for explosives.

Bomb Makers, Blenders and Cooks

Bomb makers, blenders and cooks come in a variety of levels of sophistication. From guys pouring gun powder into steel pipes to techs making advanced electrical circuits.

Blenders make simple mixtures like ANFO, to full-out lab cooks manufacturing advanced explosive materials such as Acetone Peroxide, TATP or PETN.

Cooking, a term from the meth lab phenomenon, is much more complicated. In cooking, chemicals that are mixed together react to form new compounds with explosive properties. Cooking requires more chemistry skill, as materials must be processed through a series of procedures, each has unique hazards. These include toxic fumes, chemical burns, and sudden explosions.

While these people vary greatly in ability, sophistication, and intent, they do have important indicators in common that makes them easier for law enforcement to find. One indicator is that they like to test what they make. Do neighbors report sounds of explosions? Are there craters left in the ground? If you suspect a maker or lab, check for these possibilities.

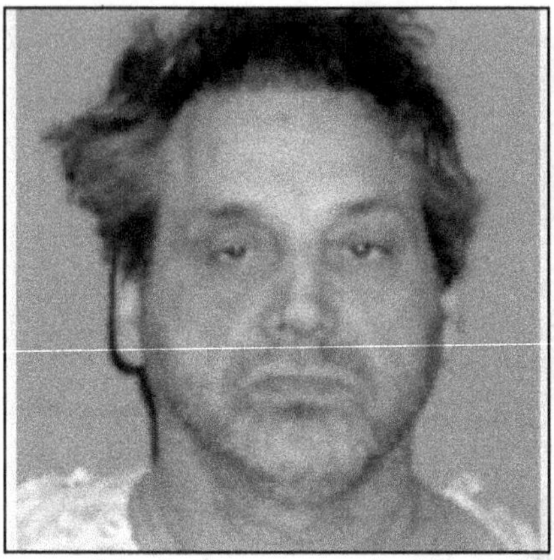

Mark Campano in the US, and Mark Tear in the UK, were both caught and arrested as bomb makers after they had injured themselves enough to require hospitalization.

The second indicator is that makers and cooks get injured. Eventually they will get burned or injured. This could be from exposure to toxic chemicals to blast injuries resulting in blown off fingers or hands. If a lab is discovered, check with local hospitals to see if they have had anyone checked in with injuries that could be consistent with this activity.

Mark Campano, a 56-year old, anti-government anesthesiologist, turned his Cleveland, Ohio apartment into a bomb factory that included 35 pipe bombs, 17 guns and hundreds of rounds of ammunition.

Neighbors heard explosions outside of his apartment and even heard him scream when he hurt himself. Materials exploded causing serious injury to his hand and arm. His mother stated that making bombs was just his hobby.

Homemade Lab Precursors

The way to confirm a drug lab, is to confirm the presences of precursors. These materials are covered in more detail in Chapter 8, but here is a list of the primary materials.

Binary Precursors

Oxidizers	Fuels
Ammonium Nitrate	Aluminum Powder
Hydrogen Peroxide	Gasoline
Potassium Chlorate	Petroleum Fuels
	Sugar

Common Precursor Chemicals

Acetone
Aluminum Powder
Ammonium Nitrate
Calcium Ammonium Nitrate
Chlorine
Hexamine
Hydrogen Peroxide
Nitric Acid
Propane
Sugar
Triacetone
Triperoxide (TATP)
Urea

A flash powder lab from Washington State. Labs that make M-80 type bombs can make more money than drug labs.

Testing for Explosive Materials

Fortunately, there is a number of chemical test kits available that can indicate if you are dealing with explosive precursors and materials. There are sprays, drops, and wipes that will cause a test paper to change color is nitrate based explosive materials are discovered. These are typically separated by:

Inorganic Nitrates	C-4
	HMX
	Nitrocellulose
	Nitroglycerin
	RDX
	Semtex
	TNT
	Tetryl
Organic Nitrates	Ammonium Nitrate
	ANFO
	Black Powder
	Flash Powder
	Potassium Chlorate

Potassium Nitrate
Smokeless Powder
Sodium Nitrate
Sulfur

It should be noted that these test kits primarily work on all materials that contain nitrogen or nitrates. Not all explosive materials include nitrate, such as ***Acetone Peroxide.*** This is why it is used by various terrorists to get on airplanes such as Richard Reid, *The Shoe Bomber*.

Mistral Security, Inc. makes a three-step explosive detection field test kit sensitive enough to detect even trace residues.

Potential Indicators of Homemade Explosive Production (from US Homeland Security)

Almost every HME manufacturing process affects its immediate environment. Although a single indicator may not be suspicious, although one or more of these indicators may point to HME production:

- Foul odors or caustic fumes coming from a room or building.
- Damage to ceilings and walls—such as corrosion of metal surfaces or structural damage—and paint discoloration from harsh chemical fumes.
- Strong chemical odors emanating from sewers and drain ditches.
- Large industrial fans or multiple fans in windows.
- Dead vegetation in the surrounding area.
- Presence of metal or plastic drums for storing explosives.

- Machinery—such as gas burners or mixers—for processing raw materials.
- Refrigerators or coolers used to store volatile chemicals and finished products.

Extreme caution should always be used when entering and investigating possible bomb labs. Besides the risk of the materials inside, there is also the possibility of entry points being booby trapped.

Islamic terrorists Farook and Malik's home in Redland, California was entered through the front garden window before the front door was breached. No booby traps, but an IED lab with18 pipe bombs were discovered inside.

15. IMPROVISED EXPLOSIVE DEVICES IEDS

Chapter Topics:

- Understand how many different types of IEDs there are.
- Understand the various components that make up an IED.
- Learn about possible physical and human indicators of IEDs.

IED Variations

IEDs can come in virtually any shape, size, style, or material. The following is a list to provide an idea of the many formats commonly encountered around the world.

Command Wire IED **CWIED**
Device Hardwired with a cable or wire

Home Borne IED **HBIED**
Building Based (booby-trapped structures)

Maritime IED **MIED**
Boat or Surface Floating (USS Cole bombing)

Radio Controlled IED **RCIED**
Controlled by cell phones or other a radio links

Under Vehicle IED **UVIED**
Booby-Trapped vehicles

Vehicle Borne IED **VBIED**
Vehicle Based (car bombs)

Victim Operated IED **VOIED**
Bomber operates the trigger (suicide bomber)

Weapons of Mass Destruction WMDs

IEDs are not limited to conventional explosives, although commercial, military or homemade materials maybe used to detonate or propel materials even more deadly that make up WMDs.

Standardized acronyms to describe these weapons

CBRN Chemical, Biological, Radiological and Nuclear

CBRND	Chemical, Biological, Radiological and Nuclear Defense
CBRNE	Chemical, Biological, Radiological, Nuclear and Explosive
WMD	Weapons of Mass Destruction
WME	Weapons of Mass Effect (create more fear than destruction)

To incite greater fear, terrorists can mix conventional explosives with radioactive, biological, or chemical materials.

Here is a list of primary WMD IEDs:

Improvised Biological Device IBD

A device incorporating biological materials designed to result in the dispersal of vector borne biological material for the purpose of creating a primary patho-physiological toxic effect (morbidity & mortality), or secondary psychological effect (causing fear and behavior modification) on a larger population. Such devices are fabricated in a completely improvised manner.

Improvised Chemical Device ICD

A device incorporating the toxic attributes of chemical materials designed to result in the dispersal of these toxic chemical materials for the purpose of creating a primary patho-physiological toxic effect (morbidity & mortality).

As well as a secondary psychological effect (causing fear and behavior modification) on a larger population. Such devices may be fabricated in a completely improvised manner or may be an improvised modification to an existing weapon. Also known as: *"al Mobtakar al Farheed."*

Improvised Incendiary Device IID

A device making use of exothermic chemical reactions designed to result in the rapid spread of fire for the purpose of creating a primary patho-physiological effect (morbidity & mortality), or secondary psychological effect (causing fear and behavior modification) on a larger population or it may be used with the intent of gaining a tactical advantage. Such devices may be fabricated in a completely improvised manner or may be an improvised modification to an existing weapon. Example: the Molotov Cocktail.

Improvised Nuclear Device IND

A device incorporating radioactive materials designed to result in the dispersal of radioactive material or in the formation of nuclear-yield reaction. Such devices may be fabricated in a completely improvised manner or may be an improvised modification to a U.S. or foreign nuclear weapon.

Improvised Radioactive Device IRD or RDD

A device designed to disperse of radioactive materials to contaminate a target area creating death, damage, and terror. Such devices may be fabricated in a completely improvised manner or may be an improvised modification to an existing nuclear weapon. Also known as a Radiological Dispersion Device (RDD) or "Dirty Bomb."

IED Structure

To help recognize IEDs, it is important to understand the various components that create them. IEDs consist of some form of ***Trigger*** that sets off an ***Initiator*** that sets off a ***Booster***, that detonates the ***Primary Explosive Charge***, then throws the ***Shrapnel***.

Triggers (What activates the IED)

- Car Alarm
- Cell Phone
- Command Wire (wire to battery)
- Door Opener
- Fuse

- Infrared Light Beams
- Motion Switch
- RC Servos
- Radio Signals
- Trip Wire

Advanced IED Trigger - Switches

Anti-Disturbance Switch

Circuit is complete through movement, typically trough a mercury switch.

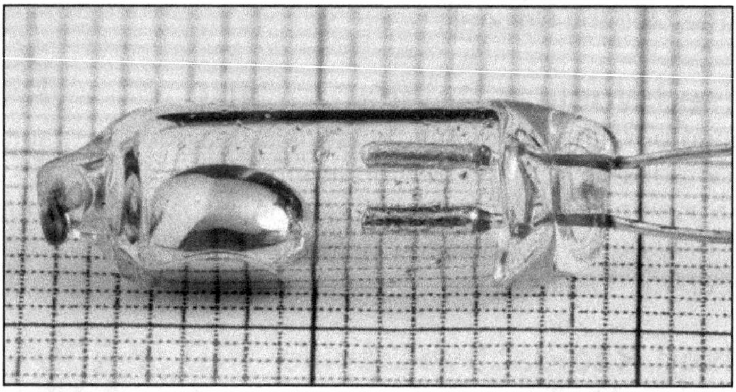

This is why you don't pick up suspicions packages.
A mercury switch makes an electronic connection when moved.

Anti-Probe Switch

Circuit is compete when a knife or metal probe pierces two sheets of foil.

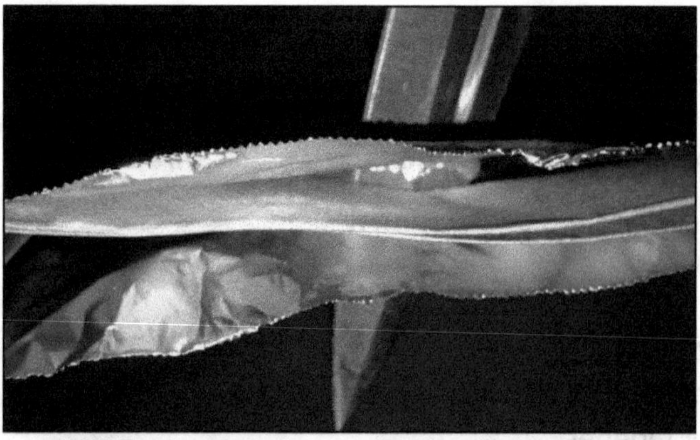

Anti-Probe switch, contact is made when a metal knife or probe pierces two sheets of foil.

Anti-Opening Switch

Circuit is complete from any opening of a lid, hatch, drawer, from a spring release or micro type switch that makes a connection from the relief of the door movement.

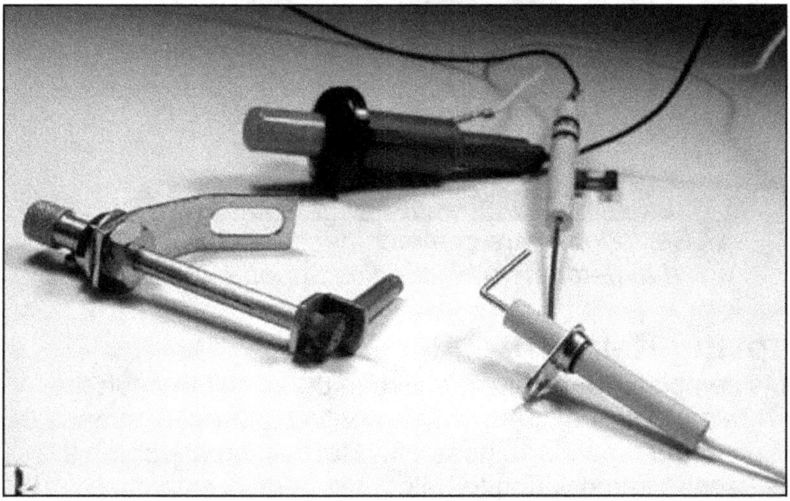

Switches can be purchased or re-purposed to meet virtually any application.

Barometric Switch

Circuit is complete when the device reaches a set atmospheric pressure or altitude.

A nightmare for aviation, a switch activated by altitude.

Cell Phone Switch

Circuit is complete when the phone is called or when the alarm goes off as the blasting cap is wired to phone's speaker output wires.

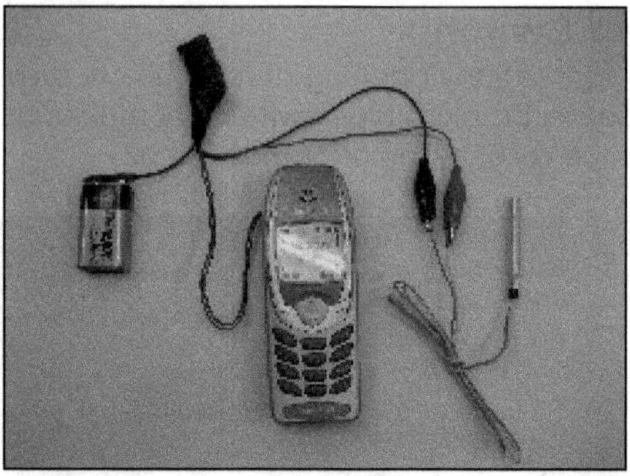

Cell phones are common because they can be wired to detonate a blasting cap upon a call or alarm.

Collapsing Relay Circuit

Circuit is complete from cutting a wire in the circuit through the use of a relay. Think of it as when a contact is broken on an alarm sensor and the alarm goes off. More elaborate bomb the makers use the same wiring to help make a device 'tamper proof.' If a Bomb Tech cuts the wrong wire, the electrical circuit is complete and the bomb explodes.

Collapsing circuits can also be used as delay devices. For example, a nine-volt battery is used to power a circuit until the battery runs out of energy (approximately 23 hours), then the circuit is open, completing the collapsing circuit and detonating the bomb.

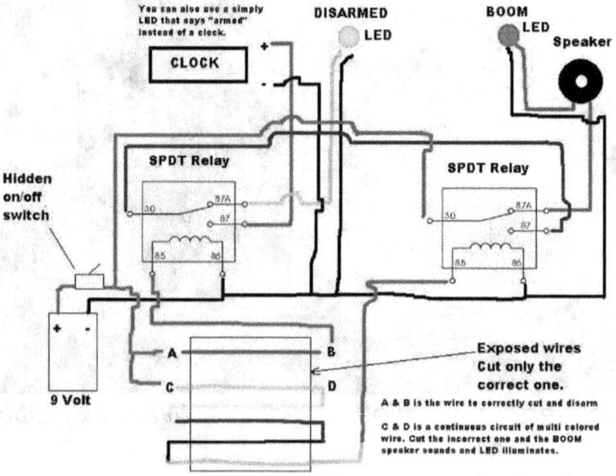

This system was created for scenario game training. This system is complicated enough, but a bomb maker may add many other circuits, relays and wires to throw a bomb tech off.

Deadman Switch

Circuit is complete when a person's thumb or finger is removed from a compressed switch. Used with suicide bombers or forced victim bombers.

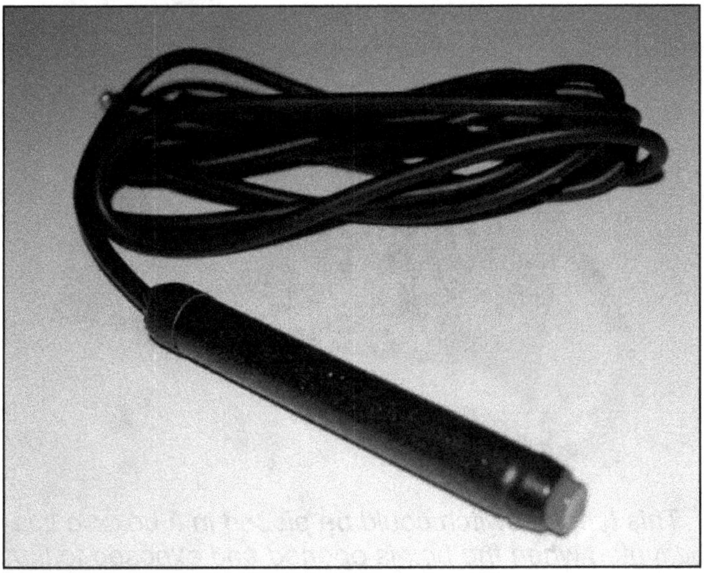

These switches keep operators from killing suicide bombers.

Magnetic Switch

Circuit is complete from any nearby passing of a metal object.

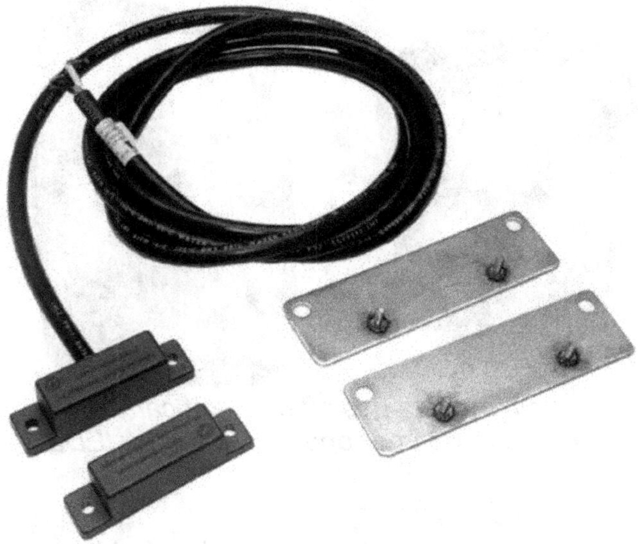

Magnetic switches used for door or window alarm switches.

Photoelectric Switch

Circuit is complete from device being exposed to light.

This type of switch could be placed in a box, so it is activated when the box is opened and exposed to light.

Radio Controlled Switch

Circuit is complete through a radio frequency transmitter such as: car alarm, garage door opener, wireless door bell.

Bomb makers use aftermarket car alarms and garage door openers to trigger IEDs.

Sound Activated Switch

Circuit is complete through an audible sound, found in car alarms, toys, or Halloween displays.

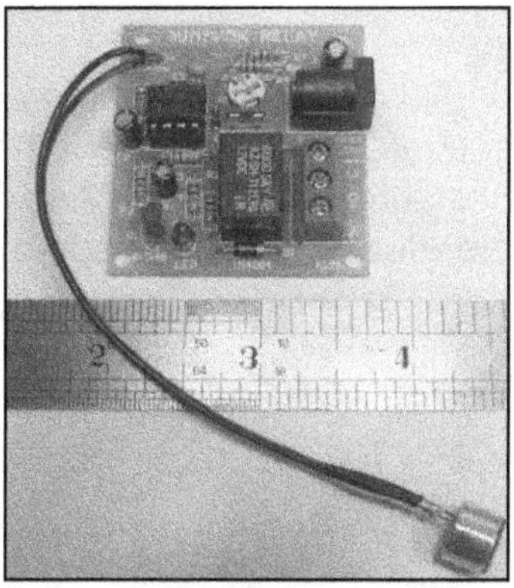

Sound sensors can be purchased or pulled from Halloween decorations.

Timing Switch

Alarms and countdown timers can provide enough voltage to trigger a device. This is done through a ***Silicon Controlled Rectifier, SCR*** circuit device. The switch has three prongs, voltage in, voltage out and gate. The low-voltage, pulse-positive wire that would be attached to a watch or timer buzzer would be attached to the gate pin. When the alarm is activated the circuit opens allowing full voltage to the blasting cap.

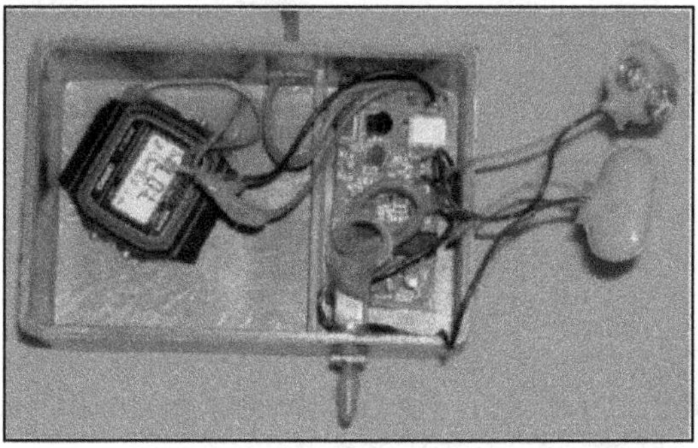

Even a Casio watch can provide enough voltage to trigger a device through the use of a SCR switch.

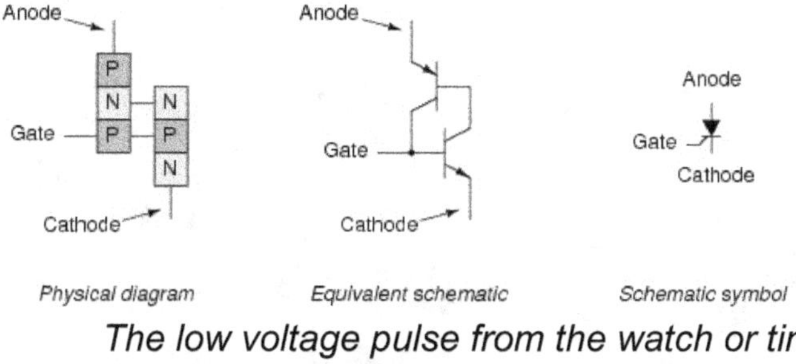

The low voltage pulse from the watch or timer is connected to the SCR gate pin to complete the electrical circuit.

Tripwire Switch

A tripwire can activate a device mechanically, which is as simple as pulling a pin out of grenade. It can also activate an electric switch like from a homemade clothespin trigger. When a tripwire pulls a non-conductive strip from the front contacts, the electric circuit is complete.

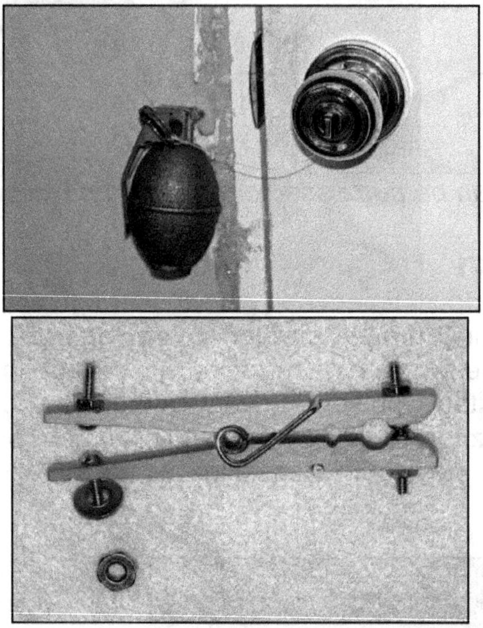

A tripwire that pulls the pin on a grenade is one of the most simplistic forms of trigger devices. The clothespin switch is activated when a tripwire pulls a non-conductive strip out between the contacts to complete the circuit.

Detonator or Initiator

The detonator is the first blast that initiates the bomb sequence. These can be electric or fuse based. Materials used can include:

- Acetone Peroxide
- Black Powder
- Blasting Cap
- Flash Powder
- Mercury Fulminate

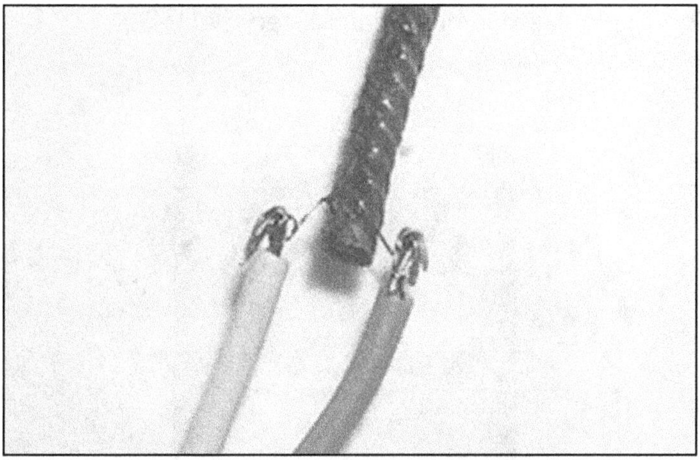

In this system, an electric pulse sets off a Visco fuse.

Booster

A booster is used to initiate the Primary Charge. Not every IED will use one, but some primary explosives will require an additional charge. For example, a propane tank needs another charge to detonate the propane gas. These materials can include:

- Acetone Peroxide
- Black Powder
- Flash Powder
- High Explosive (Commercial, Military or HME)

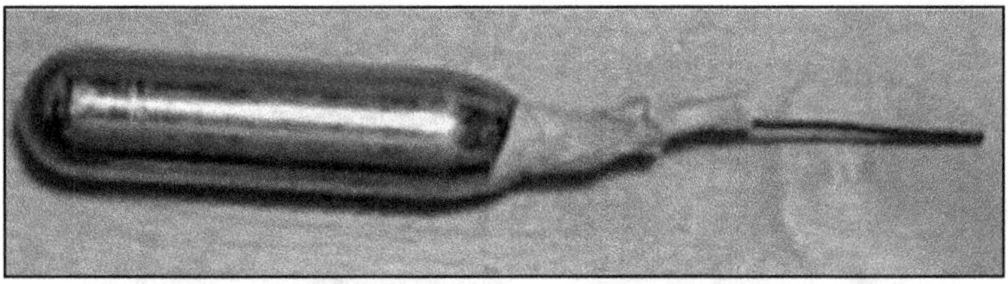

Flash Powder packed into a CO_2 capsule makes a homemade blasting cap or booster.

Primary Charge

The primary charge is the main explosive material in the bomb. These materials can include:

- ANFO
- Artillery Shell
- Gun Powder
- Gasoline

- High Explosive (Commercial, Military or HME)
- Petroleum Fuels
- Propane Tank

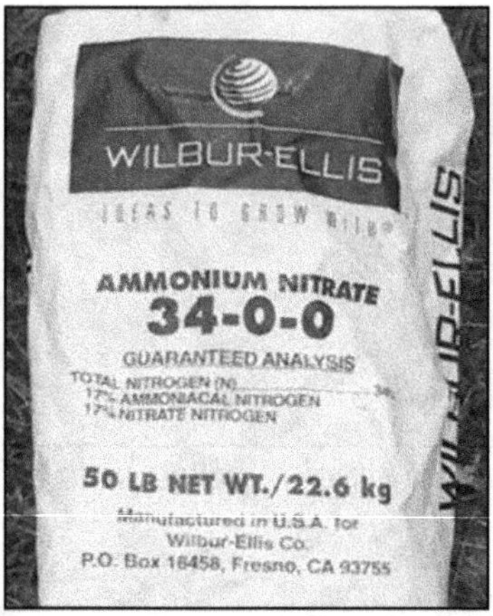

Ammonium Nitrate is a popular primary explosive due to its potential explosive power and ease to purchase.

Shrapnel

Shrapnel is the flying metal pieces projected by the bomb's blast that cause death and injury. Shrapnel can be made from the following materials:

- Ball Bearings
- Chain Links
- Glass
- Hardware-Nails, Screws
- Metal housings (Pipe or Pressure Cooker)

Ceramic ball bearings can pass through metal detectors.

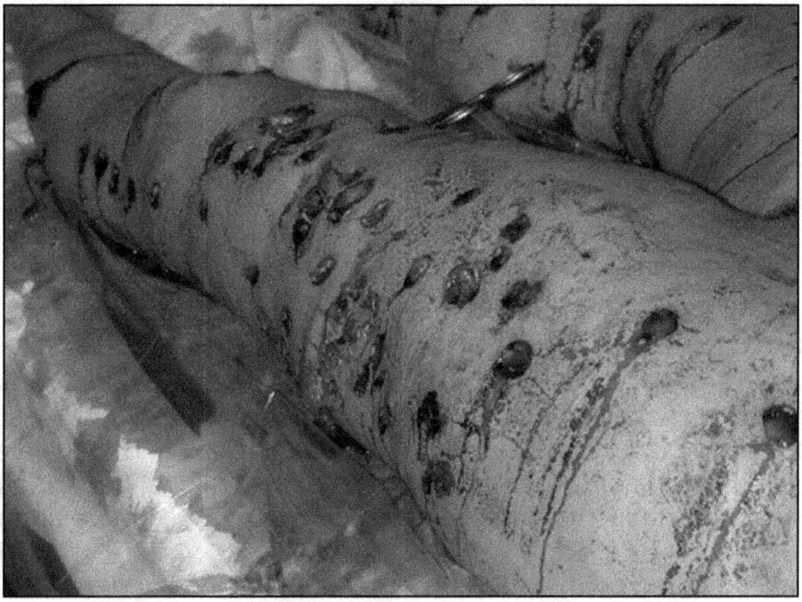

IEDs are all about causing fear, death and injury. Flying shrapnel is intended to do just that.

Pipe and Pressure Cooker Bombs

One style of bomb is so common it gets its own category. While pipe bombs and pressure cooker bombs look completely different, they operate the same. Essentially a metal sealed container that will turn to shrapnel from an explosive charge encased in the center.

Low explosives can detonate in a high yield explosion if the powder is encased in a housing. Upon detonation, pressure builds until the casing is breached and shatters. It should be noted that black powder takes on the velocity characteristics used to detonate it.

For example, a pipe bomb detonated with a blasting cap will have a greater rate for a high yield explosion than one initiated with a burning fuse. Black powder initiated by a fuse can build up pressure slow enough for a low yield detonation, only splitting open the casing before a full explosion.
If the explosive material inside fully explodes, the bomb's casing and any other shrapnel fragments will blow in all directions with a high possibility of producing death and injury.

As indicated by our IED case study, these devices are used frequently due to a number of factors:

- Cheap and easy to make
- Components can be easily purchased
- No special training needed, only tool is a drill
- Can be filled in a variety of low or high explosive material
- Simple hardware can be added for additional shrapnel
- Trigger systems can be a fuse to advanced electronics
- Can be easily hidden in packs and cases

Bomb Casings

Pipe and Pressure Cooker bombs operate the same. Extremely simply, just needing a hole drilled in the casing for a fuse or a wire. Pressure cookers have the advantage to hold more explosives and hardware material for shrapnel. Pipe bombs often have additional nails or other hardware attached to the outside of the pipe to produce more shrapnel.

It should be noted on threaded-end pipe bombs, an experienced bomb maker will grease the threads of the final capped end to help avoid any possible detonation of the powder when the final capped end is tightened down.

Pipe bomb left behind after Eric Frein was arrested for killing one and wounding two Pennsylvania State Troopers. Simple, cheap and effective, this bomb includes a short Visco fuse with extra hardware to create shrapnel.

Fill Material

These bombs are popular because they use a low explosive material, that unlike high explosives, is very easy to obtain. The other advantage is that low explosives are fuse sensitive to avoid the need for a more difficult to obtain blasting cap. Here is a quick list of what could be used to fill the bomb:

- Black Powder (can be purchased by can at gun stores)
- Gun Powder (can be purchased or removed from ammo)
- Flash Powder (made for purchased for pyrotechnics)
- Potassium Chlorate (matchheads), and sugar
- Acetone Peroxide (made by bomb cooks)

Advanced bombs are made with the powder filled loosely using a buffer or wadding material to allow the expansion inside the container.

Trigger System

These types of bombs can be initiated by a simple fuse or a more advanced electric system. While blasting caps can be difficult to obtain, homemade electric initiators can be used from light bulbs to model rocket motors. If the trigger is electric, there is no limit to the systems that can be used that includes the following:

- Command Wire
- Cell Phone
- Clock or Timer
- Radio Signal
- Motion Sensor

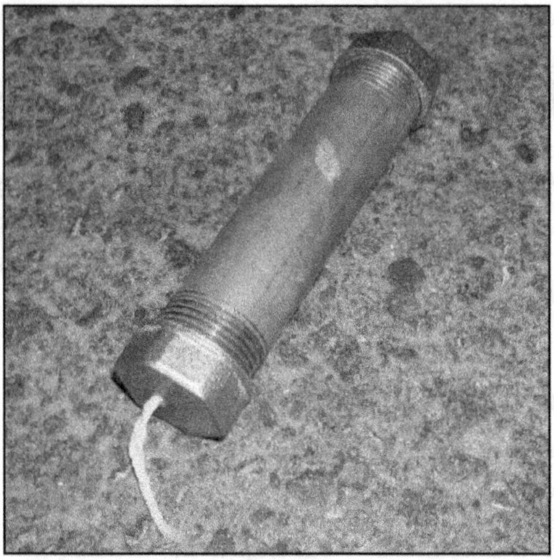

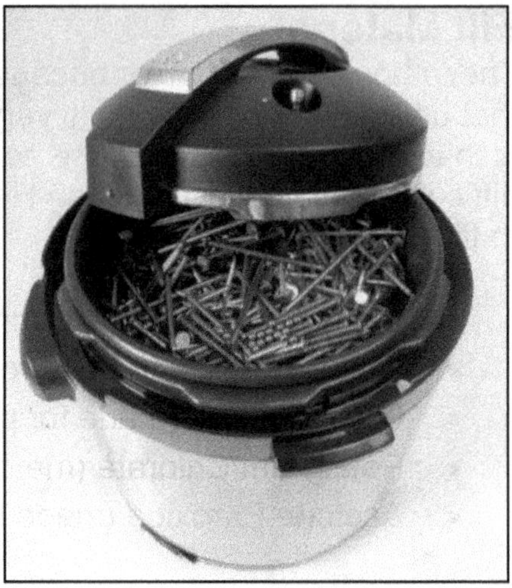

Pipe Bombs and Pressure Cooker bombs work on the same principle of providing an enclosed case for power and shrapnel.

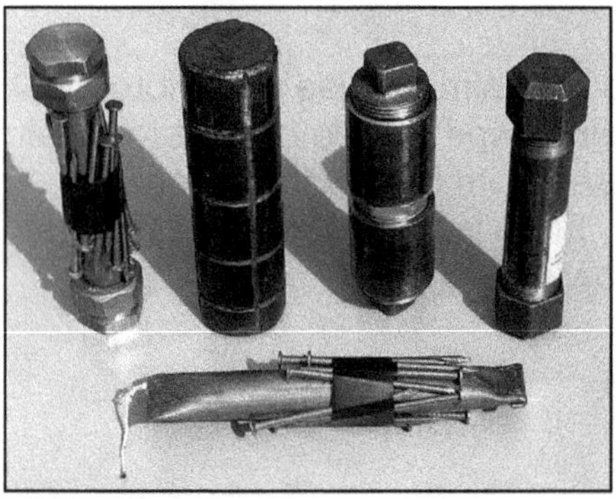

Pipe bombs shown that Include external shrapnel.

If the powder detonates too slowly, the pipe may blow out instead of shattering.

Finding a Pipe or Pressure Cooker Bomb

When encountering this style of bomb, first check to see if it appears to be triggered by a fuse or an electric system. If a fuse, is it burning? If not, it should still not be approached or touched. A fuse could be a decoy and wired to explode upon movement.

U.S. Homeland Security states the minimum perimeter distance should be 21 meters (64 feet). Bomb Techs may choose to x-ray to determine to remove or blow them in place.

IED Indicators

Physical visual signs that may suggest the presence of an IED

Trust your instincts, if something does not look for feel right, it may not be!

- Abandoned vehicles (vehicles weighted down)
- Animal carcasses
- Containers that seem out of place
- Garbage piles
- Hatches and panels recently removed
- Turned-over soil
- Wires hidden or buried

Human visual signs that suggest the presence of an IED

Look for trigger behavior and body language to indicate something is wrong!

- Locals have vacated the area
- Moving away from you or out of your area
- People watching you
- People looking nervous or stressed
- Video recording or photographing you as if they know something is going to happen
- Remember the suspect is most likely watching and needs a line of sign view

16. IED SCENARIOS AND LOCATIONS

Chapter Topics:

- Obtain a better understanding of possible terroristic IED scenarios.
- Understand locations where bombs or IEDs could be hidden or placed.

The purpose of this chapter is to inspire top of mind awareness of possible IED scenarios and locations. Terrorism is about inciting as much fear as possible. Terrorists can maximize fear through deception. Any device located could be a deadly, a fake, a decoy or a secondary. Once you learn about possible scenarios, it is easy to almost become paranoid. It is a fine line. We want you to become hyper-aware of real-world possibilities without becoming overly suspicious.

Every day first responders have to enter environments such as this. The idea is to find the balance between being hyper-aware without being paranoid.

Possible IED Scenarios

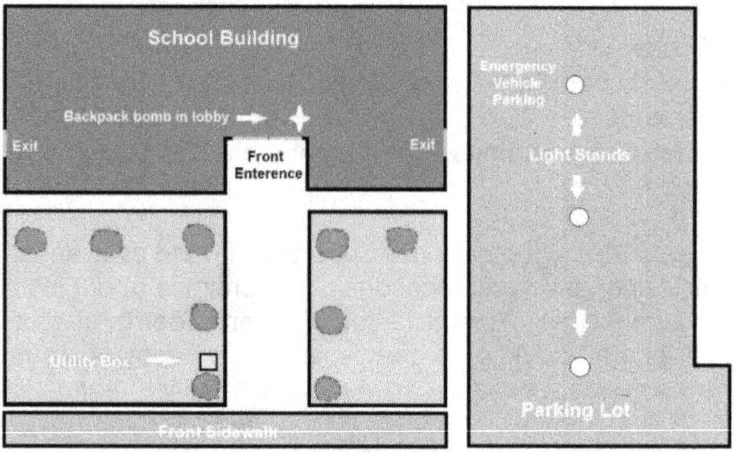

In this scenario a backpack is discovered in a school's lobby and the following is an example of a chain of events that follow:

Chain of Events

0925 A backpack was discovered in the school lobby. Backpack feels heavy and it smells like oil.

1032 Backpack is still not claimed so a janitor picks it up and brings it into the school office to search it for ID. No markings or name tags are located on the outside so it is unzipped by the vice principle who discovers it is full of pipe bombs. The pack is dropped and the administration staff is evacuates the office area through the front doors. On the way out, the fire alarm is pulled to evacuate the rest of the students and faculty.

1040 Based upon fire drill protocol, students, and faculty line up on the front sidewalk. 911 was called and emergency vehicles start to mass in the side parking lot next to the school building. The terrorist pulled the fire alarm two months prior to confirm what the response would be.

1053 The backpack in the office explodes sending a wave of shrapnel through the office. The windows are blown out, but no one is injured due to the area being evacuated first. After the blast, the security guard the SWAT members quickly evacuate the school building and rejoin the rest of the personnel in front and to the side of the building.

1055 The light post stand in the north section of parking lot explodes sending a wave of shrapnel through the area next to the building were the emergency personnel were staged.
Officers are down and there are casualties. Surviving emergency personnel extract the wounded and evacuate away from the building and the other two remaining light pole stands in the parking lot.

1056 A bomb tech unit arrives into the parking lot just after the light pole stand blast. They activate radio jammers to help prevent any further remote switch IEDs from detonating.

1057 The students and faculty are evacuated to the center of a nearby football field while police search for secondary devices.

1137 Bomb techs discover a large IED in the utility box located in the lawn next to the front sidewalk. The cell phone trigger failed to work due to the radio frequency jammer. The bomb was hit with an IED disrupter to render it safe.

Debrief: This was a tragic scenario that can easily happen at any school facility. As bad as it was, it could have been much worse with some actions done right and some not.

Let's review this case to determine what can be learned. The backpack was first discovered at 0925 and not dealt with until 1032. Not unusual for a student to lose a backpack, but the pack should have been brought to the security guard's attention when the pack was considerably heavier than a normal and it smelled of oil.

1032 The fire alarm was pulled out of instinct which brought students and faculty to the front of the school just as they have trained for. Emergency event managers have to realize that fires are much different than bomb threats or mass shooter events.

There needs to be a level of flexibility to evacuate students or have them lock down in place. If the building walls are constructed of cinderblock, it may have been an option to keep the students locked down in the building in rooms away from the office. From this example, automatically sending students out to the front of the building could have been very disastrous in this case or during an active shooter event.

1032 Once the backpack was confirmed as a bomb, besides the safety of the students, the focus needed to be directed to searching for secondary devices. Fastening screws had been left out of the light post stand and the utility box, but they were not checked.

1056 The bomb techs deploying the radio frequency jammer prevented the front utility box IED from exploding. This saved the lives the hundreds of students that were lined up in front of the bomb.

1057 It was smart to get the students and faculty out of the area and onto an open space, but this is a risk with any possibility of an active shooter event. A possible better solution would be to secure the students and faculty into a nearby building until they can be bussed out of the area.

Now is a good time to review your agencies standard operating procedures when it comes to these mass threat terroristic events.

Possible IED Locations

Review the following locations to become more aware of possible IED hiding locations. Examine the first photo to see what locations you can find before reviewing the second photo.

School Front

Planters for concealment
Overhangs and vaults
Irrigation access
Bushes or cover
restricing approach
Bushes for concealment

House Front

Choke points for entry
Points of consealment
for devices
debris near doors
Trash cans
Discolored earth

Main Street

KING'S PALACE
CAFE
BLUES

KING'S PALACE
CAFE
BLUES
Shrubs
Lamp post removable base
News paper box
Garbage can
Sewer
drain

Shopping Mall

sleep number
macy's
macy's

sleep number
macy's
Charge here throws glass debris
Baby stroller
Out of place planter
Plants
Backpack behind planter

Urban City Alley

Review these scenarios with your department. It is a great way to start discussions to increase awareness and highlight would special considerations you may have in your jurisdiction.

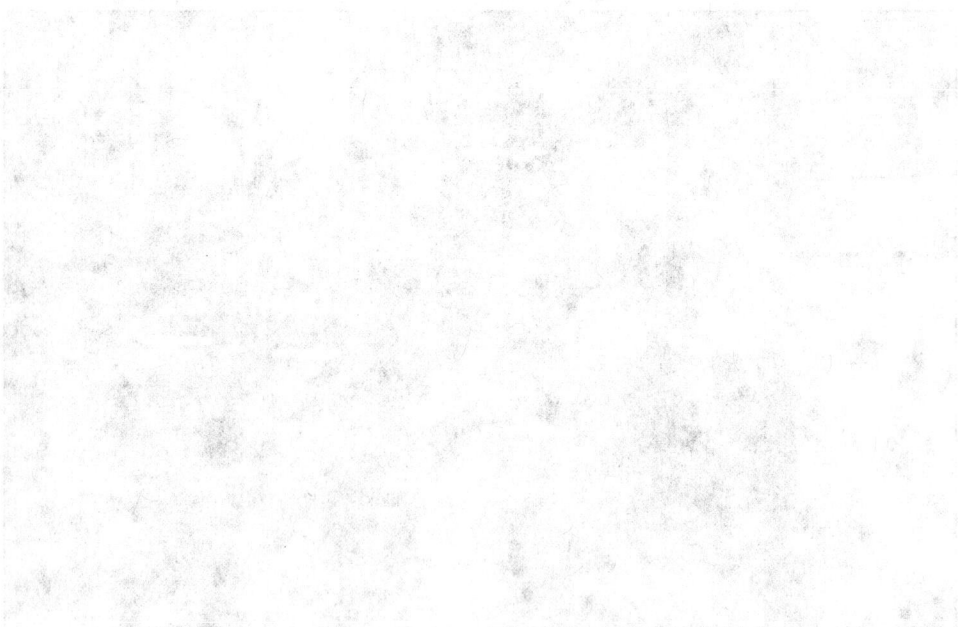

17. IEDS USED WITH ACTIVE SHOOTERS AND RIOTS

Chapter Topics:

- Most mass casualty events combine explosives and firearms.
- Learn critical facts and considerations for Active Shooters.
- Learn how IEDs and weaponized fireworks are used in riots.
- Understand common response terminology.
- Understand possible responses by First Responders.
- Learn about possible bomb tech responses to IEDs.

Special Considerations for Active Shooter Combined Events

Much has been discussed and written on Active Shooters in recent years with enough acronyms and lists of responses to make anyone's head spin. Our goal is to provide the most relevant and lifesaving information possible in a way that can be remembered and adapted to your agency.

Mass casualty events more often than not include both threats from explosives and firearms. At the very least, if you have an Active Shooter, consider there maybe the use of threat of explosives and if you have IEDs, understand there could be a shooter nearby.

Much as been learned on the responses to combined IED and shooter events that include:

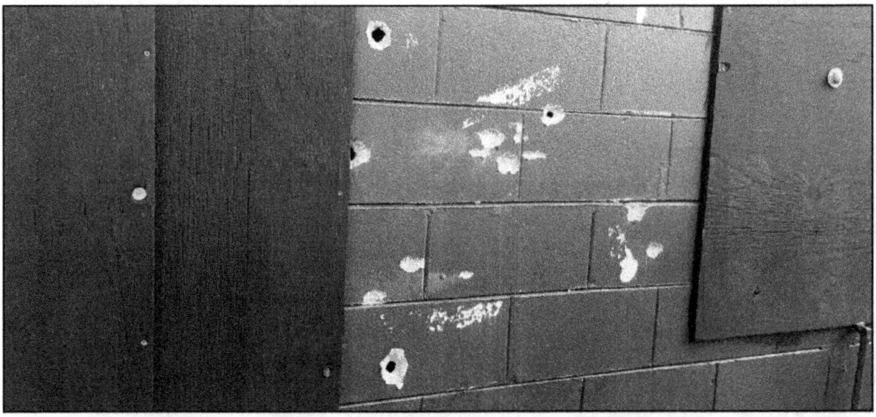

Much was learned after the Pulse Night Club shooting. A cautious response by police after the terrorist threatened to blow up victims bought additional time by the gunman to kill and wound more people. This photo shows the breaching points were SWAT blew though a brick wall to access and kill the shooter.

Pulse Night Club Shooting, Orlando, Florida 12 JUN 2016
The suspect told police he had victims attached to bomb vests, causing the police to back off. This bought the shooter enough time to kill 49 victims and wound as many more.

Black Lives Matter Police Shooting, Dallas, Texas 07 JUL 2016
The suspect also said he had explosives. Police learning from the massacre in Orlando the month before, they took no chances and immediately sent in a robot with a pound of C-4, killing the suspect.

Concert Hotel Shooting, Las Vegas, Nevada 01 OCT 2017
Explosives were not used in the attached, but the suspect had 50 pounds of explosive materials in his vehicle. From this it could be assumed that the suspect would have used the explosives if they worked and was possible or convenient for him to do so.

Learning from Active Shooter Statistics

A shooter with even moderate weapons training can kill an average of seven victims per minute.

An average response time for armed responders (police or security) can easily be 14 minutes. Based upon this, a shooter could kill 98 victims. This is exactly why a rapid response is so critical, every minute saved could mean saving seven people!

Active Shooter Statistics for the U.S. for 2000-2016

Total Events	220	
Total Casualties	1,486, out of which 661 dead, 825 wounded	
Locations:	Commerce	43%
	Education	21%
	Open Areas	13%
	Government	10%
Residence, Church, Health Care		11%

Only 1% of gun murder victims are from Mass Shootings

Hartford Consensus 2013 – The Takeaway

Following the Sandy Hook School shooting, a group of medical professionals established a conference to help increase the survivability of victims in mass casualty active shooter events.
The group states that "no one should die from uncontrolled bleeding" and developed the acronym **THREAT**

Threat Suppression
Hemorrhage Control
Rapid Extrication to Safety,
Assessment by Medical Providers
Transport to Definitive Care

We support their conclusion for the following reasons:

1. **Threat Suppression** must be the first priority, considering a shooter can kill seven victims a minute.

This is done by a rapid and aggressive response by armed First Responders trained and ready to neutralize the shooter as soon as possible.

This is ideal for police or SWAT, but case study has shown that response from an armed civilian can also result in neutralizing the suspect by shooting them or the the presence of an armed challenge often can cause the suspect to kill themselves.

Ultimately, this could be the best outcome because it ends the event and no one else is required to take the life of the shooter. For example, a shooter at a shopping mall near Portland, Oregon took his own life after being confronted by an armed concealed weapons license holder.

2. **Hemorrhage Control** saves lives. This had been proven time and time again by battlefield medics. The use of hemostatic bandages and tourniquets can stop the bleeding efficiently enough to improve the victim's odds of survival.

Hemostatic bandages and tourniquets save lives and should be in every Police, Fire and First Responder's medical kit.

3. **Rapid Extrication, Assessment and Transport** all have to do with medical response. Medical personnel need to be part of the response Contact Team, Rescue Task Force.

With medical technicians imbedded into the response team, they can immediately triage victims. This includes applying bandages and tourniquets as the wounded are assessed, treated, and extracted out of harm's way.

This responsibility means that firefighters and EMTs need to train for being in an active shooting zone, knowing that the suspect could be waiting for them around the next corner. Medical personnel need to consider carrying and training in ballistic helmets and vests.

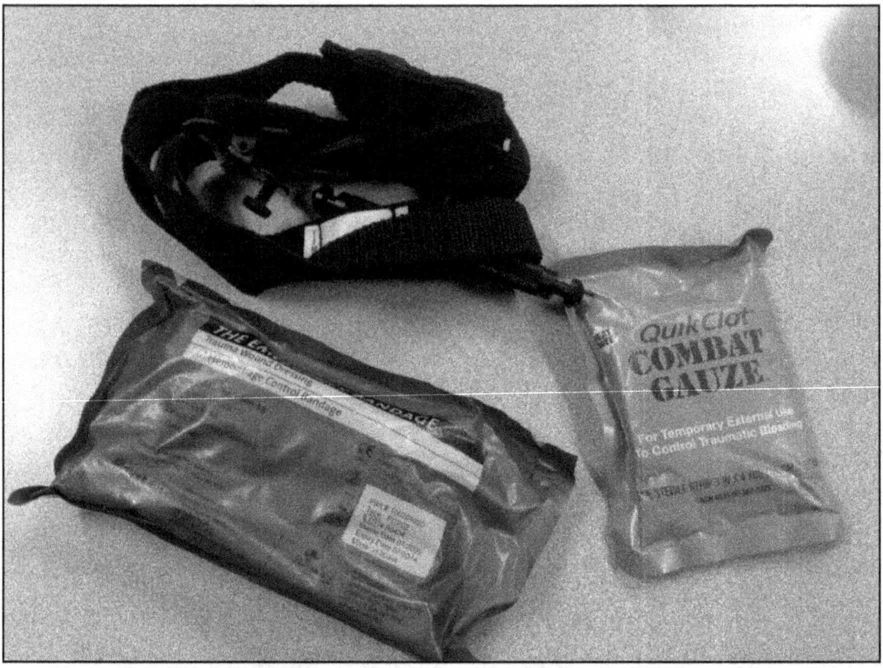

Hemostatic bandages and tourniquets save lives and should be in every Police, Fire and First Responder's medical kit.

Common Response Terminology

From FEMA, National Fire Protection Association, and other sources.

ASMCTE

Active Shooter & Mass Casualty Terrorist Event

CCP

Casually Collection Points, locations where triage can be performed.

Contact Team

Four Officers for Rapid Response

Incident Commander (IC)

The individual responsible for the management and coordination of all incident operations.

Lockdown

An emergency protocol used to protect people inside of a facility.

RTF
Rescue Task Force

TEMS
Tactical Emergency Medical Support

Hot Warm and Cold Zone Definitions
By the Los Angeles Police Department

Hot Zone - Where a direct and immediate threat exists based on the complexity and circumstances of the incident as determined by law enforcement. An area within range of direct gunfire or explosive devices or an unsecured or unsearched area where a suspect could be hiding is considered to be a Hot Zone. The Hot Zone is an Immediately Dangerous to Life and Health (IDLH) zone. Law enforcement resources (Contact Teams, SWAT teams, TEMS Specialists) should be the only safety personnel operating in the Hot Zone.

Warm Zone - Where a potential threat exists, but the threat is not direct or immediate. An area that has already been searched and secured by law enforcement is considered to be a Warm Zone. The threat still exists elsewhere in the building or venue, but law enforcement has cleared and secured an area to which fire and EMS personnel may be brought in to render Life Saving Intervention (LSI) to injured victims.

Cold Zone - Where no significant danger or threat can be reasonably anticipated. Determined by utilizing distance, geographic location, or terrain with respect to the type of firepower or explosive potential, the Cold Zone is the appropriate location for the Incident Command Post, Treatment Areas, Staging and logistical functions of the incident.

IEDs Used in Riots
The use of explosives is nothing new in political protests and riots. In modern times, it was used by the *Irish Republican Army* against the *British Army*. In the United States it was used by left wing groups to protest the Vietnam war. In 1975 the *Weather Underground* detonated a bomb that rocked the headquarters of the U.S. State Department in Washing D.C. They took credit for 25 other terroristic bombings and even accidently blew up their own headquarters killing three of their own in 1970.

Also, in 1970 a group of four men protesting the support of the *University of Wisconsin-Madison* to the *U.S. Army* during the Vietnam war. They detonated a van full of ANFO in front of Sterling Hall to destroy an Army Mathematics Research Center. The bomb killed one and injured three.

The difference from the 1970's and now is that back then, high explosives was loosely regulated and about anyone could find a way to access dynamite, ANFO and blasting caps. The ATF and other agencies started to more strictly controlling the sales and regulation of explosive that thankfully, makes it much more difficult for these materials to fall into the wrong hands. As mentioned in the beginning of the book, terrorist use what they can make, buy, or steal.

It is very difficult for terrorists to buy commercial or military high explosives, but they can steal them, and they do. The black-market demand for high explosives and blasting caps make them highly profitable and desirable to obtain. A much easier target is fireworks. We have seen in the 2020 United States riots, groups like ANTIFA and BLM use and weaponize fireworks.

A rioter in Portland, Oregon nearly blows himself up after a backpack of pyrotechnics explodes.

Weaponized Fireworks

In the United States, fireworks regulation is confusing considering every state has its own rules of what is considered off-the-shelf consumer grade fireworks. These fall into the hazmat 1.4G category. Many states have reduced the limits of the pyrotechnic powder in consumer fireworks that make them quite tame. Nothing can shoot through the air, limiting products like smoke bombs, whistling charges, and sparklers.

These products, however, can still be made into an IED. When I was a kid, we took two *Piccolo Pete* whistling charges, removed the powder the placed it in a two-liter plastic pop bottle. What little power was in the bottle created a loud enough boom to rattle windows two blocks away. It does not too much imagination for some to extract the powder and fuse to make a charge much bigger and more deadly.

Moving up the fireworks food chain, there are larger professional public display grade hazmat category 1.4S, 1.4Pro and 1.3G public display products. This includes flying and exploding shells such as bottle rockets, Roman candles, and mortar rounds. Many of these products are in ***Repeating*** package know as ***Cakes***. For example, there are 200-gram and 500-gram cakes that include a series of pre-loaded mortar tubes within a cardboard box. They are repeating because after a single fuse is lit, 9 to 24 mortar shells are fired one at a time.

The shells come in various sizes and pyrotechnic effects typically ranging from one-inch to three-inches. For example, a 1.75-inch shell can fly 120-feet (36 meters). A popular sized cake is 500-grams that can include six to nine, three-inch mortar tubes. A three-inch mortar shell can fly 210-feet (64 meters). These cakes can be shot horizontally and aimed at a target. Being on the receiving end of these shells can cause series injury as hundred of public safety personnel have be injured in the United States during the 2020 riots.

Hazmat classification 1.3 public display fireworks can include mortar shells that are four to six inches. These larger shells are fired from buried mortar tubes making them difficult to be used in riots. If these larger shells were stollen and detonated, they would make a deadly flying bomb.

500-gram cake with nine three-inch preloaded mortar tubes.

Access to Professional Display Grade Fireworks

To legally purchase these public display fireworks in the United States requires a license through the ATF. These larger fireworks are obtained in other ways, however. Indian Reservations sell various categories of larger fireworks over the counter. These reservation fireworks stands have become very popular since states of greatly restricted the power of consumer grade fireworks. These stands also sell all year around and not limited to the 4th of July timeframe.

Others obtain these materials on the black-market. Fireworks dealer could sell to friends and family then in turn get sold or stolen. Most of these fireworks are from China, which could also be smuggled in and sold on the black-market.

Flash powder is an extremely sensitive and powerful pyrotechnic substance that can easily be manufactured. This is the same material use in bombs like M-80s. While flash powder is a low explosive, getting enough of it together and placed in a container will cause it to detonate much more like a high explosive.

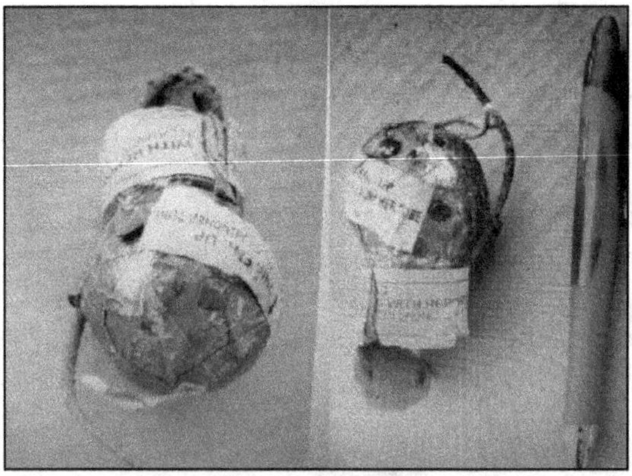

Mortar shells with nails in Atlanta to Molotov cocktails with 30 round mags in Portland. First Responder need to be prepared to face third world battlefield guerrilla tactics and conditions.

Turning Fireworks into IEDs

The report from a pyrotechnic round or shell can cause skin, eye, and ear burns and damage. Its smoke also causes irritation to the eyes, nose, sinus passages and lungs. Now adding metal to these charges turns them into deadly, flying shrapnel grenades. Officers in multiple cities like Seattle, Portland and Atlanta have found mortar shells imbedded with nails. The thee-inch shells can fly 210-feet then explode releasing the nails into a potential kill zone.

Adding flash powder, gun powder or any other pyrotechnic into a metal pipe or container creates a pipe bomb where the container shreds apart throwing deadly shrapnel throughout the air. The explosive substances used are typically fuse sensitive, which makes them easy to light and place or throw.

It should be notes that anyone making or possessing IEDs is a felony. If they are used in a crime where someone is hurt, the charges should be related to *Assault with a Deadly Weapon* which could get the user a lengthy prison term.

Riots are now Warzones

We have watched the rapid escalation from peaceful protests, to more aggressive protests, to riots to all out carefully planned guerrilla tactical warfare. This means that rioters are using strategically planned, well-funded attacks using a variety of weapons, firearms, explosives, protective gear, and shields.

Public safety personnel or anyone that finds themselves in this circumstance needs to be hyper-aware of potentially anything. Assume there will be shots fired. Rioters could be shooting directly at police and/or apposing political sides (the Right vs. the Left) could also be exchanging gunfire. Assume you will have fireworks shot at you as well as dangers objects thrown at you from bricks, to bombs, to feces.

Remember to consider deceptive and diversionary tactics. Do not let a mob separate you where you become more susceptible to assault. Do not let a mob move you or your group into a more isolated area that could be a potential ambush or IED kill zone. In these extreme battlefield scenarios, leadership, teamwork, and communication have never been more critical. Cover each other's six and go home safe.

Possible Reactions to Potential IEDs for First Responders

A First Responder's duty first and foremost is to keep others safe by helping keep them from being exposed to possible explosives or an IED. First Responders should not approach, handle, or disarm any possible device without extensive training. Doing so could put yourself and others at serious risk of death or injury.

The following are 11 actions First Responders can perform upon encountering a possible IED based upon the recommendations from our own team of explosives and anti-terrorism specialists.

1. Establish an initial exclusion zone based upon the potential threat.

2. Establish security by restricting access into the exclusion zone.

3. Do not let any non-bomb tech personnel to approach or move the device.

BOMB THREAT STAND-OFF CHART

Threat Description Improvised Explosive Device (IED)	Explosives Capacity[1] (TNT Equivalent)	Building Evacuation Distance[2]	Outdoor Evacuation Distance[3]
Pipe Bomb	5 LBS	70 FT	1200 FT
Suicide Bomber	20 LBS	110 FT	1700 FT
Briefcase/Suitcase	50 LBS	150 FT	1850 FT
Car	500 LBS	320 FT	1500 FT
SUV/Van	1,000 LBS	400 FT	2400 FT
Small Moving Van/ Delivery Truck	4,000 LBS	640 FT	3800 FT
Moving Van/ Water Truck	10,000 LBS	860 FT	5100 FT
Semi-Trailer	60,000 LBS	1570 FT	9300 FT

1. These capacities are based on the maximum weight of explosive material that could reasonably fit in a container of similar size.
2. Personnel in buildings are provided a high degree of protection from death or serious injury; however, glass breakage and building debris may still cause some injuries. Unstrengthened buildings can be expected to sustain damage that approximates five percent of their replacement cost.
3. If personnel cannot enter a building to seek shelter they must evacuate to the minimum distance recommended by Outdoor Evacuation Distance. These distance is governed by the greater hazard of fragmentation distance, glass breakage or threshold for ear drum rupture.

This Homeland Security chart shows evacuation distances based upon pounds of explosives. For example, 400 yards for a pipe bomb. This makes sense for the public, but as First Responders, how do you establish a perimeter from this distance? What are your agencies SOPs?

4. Search secure area for possible secondary explosive devices.

5. Does the device threaten a critical asset? This may provide clues to other placements.

6. Understand that the first device can be a diversion to group responders into a new kill zone.

7. Search for and identify potential suspect observation-vantage points.
8. Assume the suspect is watching, potentially waiting for the ideal time to detonate device.

9. Take protective measures, maintain cover to protect from possible blast.

10. Follow communication procedures without using radios or cells in secured area.

11. Continue to collect and report accurate and current intelligence.

Can you see the devices at a safer distance through binoculars? Report anything that could be helpful to the Bomb Techs. This would include:

A. Was there a bomb threat associated with this event?

B. Any sign of:
- Wires
- Fuse
- Smoke
- Antennas
- Oily Stains
- White or Pink Ammonium Nitrate Prills

C. Does it smell like:
- Oil
- Chemicals
- Gasoline
- Propane

D. If someone picked up the device or package, was it heavy?

E. Can you or did the person who discovered it take a photo or video with a cell phone?

Possible Reactions to Potential IEDs for Emergency Agencies and Managers

Seven actions upon encountering a possible IED, based upon the recommendations from the NFPA, the *National Fire Protection Association* from the Urban Fire Form, September 2013, UFF Position Statement: ***Active Shooter and Mass Casualty Terrorist Events***

A summary from this Position Statement includes:

1. Use of the National Incident Management System (NIMS) in particular the Incident Command System (ICS). In accordance with NIMS guidance, Fire and Police should establish a single Command Post (CP) and establish Unified Command (UC).

2. Police and Fire Departments should train together. Initial and ongoing training and practice are imperative to successful operations.

3. Use of common communications terminology. Fire department personnel must understand common police terms, such as Cleared, Secured, Cover, Concealment, Hot Zone/ Warm Zone /Cold Zone and related terms (red, green etc.), and others.

4. Provide appropriate protective gear to personnel exposed to risks. Firefighter EMT's and paramedics should be provided ballistic vests and helmets if they are to participate in a rescue task force (RTF).

5. Consider secondary devices at the main scene and secondary scenes in close proximity to the main scene.

6. Acts of terror using IED, as well as active shooters often prepare or actually begin their attacks at a location separate from the area designated as the main scene.

7. For events including IEDs, consider fire hazards secondary to the initial blast. For example, in public areas such as restaurants, clubs, schools and churches, natural gas is used in food preparation and heating; therefore, responders should check to ensure that gas lines and valves have not been compromised.

Additional information on First Responders from the NFPA can be found at: http://www.nfpa.org/research/resource-links/for-first-responders

Possible Reactions to Potential IEDs Performed by Bomb Techs

Improvised devices are so diverse and made from so many different types of triggering and explosive components, it is not possible to establish specific guidelines for every possible material or scenario. Instead the focus is on the safest and most effective way to disarm and dispose of explosive material based upon the assessment of the current threat. This is known as RSPs.

One concept that is consistent with techs is LIFE before PROPERTY! If a case of old explosives is found in a barn, they would typically rather burn down that barn than to risk human life by someone moving it by hand. Most bomb techs would not try to disarm a bomb unless it threatened human life.

Bomb techs would only risk their lives to disarm only in the most extreme circumstances. Such as a bomb placed in a hospital near patients that cannot be evacuated.

Bomb Techs will attempt to obtain all of the intelligence available to assist them in making the best decisions as possible based upon their experience and the circumstances. This is known as ***Render Safe Procedures (RSP)***.

RSPs are based upon years of real world front-line experience from EOD personnel using all the appropriate measures, tools and procedures to safely disable and disarm an IED or explosive ordnance. The following include methods Bomb Techs could utilize:

Command Wire Search

A search by metal detector or physical means to locate any wire that could connect to and detonate the IED through an electric charge.

A Chemring Technology Solutions metal detector is used to find buried command wires used to trigger a bomb.

X-Ray Device

A portable x-ray system can be deployed either manually or by robot to review the contents of suspicious packages. X-ray systems take time to set up and use, but at least Bomb Techs have the advantage to gain a better understanding of what they are dealing with.

Photo by Michael Sears

Mobile x-ray systems use a camera head and backing plate. Deputy Gary Nell of the Milwaukee Co., Wisconsin Sheriff's Office tests the contents of a suspicious package.

IED Water Disrupters

An explosive charge within or behind a water bladder that sends a jet of water through the device, destroying the bomb components enough to prevent detonation while still preserving the physical evidence such as fingerprints, the cell phone, or any other triggering device.

A ***PAN (Percussion Actuated Nonelectric) Disrupter*** also known as a ***Pig Stick***, is a more surgical version shooting a 12-gauge water based or metal projectile to breach and disrupt the bombs components.

An AEG Dragon water disrupter destroys a suitcase and the bomb hidden inside.

An AB Precision disrupter is set to blow a hole through a suspicious backpack at an airport.

Containment

Targets can be covered in place with ballistic blankets or sandbags to help mitigate the damage from the blast and fragmentation in the event of a detonation. These covers are ideally paced by a robot to further reduce the risk to officers.

SAC-D bags are used to contain an explosive device in conjunction with a PAN disrupter. These bags are ideal because when activated by water, they turn into 32 pounds of ballistic gel capable of stopping shrapnel, even rifle bullets.

EOD Robot or Unmanned Ground Vehicle (UGV)

Departments large enough to outfit their own robot team have the safety advantage to have a UGV available to check out a potential device to reduce the exposure to bomb techs. Robots can be equipped with a number of tools that bomb techs would have to place physically that includes X-ray, cameras and a disrupter with the added benefit of a grappling arm that may allow the robot to physically pick the device up to move it.

This larger UGV is equipped with a PAN disrupter to blast a hole through a suspicious box.

Radio Frequency Jammers

IEDs can be programmed to be triggered by radio frequencies such as a key up on a mobile radio or a cell phone call. Jammers can be set to block UHF, VHF, cell, and other signals to prevent the remote triggering of a device. These jammers can be vehicle mounted, portable or even backpack-sized.

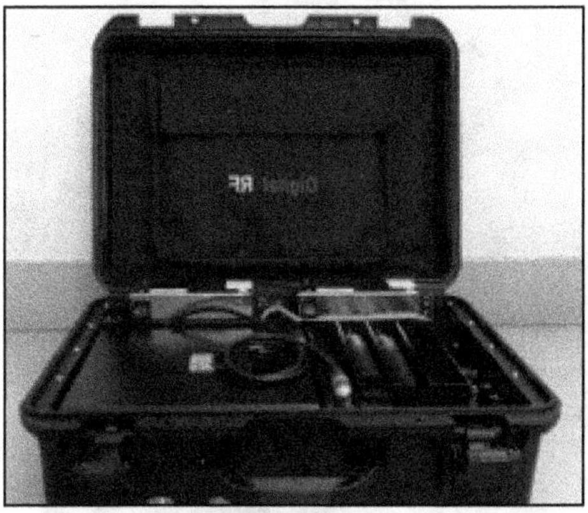

Radio jammers come in briefcase or vehicle mounted systems.

K-9s can detect virtually any explosive substance and assume a tell indicator to let their handler know they found something.

EOD K-9s

Various agencies and private companies train and use dogs to detect explosives. Their extremely sensitive sense of smell allow them to be trained to pick up the scent of virtually any homemade, commercial or military explosive substance. Dogs are trained to assume the sit position or some other tell once they detect an explosive.

Physically Disarming the IED

EOD bomb techs suit up to approach the device to disarm it by cutting out the detonator-blasting cap or other means to disarm to prevent detonation. Again this would only be attempted by highly trained bomb techs who feel it would be necessary typically only to help save human life.

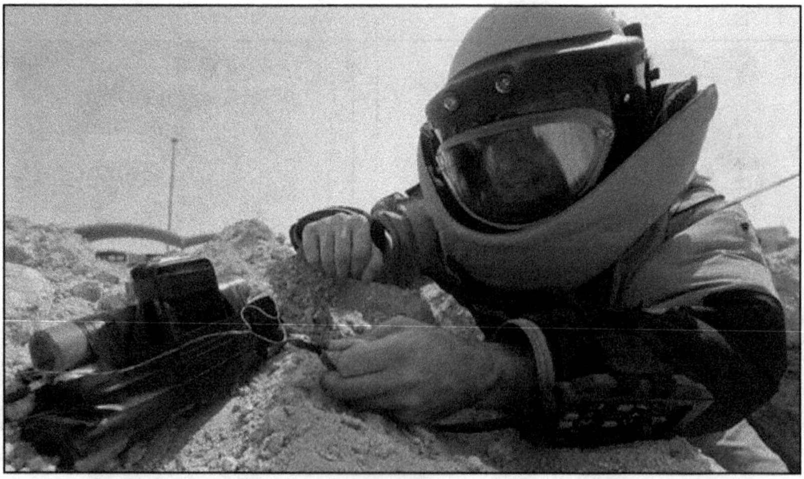

A U.S. Airforce EOD Tech cuts a wire to disarm an IED.

If a bomb tech decides to detonate explosives, they must consider its yield and possible damage it may cause. Ordnance that may be detonated is categorized in two categories:

High Order Detonation

A detonation of the material's full explosives power.

Low Order Detonation

A detonation of low or limited explosive power through detrition, control or malfunction.
Once a bomb tech makes the choice to destroy ordnance through detonation, they can do so by the following two methods:

Blown in Place BIP

Ordnance is too dangerous to move, destroyed on site.

Safe Detonation Area SDA

Safely moved and detonated in a designated blast area. This could be in an open field or bomb teams can utilize their own ***Bomb Disposal Chambers or Bomb Containment Vessels*** to safely contain the blast.

EOD Bomb Disposal Chambers are ideal for disposing of a potential threat on site without the added risk of moving it to another location.

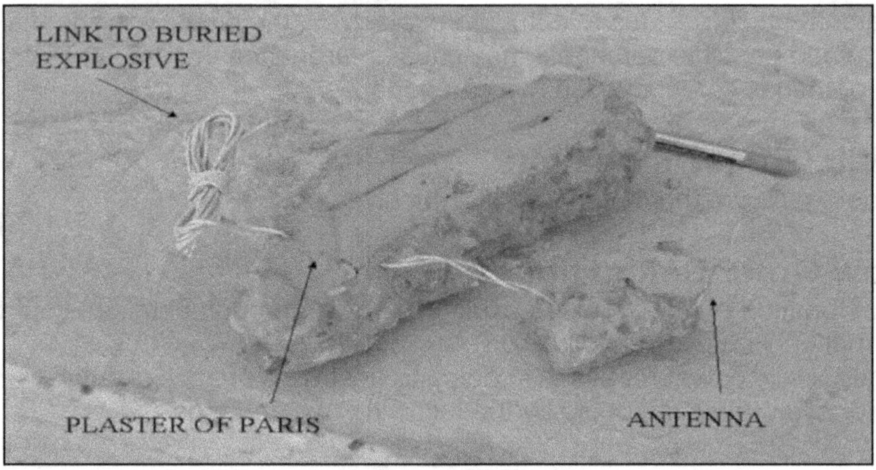

In IED can look like anything, even a rock.
This one was found and disarmed in Iraq.

Bomb Containment Vessels are ideal for safely securing IEDs or even suspicious packages. Our company tests NABCO vessels with ten different 8 KG explosive charges with no sign of failure. In this photo, a bomb team tests using their robot.

18. IED U.S. CASE STUDY

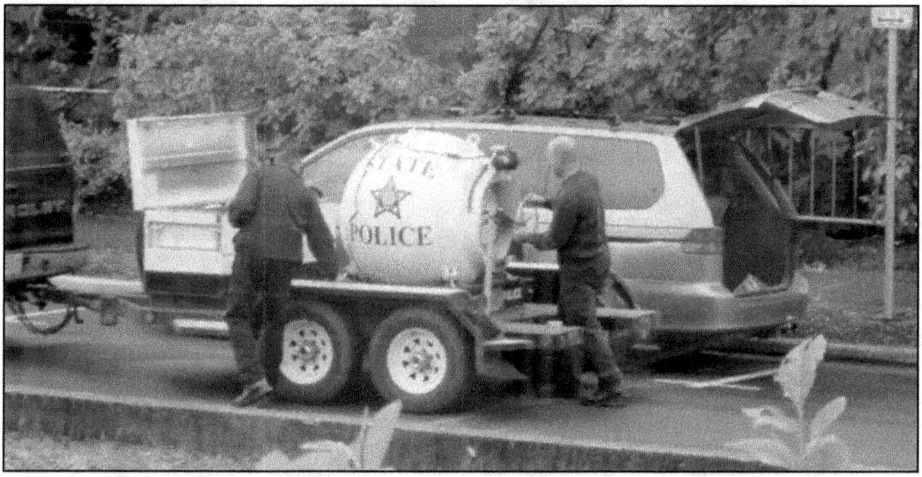

There are thousands of examples of failed IED, bomb and terroristic attacks in the United States alone. The following list of eleven attacks was selected for this study do to the following three criteria:

- The attacks had some level of success
- The diverse makeup of the suspects and their ideology
- The wide variety of explosive materials and tactics used

The prior use of tactics and explosives is certainly no guarantee that they will be used again, but it is important to understand that there are many consistencies from various historical attacks. Terrorists are highly motivated to use what has been proven effective in the past based upon what explosive materials and weapons they have access to.

While much of the attention is currently being placed on *ISIS, ISIL, Al Qaeda* and other radical Muslim terrorist groups, as indicated by this case study, bombers can have strong motivation based upon a variety of other political, religious or criminal intent.
The bottom line is that investigators and first responders must keep an open mind while gathering the facts needed to address any possible explosive-based threat.

Case 01 Seattle Police East Precinct Bombing

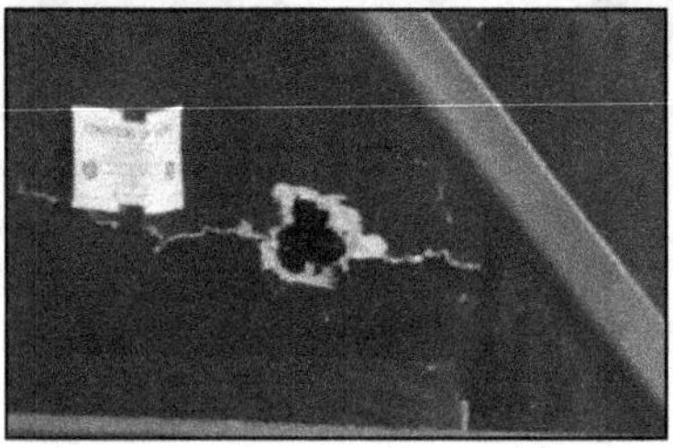

Date	July 25, 2020
Location	12th Street, Seattle, Washington
Suspects	Leftist riot/protest groups that most likely include member of ANTIFA and BLM.
Summary	Rioters breached a security fence and proceeded to burn a building at the *King County Youth Services Center* construction site. The mob moved to Seattle Police Department's East Precinct. Security cameras were disabled with spray paint, then their security fence was breached. Moments later a bomb was detonated leaving an eight-inch hole in the precinct wall. "The crowd threw bottles, balloons filled with liquid, shot mortars fireworks and threw explosives at officers." Seattle.gov On July 29th, a van whose occupants were supplying riots with pyrotechnics and weapons was seized. IEDs were found including mortar balls imbedded with nails to make shrapnel.
Material	A mixture of fireworks, illegal and homemade IEDs from unknown and firework materials.
Outcome	21 officers injured from this event, 59 officers injured in total. 47 rioters arrested. Case remains under investigation by arson/bomb detectives.

Case 02 **Pulse Nightclub Shooting**

Date	June 11, 2016
Location	Pulse Nightclub, Orlando, Florida
Suspect	Omar Mateen, 29. Islamic, called 9-1-1 to state the attack was in retaliation for the U.S. killing Abu Waheeb, an ISIL commander in Iraq.
Summary	Mateen walked into a packed gay nightclub and opened fire, killing and wounding as many patrons as he could. After a brief firefight with an armed off-duty officer, he retreated deeper into the building and took hostages. He called 9-1-1 to confess to being the shooter and swore allegiance to the leader of the Islamic State of Iraq. He told 9-1-1 that he was wearing an explosives vest and there was a car in the parking lot filled with enough explosives to level city blocks. This delayed the police's aggressive response, giving Omar more time to shoot additional victims. Eventually, SWAT breached the rear wall and after a firefight, Mateen was killed by police.
Material	Rifle and handgun. No explosives, but the threat of explosives delayed the police response.
Outcome	49 people dead, 53 injured, Mateen shot dead. Tactical personnel and active shoot specialists debated the decision to delay their attack on the shooter despite the extreme potential danger of the suspects threat to use explosives. From this event it was confirmed that eliminating the active shooter as soon is possible saves lives despite the extreme risk of entering an unknown IED threat.

Case 03 San Bernardino Shooting-Bombs

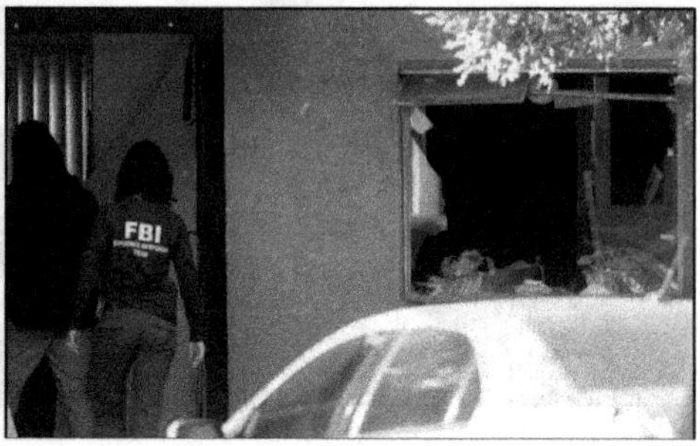

Date	December 2, 2015
Location	San Bernardino, California
Suspects	Syed Rizwan Farook and Tashfeen Malik, an Islamic terrorist married couple. Possibly an arranged married as part of their sleeper cover including the couple having a six-month old baby daughter. Couple allegedly inspired and or backed by ISIS. Unknown status of a possible third suspect.
Summary	The couple opened fire on co-workers during a Christmas party at a county office building, the Inland Regional Center in San Bernardino. A pipe bomb with a remote triggering device to kill first responders. Fortunately, the bomb did not go off. Pipe bombs were used during police vehicle pursuit, and one dozen pipe bombs were found in the terrorist's Redlands, California home.
Material	Bomb making lab in the couple's home to produce pipe bombs, but bombs used during the attack failed to detonate or were empty of a primary explosive material. The home bomb lab included 18 pipe bombs, gun powder and RC cars. Bomb left behind at the office building consisted of three pipe bombs attached together on a remote-control car hidden in a canvas bag. The design is believed to be copied from a design published in Al Qaeda's *Inspire* magazine.
Outcome	14 people dead, 21 injured, both terrorists shot dead.

Case 04 **Boston Marathon**

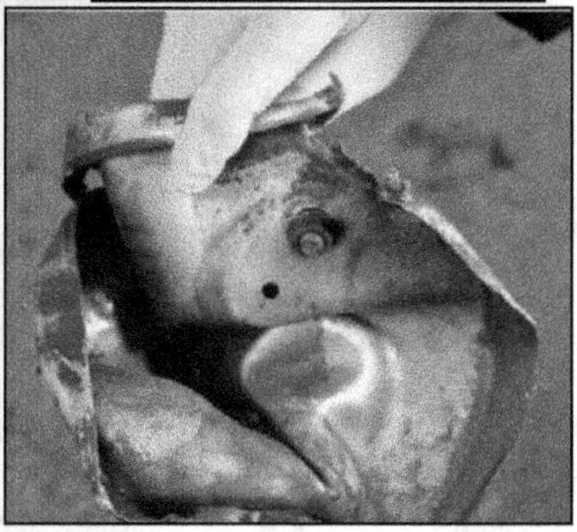

Date	April 15, 2013
Location	Boston, Massachusetts
Suspects	Dzhokhar and Tamerlan Tsarnaev, radicalized Muslims
Summary	Two bombs hidden in backpacks explode in the packed streets near the finish line of the Boston Marathon.
Material	Homemade pressure cooker bombs. Brothers learn to make from al-Qaeda magazine *Inspire*, "Make a Bomb in the Kitchen of Your Mom." Pressure cookers filled with black powder, nails, and ball bearings. Initiated with light build filament activated with a remote detonator. The pressure cooker container contains and intensifies the power of the low explosive, (black powder).
Outcome	Three people dead, 246 injured. One brother dead, the other convicted and sentenced to death.

Case 05 Medford, Oregon DA's Office

Date	November 13, 2013
Location	Medford, Oregon
Suspects	None known or convicted
Summary	Propane tank IED bomb left in front of the DA's Office. Booster charge was set on fire and blew out a window without detonating the propane tank.
Material	Propane tank with most likely a black powder charge for a booster.
Outcome	Minor property damage, no injuries. Would have been much worse if tank would have exploded.

Case 06 **Martin Luther King Day Parade**

Date	January 17, 2011
Location	Spokane, Washington
Suspects	White supremacist, Kevin Harpham, serving life in prison.
Summary	Meant to disrupt a civil rights march, the bomb was found by a security guard and police disarmed before it was detonated.
Material	Pipe bombs protected by a motion sensor car alarm.
Outcome	Bomb disarmed, no damage or injuries.

Case 07 West Coast Bank, Woodburn, Oregon

Date	December 12, 2008
Location	Woodburn, Oregon
Suspects	Anti-Gov extremists, Joshua Turnidge, son, Bruce Turnidge, father.
Summary	Botched bank robbery. Wells Fargo Bank receives a bomb threat and is instructed to pick up a cell phone hidden out front for further instructions. Experts search and determine there is no bomb. Later in the day, a device was located at a bank next door, West Coast Bank. State bomb technician concludes it is a hoax and brings it into Wells Fargo Bank. At 5:24 PM it explodes, killing Oregon State Police Senior Trooper William Hakim and Woodburn Capt. Tom Tennant, critically injuring Woodburn Chief Scott Russell and cutting a bank employee's leg.
Material	Unknown
Outcome	Two officers dead, two others injured, suspects convicted and on death row.

Case 08 Time Square Vehicle IED

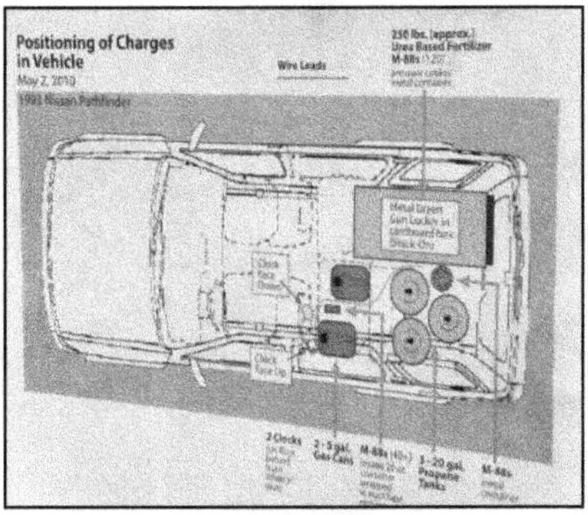

Date	May 1, 2010
Location	Manhattan, New York
Suspects	Pakistani Muslim, Faisal Shazad, convicted, life in prison.
Summary	Nissan Pathfinder packed with explosives left in Times Square. Street venders spot smoke coming from vehicle and the bomb was disabled with the help of a bomb robot before the primary charges were detonated.
Material	Two travel alarm clocks with batteries that apparently were fashioned as triggering devices, connected by electrical wires to two red, full 5-gallon cans of gasoline, sandwiching 120 M-88 consumer-grade firecrackers inside a 20-ounce metal container, gunpowder, three full 20-gallon propane tanks, and metal gun locker that contained: a metal pressure cooker pot with wires connected to the alarm clocks and 250 pounds (110 kg) of urea-based fertilizer.
Outcome	No damage or injuries. If the bomb would have detonated, there would have been a great deal of blast and shrapnel that would have most likely killed and wounded many.

Case 09 Underwear Bomber

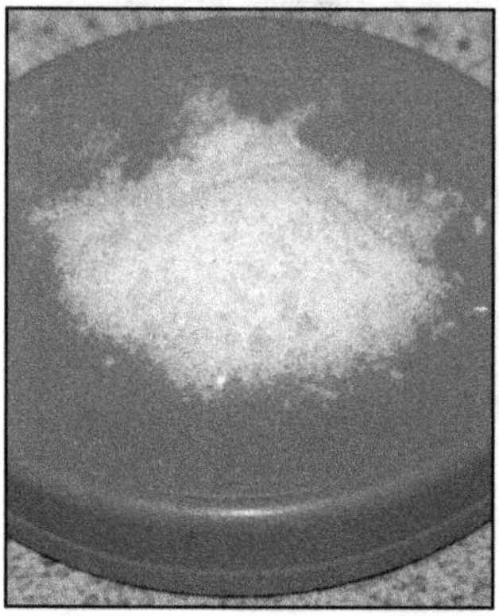

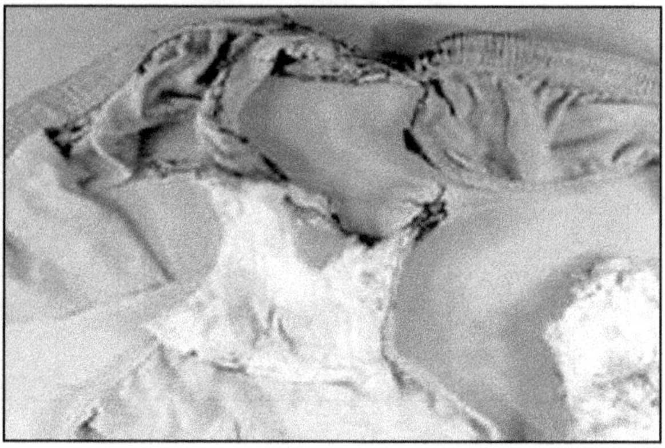

Date	December 25, 2009
Location	Air France Flight 447 from Paris to Detroit
Suspects	Nigerian, Umar Farouk Abdulmutallab, convicted, life sentence.
Summary	Suspect attempts to detonate a bomb by injecting an acid filled syringe into an explosive material sewn his underwear. This created a chemical reaction, small detonation and fire, but did not detonate the primary explosive. Passengers and crew on the plane subdue him.
Material	80 grams (2.8 oz) of pentaerythritol tetranitrate (PETN), a crystalline powder that is often the active ingredient of plastic explosives, the high explosive triacetone triperoxide (TATP).
Outcome	Suspect severely burned, one passenger received minor burns. No structural damage to plane, but a full detonation would have most likely breached the hull and depressurized the plane.

Case 10 The Unabomber

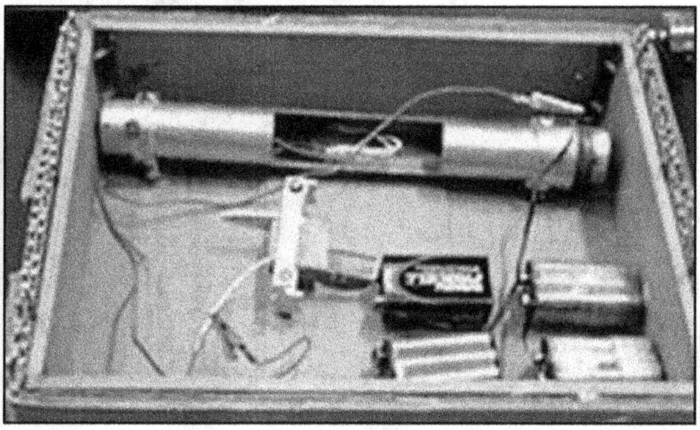

Date	January 22, 1998, guilty conviction for spree 1978-1995
Location	Nationwide, arrested in Lincoln, Montana
Suspects	Leftist anarchist, Theodore Kaczynski
Summary	Placed or mailed 16 separate bombs to various professors, engineers, and executives to protest the advancement of technology. Got his name from the FBI for initially targeting Universities and Airlines.
Material	Black powder pipe bombs often filed with shrapnel in boxes with physical or electronic trigger devices.
Outcome	16 bombs left three people dead, 23 injured. Suspect was arrested after the release of his manifesto through the assistance of his brother David. Convicted, life in prison.

Case 11 — Centennial Olympic Park Summer Games

Date	July 27, 1996
Location	Atlanta, Georgia
Suspects	Eric Robert Rudolph, Anti-Abortion protester, convicted, life in prison.
Summary	Security guard, Richard Jewell discovered an army backpack under a concert stage containing three pipe bombs and cleared the crowed prior to detonation. Jewel was falsely implicated by the FBI for the crime.
Material	U.S. military ALICE backpack containing three pipe bombs triggered by an alarm clock surrounded by three-inch-long (7.6 cm) masonry nails, which caused most of the human injuries. A steel plate was used as a directional device.
Outcome	Two people dead, one from injury, one from a heart attack, 111 injured.

Case 12 Alfred P. Murrah Federal Building in Oklahoma City

Date	April 19, 1995
Location	Oklahoma City, Oklahoma
Suspects	Timothy McVeigh and Terry Nichols
Summary	Rental delivery box truck parked in front of building packed with explosives.
Material	Ammonium nitrate as the oxidizer and Nitromethane as the fuel
Outcome	168 people dead, more than 500 injured

Case 13 World Trade Center (first attack)

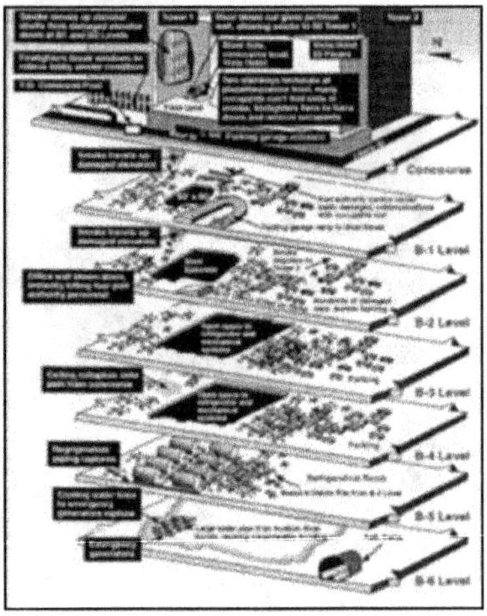

Date	February 26, 1993
Location	Manhattan, New York
Suspects	A cell of five Muslim extremists, convicted, life in prison.
Summary	A rental delivery truck packed with explosives detonates in the underground World Trade Center garage under the North Tower.
Material	A 1,310-pound bomb, which was made of a urea nitrate main charge with aluminum, magnesium and ferric oxide particles surrounding the explosive. The charge used nitroglycerine, ammonium nitrate dynamite, smokeless powder and fuse as booster explosives. Three tanks of bottled hydrogen were also placed in a circular configuration around the main charge, to enhance the fireball and afterburn of the solid metal particles.
Outcome	Six people dead, over 1,000 injured.

19. EXPLOSIVES DOOR BREACHING

Chapter Topics:

- Understand various techniques for door breaching.
- Learn how to breach doors and walls with det cord.
- Learn to use two styles of *Dragon* water impulse charge door breaching bags.
- Understand the tactical advantage of multi-breach operations.

Door breaching is as old as warfare itself as ancient armies developed battering rams to bust through fortress doors and walls. Things have not changed much. Chances of survival increase when breachers can go undetected and with as little time as possible in front of the door, the 'Fatal Funnel.' Referred to as the fatal funnel because once the bad guys believe there are intruders at the door, the odds are good that a spray of bullets could quickly follow.

To introduce you to breaching we will be introducing you to breaching terms as the different types of breaching followed by various door breaching techniques. Then we will over for team specific actions that include room clearing principles, weapons control and safety considerations for team members.

Breaching Terminology

Breach Area
It is the area where a breaching operation occurs. It has to be large enough to safely accommodate the entry team and support personnel.

Bypass
The ability to maneuvering around an obstacle to maintain the momentum of advance.

Clearing
The total elimination or neutralization of an obstacle.

Deliberate Breach
A breach conducted on a known obstacle where there is generally advanced knowledge and planning.

Farside Objective
The purpose of the breach and the mission once the obstacle has been cleared.

In-Stride Breach
A breach conducted on an unexpected obstacle such as a cable across a vehicle access point.

Lane
The safest proposed route to take through a breached area.

Obstacle
A man-made obstruction that is needed to be breached, such as a door, gate, window or wall.

Point of Breach
This is the location at an obstacle where the creation of a lane is being attempted.

Proofing
A lane for movement that has been cleared of mines or booby-traps.

Different forms of Breaching

There are four primary ways to breach doors, gates, walls and other obstacles:

Ballistic

Special 12-gauge powdered steel rounds to blow through locks and hinges. Any rounds will work, but powdered ones are used to help avoid injury from ricochet.

A disadvantage of this method is that if the deadbolt and primary lock are positioned too far away from each other, it could require two shots to beach the door.
Another issue is that the point breacher will have to carry two weapons or two type of ammunition as they transition from breaching to needing a primary weapon.

Mechanical

Crow bars and battering rams are used to pry open or bash through doors and locks. This method is low tech, simple and effective, but is noisy and could require two or more strikes to breach.

Thermal

A torch is used to burn through door locks and hinges. Effective and less noise than other forms of breaching. The disadvantage is that it puts the door breacher in harm's way with acetylene and oxygen tanks.

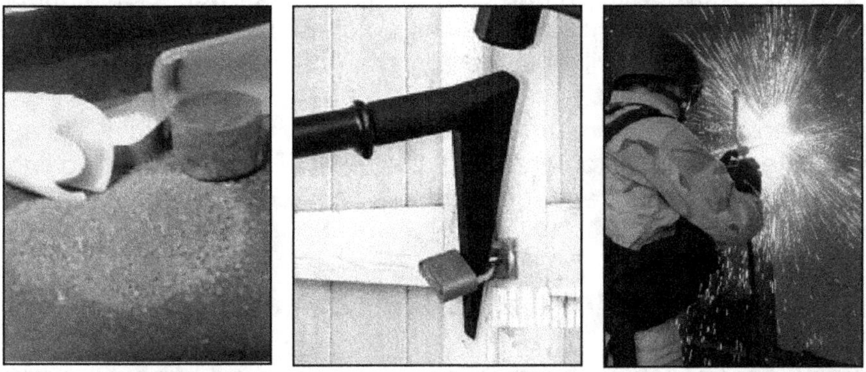

Alternatives to explosives breaching; 12 gauge rounds filled with metal powder, pry breach bars and thermal torch.

While all these forms of breaching have their place, we will be focusing on the use of explosives. While using this method of breaching should only be used for the most extreme circumstances, is probably the safest and most effective method. Why, because the biggest advantage the entry team has is speed and surprise.

The longer the delay at the door, the greater the risk to the team. Explosive breaching provides the opportunity to remove a door, stun and surprise the bad guys inside, all while doing so with limited exposure to the entry team.

Explosive Charges

Here are a number of techniques used to breach doors and obstacles using explosives. Door hangers and 'C' charges blow door knobs out of doors or ***Water Impulse Charge Breaching Bags*** can blow even the heaviest doors right off the hinges.

Explosives breaching can be the safest despite blast overpressure and flying debris. Setting a door breach charge, as tricky as it could be, is still quieter and less evasive than most other methods of breaching. Most effective also because based upon the circumstances, the breacher can decide to drop the door off the hinges or blow it through the room creating additional 'shock and awe' to stun and completely overwhelm any hostiles inside.

Explosives breaching is an extreme measure for the most extreme of tactical circumstances. Liability can be great as there is a possibility of injury to the occupants inside as well as the breach team.

Be sure to review, train on and carefully follow your agencies standard operating procedures. It should also be noted that breaching can fall into two categories: Civilian law enforcement and full military operations.

In a civilian law enforcement operation, great care will be taken to avoid any collateral damage to persons or property. This means using lighter charges and using just enough materials as necessary to get the job done.

Explosives Door Breaching

Learning door beaching is simply a matter of trial and error with various techniques and amounts of materials. We used various techniques and will break down door breaching using the following methods starting with the smallest charges first.

Doorknob Charges

These charges are simple, easy to make and effective for most light-to-medium constructed wood or metal doors.

Door hangers are easy to make from det cord and plastic and very effective for most light-to-medum weight doors.

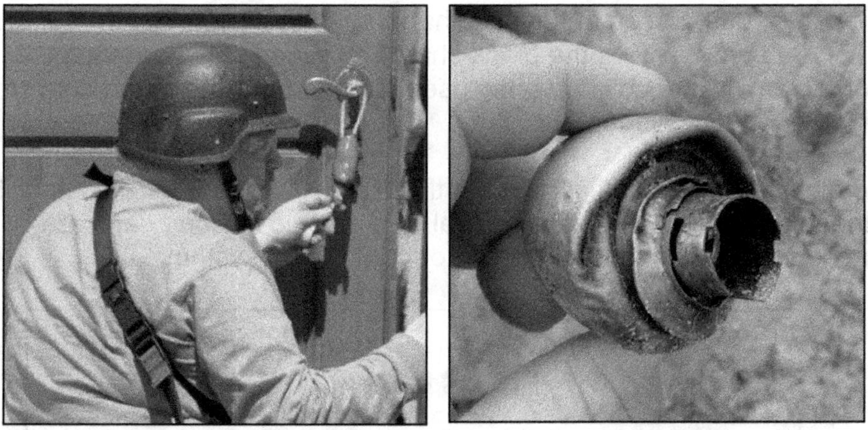

Simply hanging them on the door knob makes them quick and easy to deploy. Watch for flying door knobs.

They are made from a roll of det cord or det cord supplemented with a quarter to half pound block of plastic explosive. There are several advantages to using this style of breach. Door hangers are easy to make using det cord with the option of some additional plastic if it is determined there is a need for some extra punch.

They are also easy to deploy by simply one person hanging on the doorknob. This creates minimal noise and exposure for the breacher to hang the device and get out of the way before there is a large gaping hole where the doorknob used to be. Watch out for flying doorknobs.

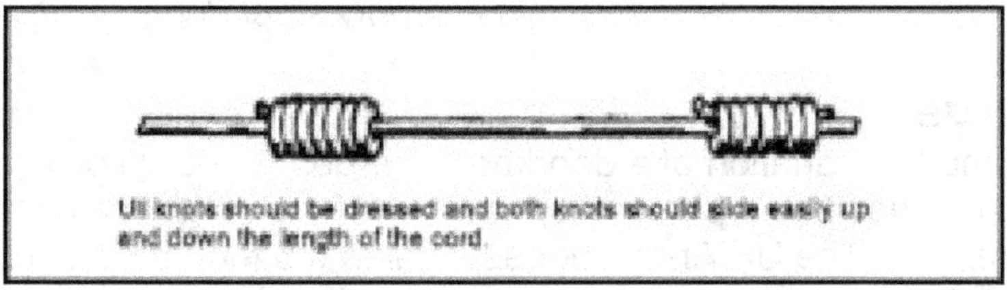

U.S. Army

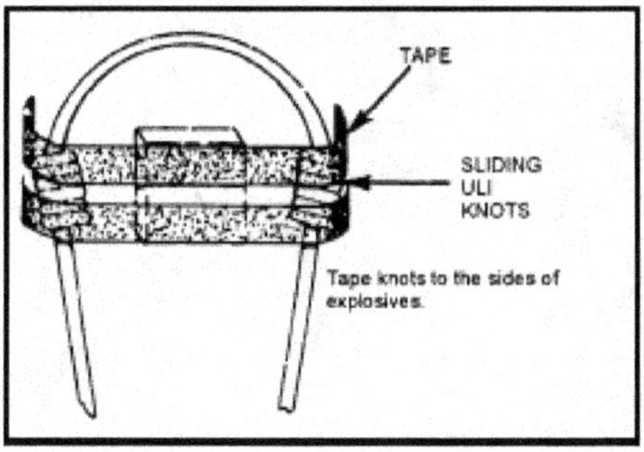

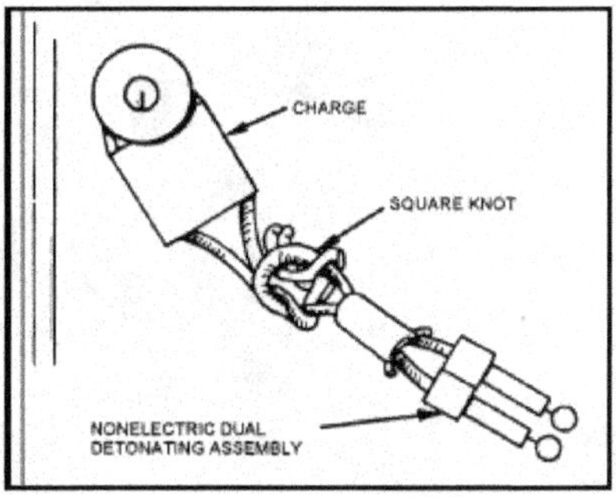

U.S. Army

The basic construction of the door hanger is the ***Uli*** knot made from a coil of det cord allowing the block charge to slide tight up against the doorknob. Uli knot coils are also used to slide on a line of det cord to be adjusted for door hinges.

The block of explosives is taped to the uli knot allowing for adjustability in the top loop. In the diagram, dual non-electric blasting caps are attached to the det cord tail for a redundant firing system.

Door hanger with a quarter pound of C-4 easily rips a large whole in a hollow steel door.

C Charge

This is another variation of a doorknob charge. A square piece of cardboard is used as a platform to secure det cord onto, then attached to a doorknob. The US Army suggests using 6.5 feet of 50 grain det cord loops at least three times around the cutout for the doorknob.

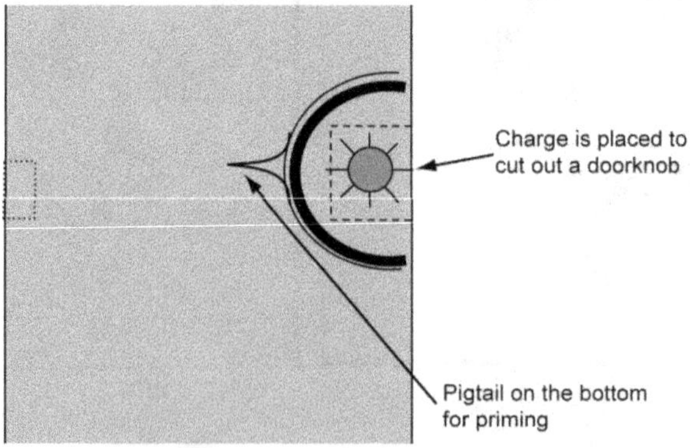

Det Cord Charges for Doors and Walls

Det cord will easily burn through doors. Det cord can be taped directly onto the door or onto cardboard, then taped to the door using double-sided tape.

Here is a chart to estimate the amount of det cord needed based upon 50 grains per foot:

Wooden Door Hollow	One wrap
Wooden Door Partial Filled	Two wraps
Wooden Door Solid	Three wraps
Wooden Door Solid Heavy	Four wraps
Plywood ¼ inch	One wrap
Plywood ½ inch	Two wraps
Plywood ¾ inch	Three wraps

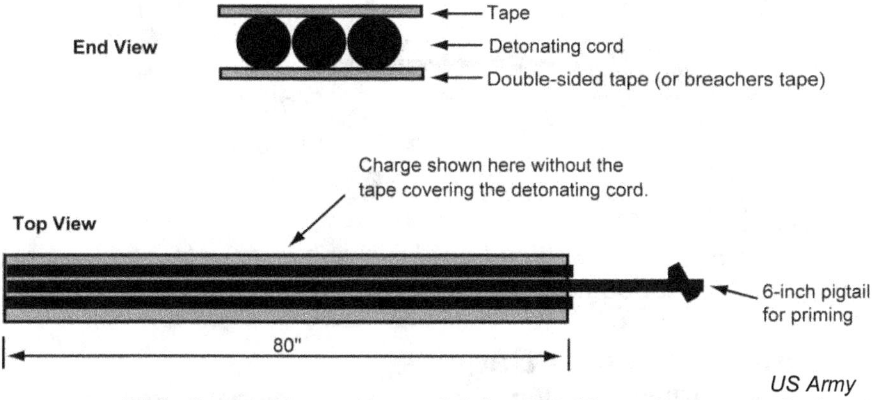

This linear charge uses 21 feet of 50 grain det cord. It will cut right through most wooden doors and walls.

US Marines cut a perfect hole in a wall by taping det cord to a folding cardboard silhouette targets.

Det cord can be attached to cardboard in any shape to make sniper or entry holes.

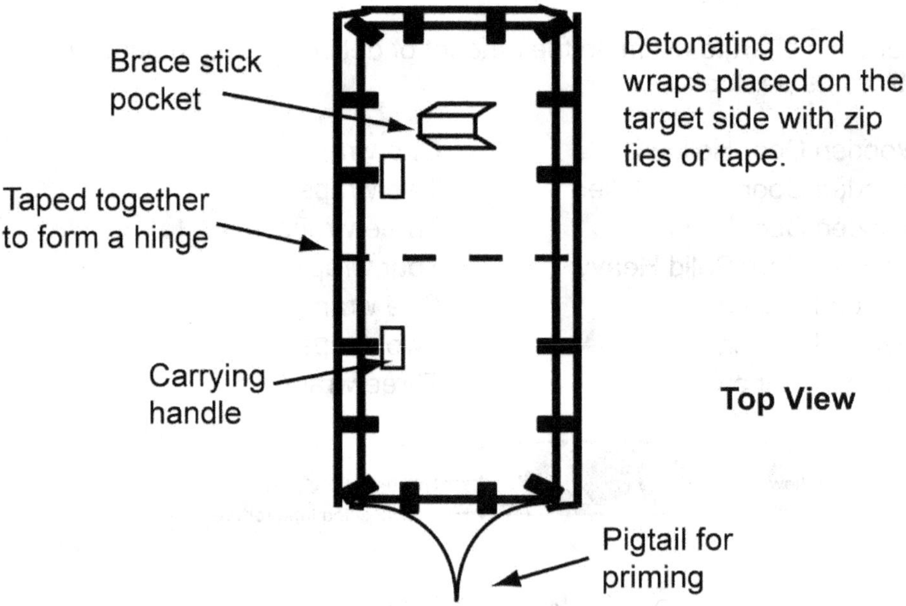

This wall breaching board is made from det cord taped to silhouette target cardboard.

Water Impulse Charge Bags

Plastic bags filled with water stem the explosive material extremely well due to that water does not contract. The water bag creates a hydraulic knockout punch to fold a door in or blow it off the hinges. Water multiplies the explosive's effect through hydraulic force and tamping. Water makes the perfect tamping material because water does not compress.

AEG Dragon Tail™

This is a linear water bladder device with a pocket for strands of det cord. Three strands, approximately 21 feet will take hollow metal door and neatly fold it in half and drop it off its hinges.

The DRAGON Tail filled with det cord is perfect for heavy wood or hollow steel doors.

Bag Water Impulse Charge

Water bag charges have been used for years, originally made from IV medical bags, with det cord or plastic placed between two IV bags filled with water and hung on a door. A U.S. Army manual suggests using 11 feet of 50 grain det cord.

The challenge to using bag water impulse charges is hanging them or attaching them to the door. Because they are filled with water, they are heavy and can be difficult to attach, especially when the breachers are trying to work without tipping off the itchy, trigger-fingered occupants inside.

Bags can be hung with Paracord from a hook or nail placed in crack above the door. Double sided tape, breachers or carpet tape may be strong enough to hold the weight. Another option is to use a prop-up stick to hold the bags against the door.

Jack showing off what's left of a door after an AEG Dragon Tail™ with 21 feet of 25 gr det cord folds and drops it perfectly.

Charge Construction (Side View)

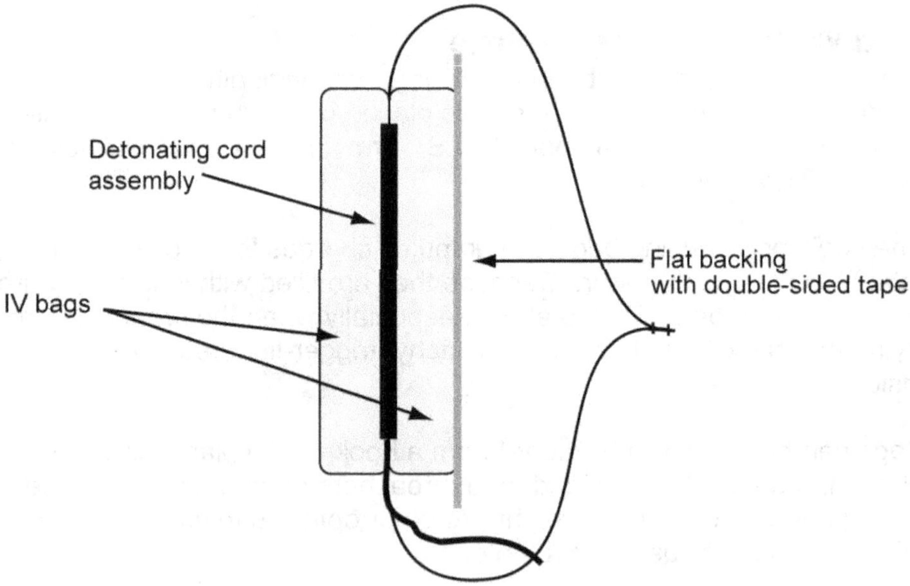

U.S. Army

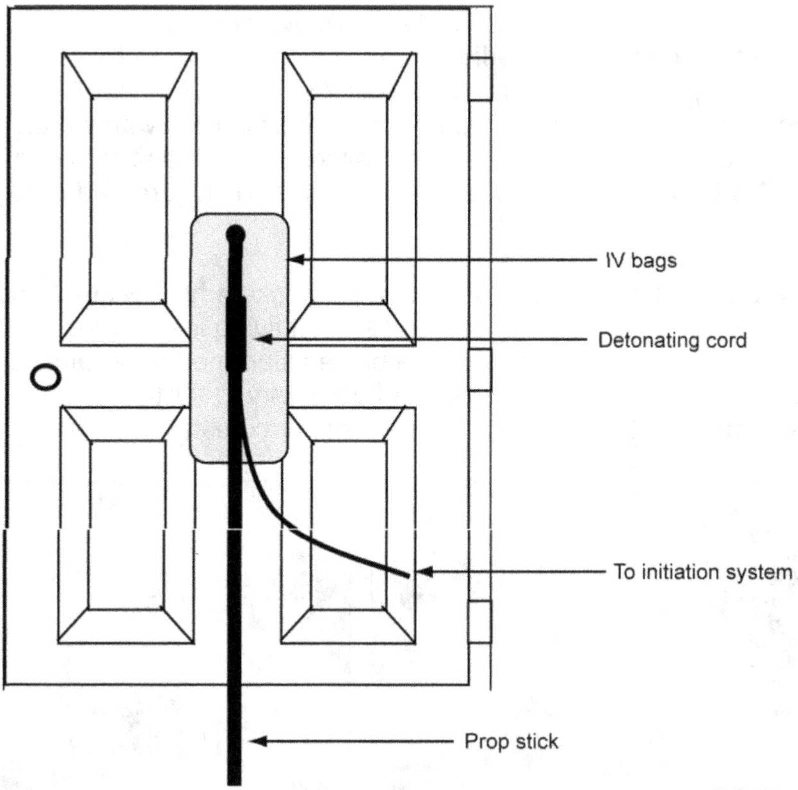

U.S. Army

AEG DRAGON C-4 Bag™

We have taken the idea of the IV bag and stepped it up to a professional level.

The C-4 Dragon bag is a water impulse charge

with a pocket for the explosive charge.

Instead of taping together medical bags, we offer solution that is mission- ready out of the box. The *DRAGON™ C-4 Bag* has two chambers. First, unscrew the plastic caps and fill them with water. Next fill the pocket with any explosive from coiled det cord, a stick a dynamite to a C-4 M112 block. Then seal the with a Velcro closure and ready to hang.

It should be noted that one pound of C-4 will take a hollow steel door and not only blow it off the hinges, but send it flying into pieces. In this test, the door flew 15 meters until the pieces slammed up against a rock wall. This method of breaching should be reserved for the most reinforced heavy doors in the more extreme circumstances.

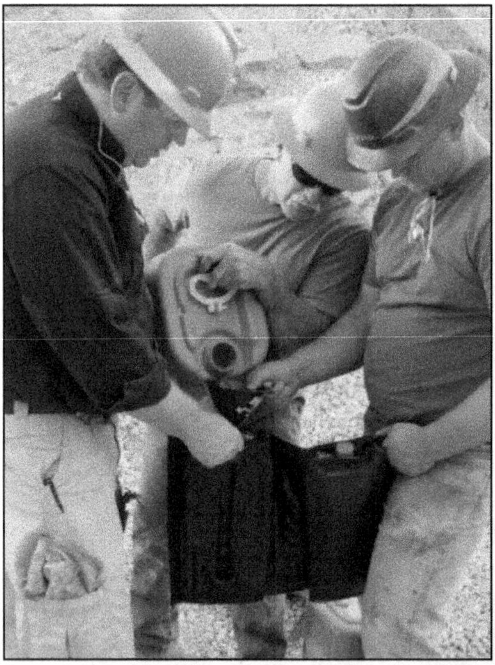

Our DRAGON C-4 bag is mission-ready out of the box. Fill with water, load explosives and hang for only the heaviest doors.

This method is overkill except for the heaviest doors in the most extreme circumstances. One pound of C-4 will send a metal door flying into pieces.

Some breachers will double this up by hanging two at a time, but it would have to be an extremely solid door to need that kind of knockdown power.

Deploying Simultaneous Multi-Breach Points

There is a substantial tactical advantage to having multiple breach or access points during an operation. One point may have limited access for entry or viewing what is happening on the inside. A second location provides another option as well as a flanking position. Two breaching points going off at once also doubles the 'Shock and Awe' stunning the occupants, possibly making the operation safer for the breach team.

This this example, Breach Team A uses a water impulse bag charge on the main door. A second wall silhouette det cord charge is used for Breach Team B. The two charges can be fused together with a line of shock tube or det cord initiated by Team A or a separate initiation system fired by Team B at the same time.

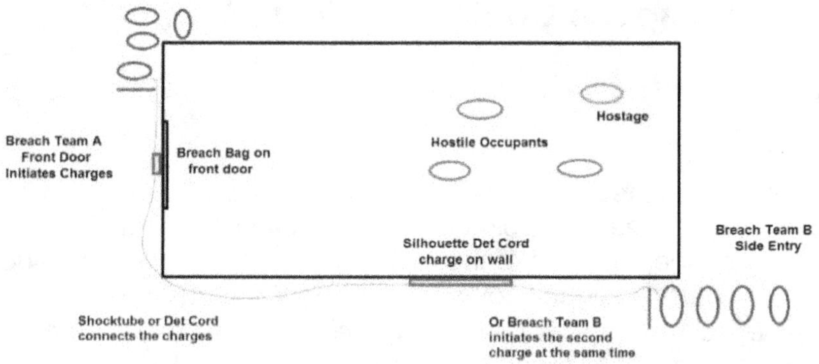

Blowing the wall out gives Team B the advantage of a critical second viewing, shooting and entry position considering there are known hostile occupants holding a hostage. The charges are made to use just enough det cord as needed to breach the door and the wall without throwing any unnecessary debris to help avoid causing injury to the hostage.

Precision Room Clearing Principles

Room clearing operations need to be conducted with absolute care to avoid firing upon entry teammates, or other friendly or non-hostile targets. Each team must do extensive training together to help ensure smooth, safe and successful operations utilizing the following three principles:

Surprise

Surprise is the key to a successful entry by distracting and startling the unfriendly occupants inside.

Speed

Speed provides a measure of security to the clearing unit. It allows team members to use the first few vital seconds provided by surprise to their maximum advantage. In precision room clearing, speed is not how fast you enter the room, rather it's how fast the threat is eliminated and the room is cleared.

Controlled Violence of Action

Controlled violence of action neutralizes hostile targets while giving them the least chance of inflicting friendly casualties. It is not limited to the application of firepower only, but also involves a mindset of complete domination of the room and its occupants by team members.

Weapons Control for Team Members

Clearing team members must move tactically and safely. This includes proven and standardized techniques as follows:

- When moving, team members maintain ***Muzzle Awareness*** by holding their weapons pointed in the direction of travel. Team members keep the butt of the rifle in the pocket of their shoulder, with the muzzle slightly down to allow unobstructed vision.
- Both eyes are open as they swing the muzzle as they turn their head, so the rifle is always aimed where they are looking.

- This procedure allows a clear view to see what or who is entering their line of fire.

- Team members avoid ***Flagging*** or leading with the weapon when working around windows, doors, corners, or areas where obstacles must be negotiated. Flagging the weapon gives advance warning of the breaching team members making it easier for a hostile to grab a weapon.

- Team members handle their weapons safely that includes muzzle direction control and having their trigger index finger outside of the trigger guard until a hostile target is identified and engaged. The use and timing of a weapons' SAFE switch is based upon your agency's SOPs.

- If a team member has a weapons malfunction during room clearing, he should immediately announce '*Gun-Down*' and drop to one knee and conduct immediate action to reduce the malfunction.

- The other members of the team should engage targets in his sector. Once the weapon is operational, he should announce '*Gun-Up*' and remain in the kneeling position until directed to stand-up by the team leader.

Safety Considerations

Extreme caution must be exercised around the handling and use of all explosive materials. Every detonation has some level of ***Fragmentation*** and ***Overpressure***. All team members must understand basic safety principles as follows:

- Each team has a designated Blaster in Charge (BIC) who supervised explosive operations.

- Team members use and understand clear pre and post blast signals and communication as provided by the Blaster in Charge.

- Team members must understand and follow safe distance stand-off from explosive charges based upon their size and other circumstances that include possible fragmentation and difference in indoor and outdoor air blast overpressure.

- Team members understand procedures to abort the detonation if individuals enter the blast zone.

- Team members are ideally stacked behind a blast shield or blanket and wearing helmets, eye, ear, and body protection.

- Misfires are handled with extreme care and supervised by the Blaster in Charge.

- Do not carry explosives and blasting caps together in the same pocket, bag, or storage magazine.

20. EXPLOSIVE OBSTACLE BREACHING

Chapter Topics:

- Understand various techniques for obstacle breaching.
- Learn how to breach various obstacles from concrete, chains, pipe, cable, steel sheets and I beams, even trees.
- Learn to make a *Hasty Breach Charge* to blast through about anything.

Tactical operations are all about speed and surprise. That requires the ability to move a team through an area with many possible obstacles some are known, some unknown. We want you to have a reference for the ability to breach about anything that come in your way.

Concrete and Masonry walls

Brick and concrete walls can be breached with a surprisingly low amount of explosive materials to create a ***Spider Hole***, a small hole used to view or shoot through. For example, a sniper may create a small hole in a wall to shoot through to avoid silhouetting through a window or over a wall. Another application is making a larger hole, just big enough to strategically crawl through called a ***Mouse Hole***, to a full-sized access point for a breach team.

Det Cord Charge

For a wall 4-6 inches think, try 5 strands of 50 grain det cord attached to a cardboard or wood frame. Braiding the det cord keeps it together and seems to give it a little more punch.

Bulk or Block Explosives

Use at least one pound of RE 1.0 materials per one inch of wall thickness. Efficiency can be doubled if there is a way to stem the charge with sandbags.

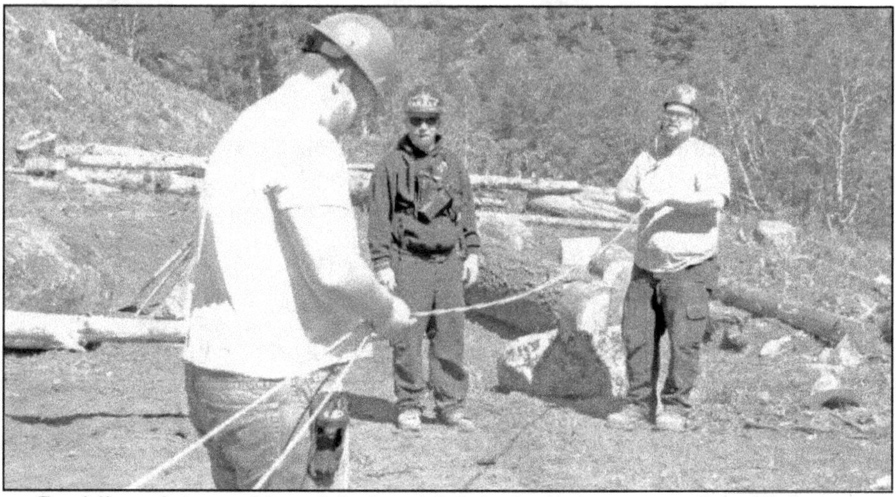

Braiding det cord is a Marine trick to help increase its efficiency.

Shaped Charge

For a smaller and for strategic breach, a shaped charge is ideal. A spider hole can be made with a small strategic blast, the sound can be masked during gunfire. This is ideal for snipers and tactical teams who need a more covert viewing and shooting solution.

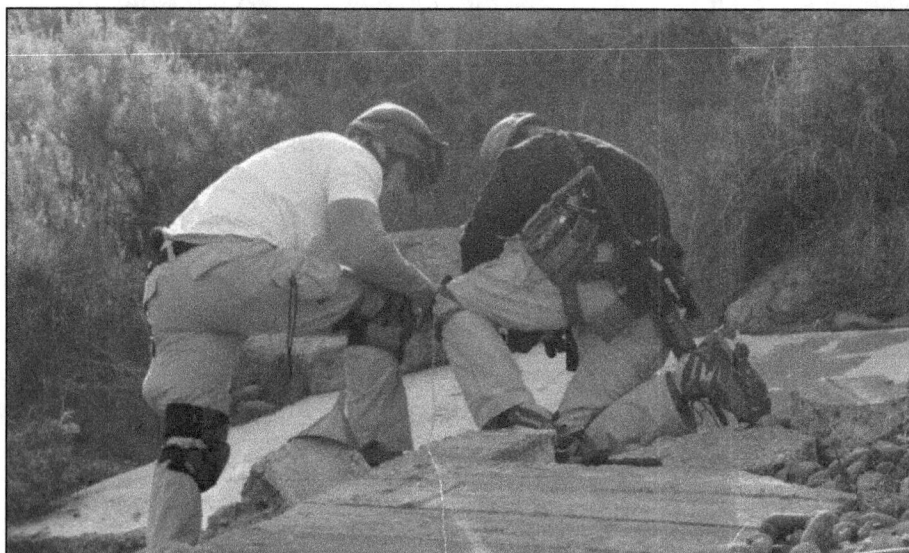

SWAT Team members use a funnel to make a ¼ lb C-4 shaped charge to punch a hole in a concrete wall.

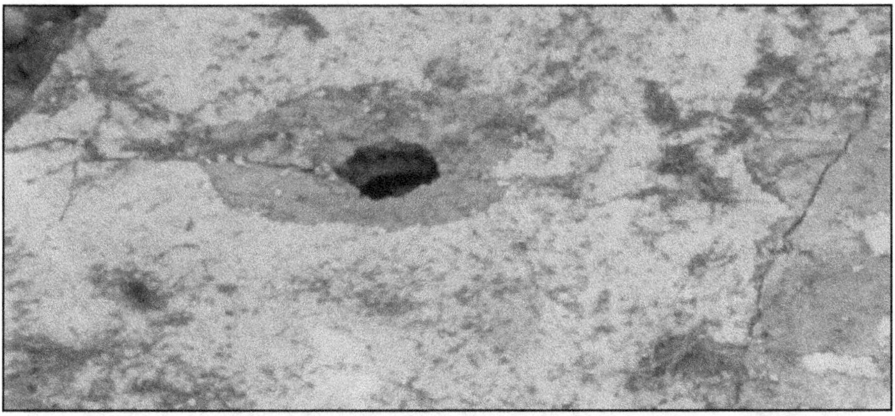

The shaped charge made a perfect 5-inch hole in the wall approximately 4 inches thick. This type of spider hole can be used as a viewpoint and gun port.

Pipe, Chain, Cable and Linear Obstacles

C-4 plastic is ideal for breaching metal objects. Its pliability allows it to be formed around locks and obstacles. C-4s high VOD will burn through steel like a torch.

SWAT team members breach a steel pipe to simulate a gate.

When in doubt, form the plastic into a shaped charge but be sure enough material is used to wrap around the pipe.

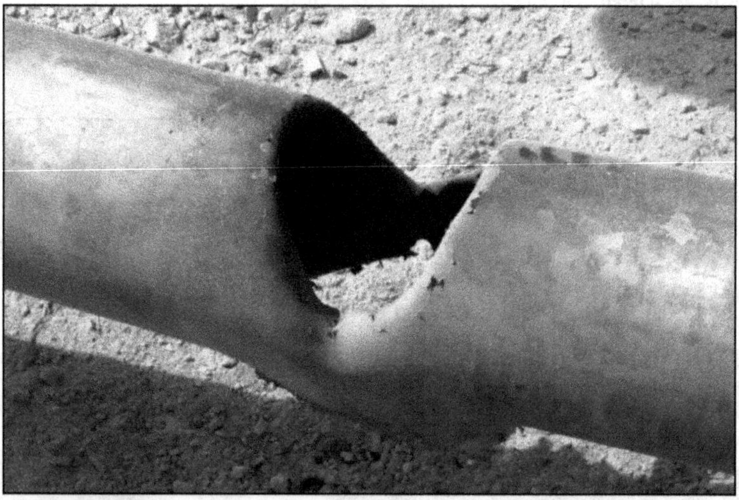

Hollow obstacles absorb an amazing amount of energy. In the case the breach team did not use enough material to make a complete breach. In a tactical situation, rarely is there time to do the same shot twice.

C-4 is very insensitive and can be dry and crumbly which can make it difficult to stick together. We suggest using enough plastic to wrap around the object or to cover the edges. Steel that is not covered may not breach. Do it right the first shot, in a tactical situation, you probably will not have time to shoot it again. Boost it with det cord and wrap it up good with tape to help ensure a complete detonation.

One solution is a flat-shaped charge that flairs and wraps around the pipe to help ensure a complete breach.

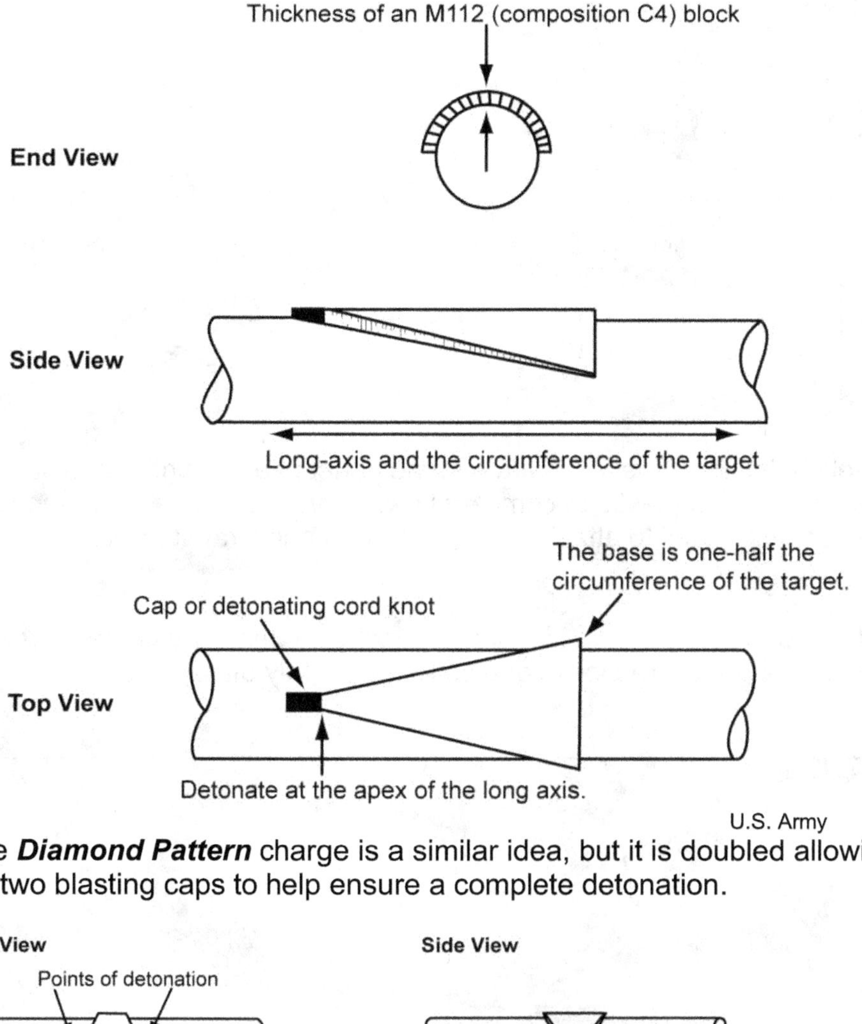

U.S. Army

The ***Diamond Pattern*** charge is a similar idea, but it is doubled allowing for two blasting caps to help ensure a complete detonation.

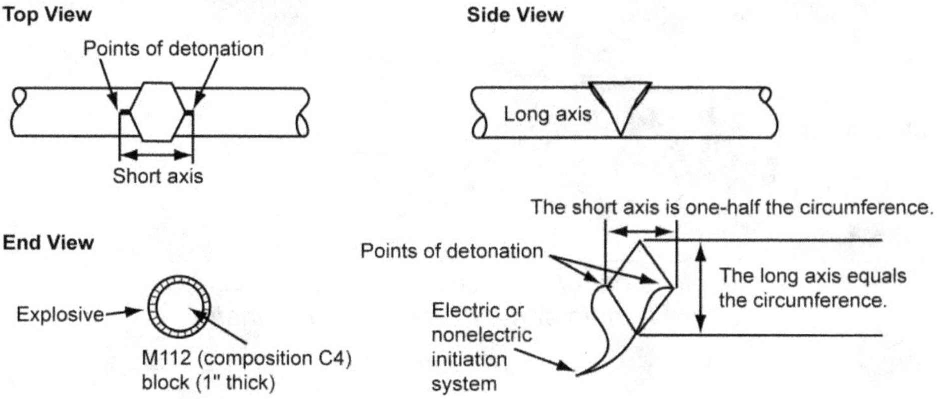

The Diamond Pattern charge has the benefit of using two caps.

For chain links, even heavy locks, fill the link up with plastic and add a few wraps of det cord with a tail to attach the blasting cap. Wrap it up good with tape to keep the charge together.

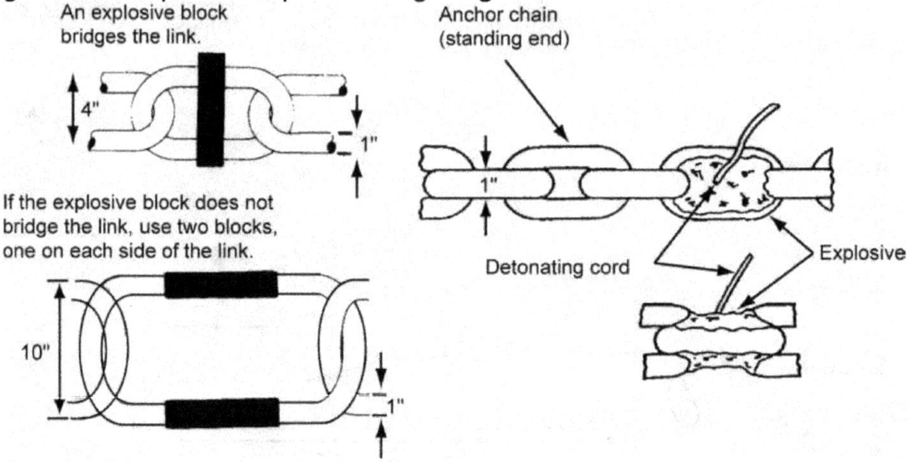
An explosive block
bridges the link.
4"
1"
If the explosive block does not
bridge the link, use two blocks,
one on each side of the link.
10"
1"
Anchor chain
(standing end)
1"
Detonating cord
Explosive

Steel cables are breached with a same concept as chain. Make sure you use enough plastic to completely wrap around the cable, prime with det cord with a tail to attach the blasting cap and wrap it up well with tape.

If the cable is larger than two or three inches, consider using a ***Counter Force*** charge where blocks of plastic are slightly offset for a slicing effect.

Make sure the cable is completely covered with plastic, then prime with det cord to help ensure a compete detonation.

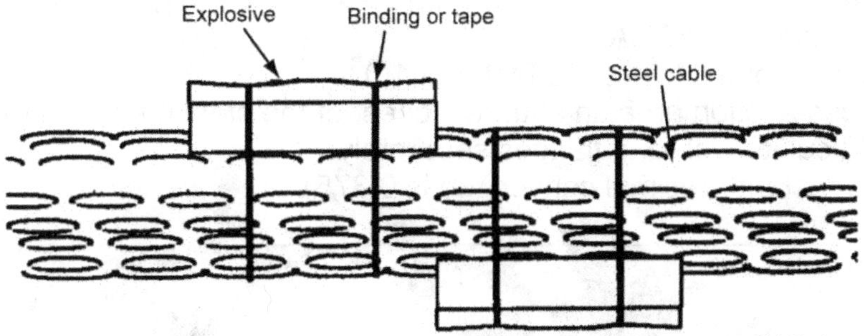

U.S. Army

Heavier cable, over 2 or 3 inches requires an Counter Force charge for a shearing effect.

Cutting Steel

Cutting steel requires high velocity explosives over a RE factor of 1.0. C-4 plastic explosives are ideal because of their 1.34 RE rating and the ability to conform directly to the shape of the steel.

Steel Plate

Use a band of plastic explosive half of the plate's thickness, but three times the width of the plate's thickness wide.

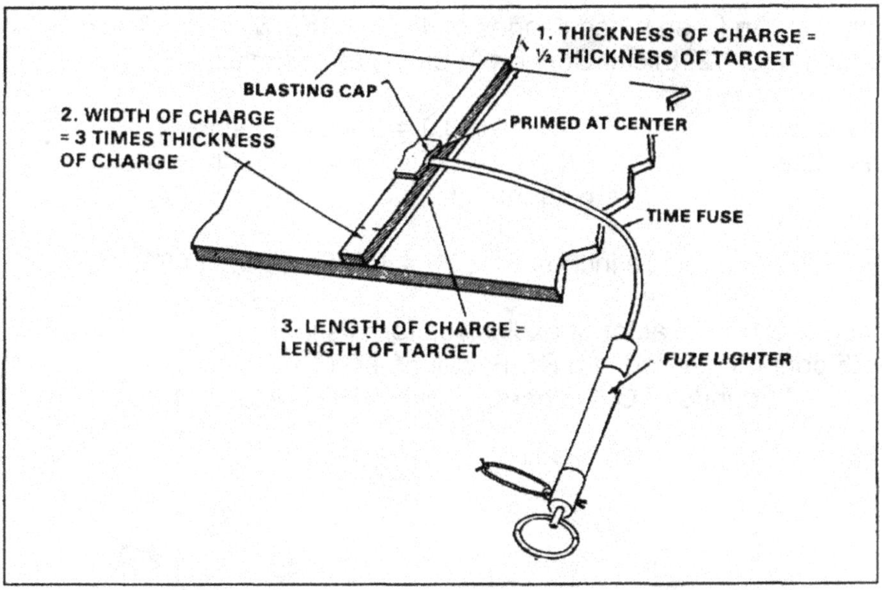

U.S. Army

Cutting plate requires a band of C-4 half the thickness. of the plate, by three times the width of the plate wide.

I-Beam
The formula is P = 3/8A
P = Pounds of explosive RE factor of 1.0
A = Cross-section area, in square inches, of the steel members to be cut. Calculate web and flanges separately.
3/8 = Constant (decimal conversion is 0.375)

The smallest band of C-4 will rip right through a ¼" steel plate.

Example: An I-beam has flanges of 4" long and ¾" thick. The web is 10" long and 1/2" thick. Convert fractions to decimals.

Area of web:	L x T	10 x 0.5 = 5 square inches
Area of flange:	L x T	4 x 0.75 = 3 x 2 for each flange
	= 6 square inches	

A = 5 + 6 = 11 square inches x 0.375 = 4.125 pounds of RE 1.0

Consider the RE Factor of explosives for this job:
4.125 pounds needed at a RE Factor of 1.0 (TNT)
Only 3.07 pounds of C-4 is needed with a RE Factor of 1.34

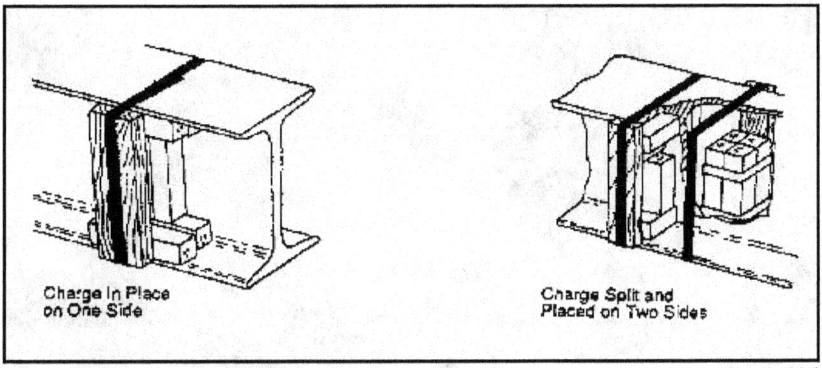

U.S. Army

Explosive charges placed on both sides of beams are off-set.

Cutting Timber

Trees, logs, and snags can often be cut faster and safer using explosives than by cutting with a chainsaw.

Bulk Explosive Method

The tree should fall to the side the explosives are placed on. Use the following formula to determine the amount of explosives necessary.

The formula is: $P = \frac{D2}{50}$

P = pounds of explosives with a RE factor of 1.0 (such as TNT)
D2 = diameter in inches squared (divided by itself)
50 = constant

In this example, the tree has a diameter of 38 inches.
38 x 38 = 1,444 ÷ 50 = 28.88 of RE factor 1.0 explosives

$$P = \frac{382}{50} = \frac{1,444}{50} = 28.88$$

Consider the RE Factor of explosives for this job:
28.88 pounds needed at an RE Factor of 1.0 (TNT)
Only 21.55 pounds of C-4 is needed with a RE Factor of 1.34

The tree should fall in the direction on which the side the explosives are placed. Keep clear on all sides anyway and watch for flying chunks of wood.

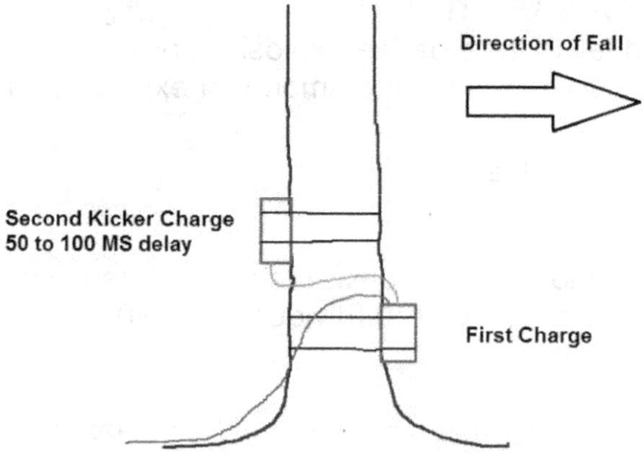

The second kicker charge pushes the tree in the right direction.

Kicker Charge

Another form that is more advanced is through the use of a kicker charge. The idea is that the first charge splits the tree and starts the fall. Then the second charge delayed 50 to 100 MS gives the tree a kick to push it in the correct direction.

Counter Force Charge

The most efficient charges are when opposing or counter force energy works against itself to provide a shearing effect. Much less materials can often be used such as on smaller fallen logs. Use four pounds of RE 1.0 materials per one-foot diameter.

Counter Force charges are detonated at the same time that provides a very efficient shearing effect.

Det Cord Charge

There is often a misconception that det cord will slice through trees. It is a very explosive fuse, but it does not have great cutting power. It will work however on smaller trees and logs if you use enough of it. Braiding it into a rope and wrapping it in a cone as a shaped charge helps increase its efficiency.

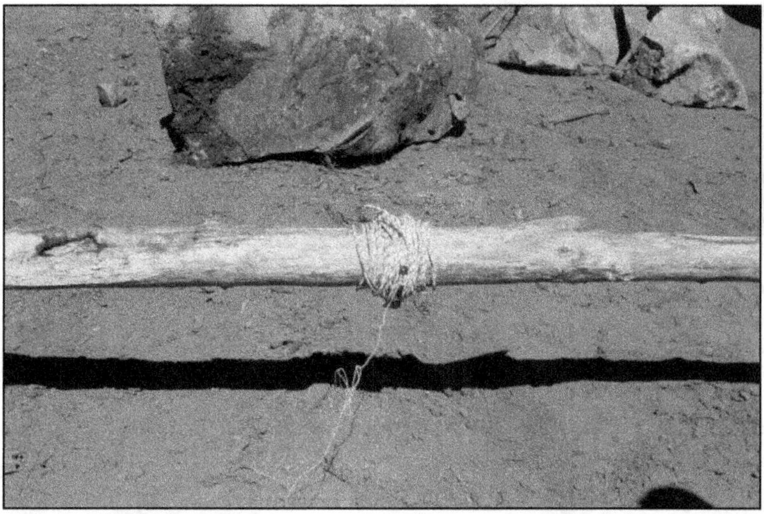

Det cord will cut a small tree or log if you use enough of it. It is not recommended unless that is the only material you have.

Creating a Hasty Charge

A Hasty Charge is designed to be a C-4 and det cord knockout punch to take out about any obstacle you can physically throw this device over. It is full or half blocks of C-4 wrapped and primed with det cord. The block that is typically used is the US Military's M112 which is 1.25 pounds (2.2 Kilograms) of C-4.
The sliding Uli knots are used to add additional det cord to prime each block. Remember that approximately eight inches of det cord equals a blasting cap so a minimum of 12-16 inches of det cord should be used for each C-4 block.

The Hasty Charge is used by military units to clear obstacles like barbed wire, mine fields, gates and booby traps. A grappling hook can be added to throw over a heavy wall or door.

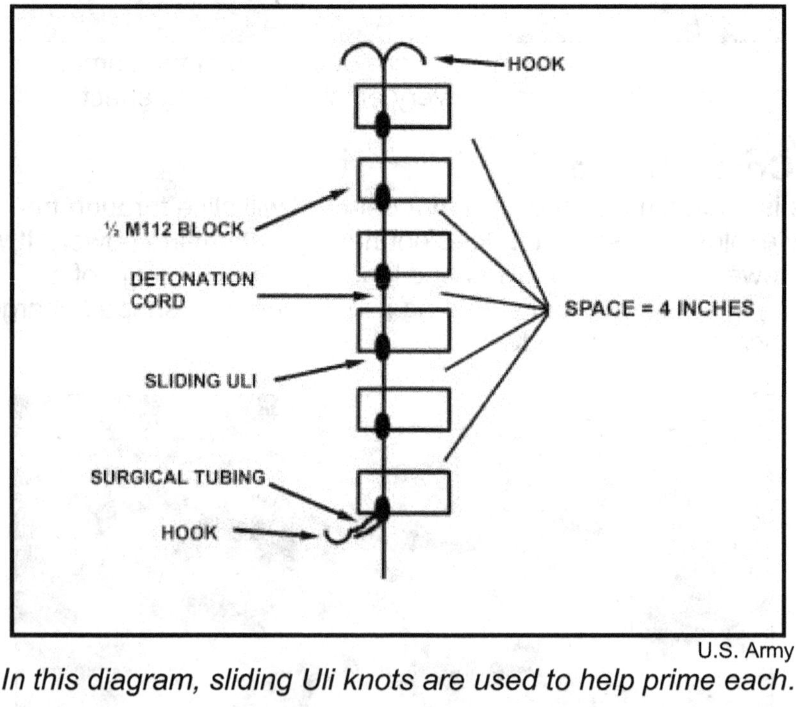

U.S. Army

In this diagram, sliding Uli knots are used to help prime each.

C-4 block. If adjustability is not an issue, its faster and more durable to just wrap each block 4 times and tape it up good to keep the line together for its deployment in extreme tactical conditions.

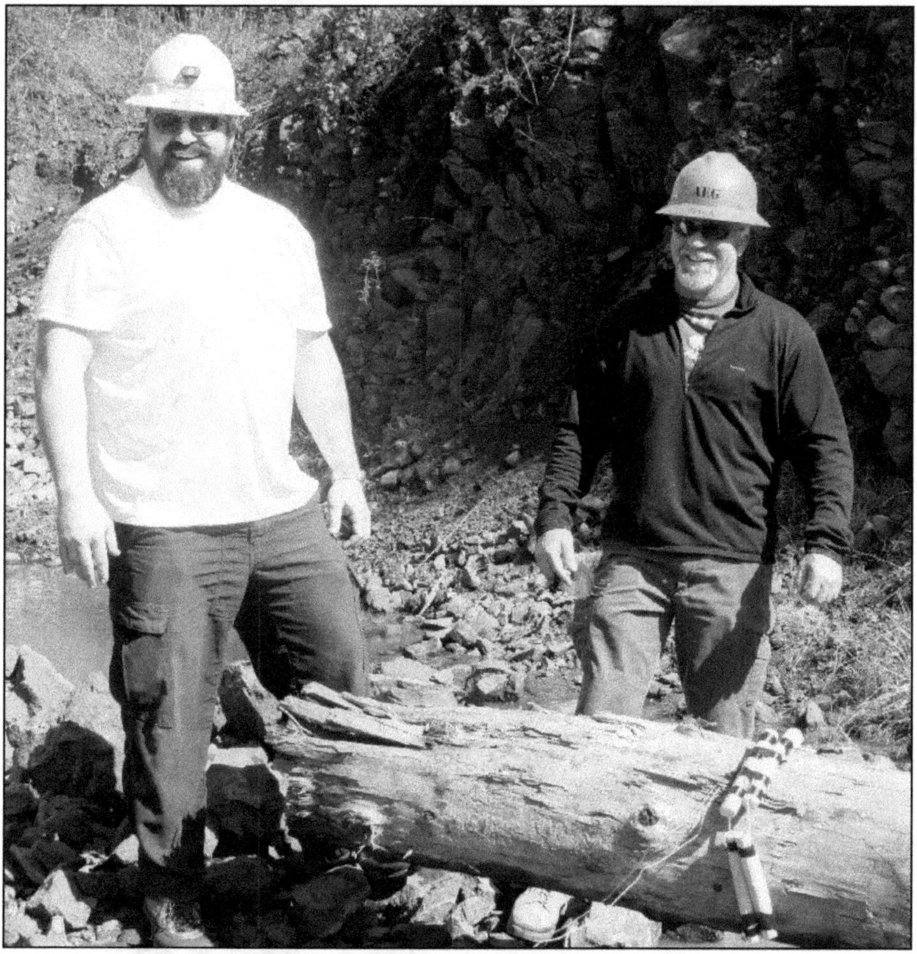

Students make a Hasty Charge out of det cord and dynamite sticks to cut a log in half.

21. BREACHING STANDOFF AND REPORTS

Chapter Topics:

- Understanding Overpressure and Fragmentation.
- Understand how to calculate the safe distance stand off for explosive breaching operations.
- Understand the need for pre and post breach planning and report writing.

No question about it, explosives breaching is an extreme measure for extreme circumstances. During training for actual operations, we want breach teams to always be thinking about mitigating liability. This includes reducing any possible risks of death or injury to the breach team or any non-combatants.

Understand if a breach operation turns out badly, every aspect of the mission and procedures will be heavily scrutinized. Our goal in this final chapter is to help ensure every breach related operation is safe and successful.

Understanding Overpressure and Fragmentation

There are two hazards from explosive detonations. One is ***Overpressure***, the air-blast shock wave created by the explosion. The second is ***Fragmentation***, which is the flying debris coming from the charge and the material being detonated.

Detonations create a ***Blast Wave***. The pressure in front of this wave is the ***Overpressure***. The wave creates a high-speed wind know as ***Dynamic Pressure***.

Once the blast wave has passed, there is a rush of air in the opposite direction known as ***Negative Pressure***.
While the negative pressure can cause injury and damage, its intensity is much less than overpressure or dynamic pressure.
The primary cause of death, injury and property damage is Overpressure. It is rated by ***Pressure per Square Inch, PSI***.

The human body can survive a reasonably high level of overpressure when experiencing ***Barotrauma***. This is an injury to an organ as a result in extreme changes in barometric pressure.

One of the first overpressure injuries is the rupturing of eardrums. For example, at 5 PSI, 1% experience a ruptured eardrums.

At 45 PSI, it happens 99% of the time. At 15 PSI the lungs will damage and collapse. A 35-45 PSI overpressure may cause death 1% of the time, and 55 to 65 PSI overpressure may cause death 99% of the time.

As dangerous as overpressure is, what causes most death and injury is the fragmentation. It is the flying debris caused by the overpressure that tears vehicles and buildings apart sending broken glass, brick, and steel through the air. This causes death and injury on two levels. The first is airborne fragments striking bodies causing lacerations and blunt trauma. Next is additional series damage by bodies being thrown, striking other structure and debris.

Damages Caused by Overpressure and Fragmentation

.04	PSI	A loud 143 db report, sonic boom, glass failure
1	PSI	Light injuries from frag, broken windows
3	PSI	Serious injuries, possible death, structure damage
5	PSI	Death and serious insures, structures destroyed
8	PSI	Eardrums start to rupture in mass
10	PSI	Most people dead, concrete buildings destroyed
15	PSI	Start of lung damage and collapse
20	PSI	Death and heavy concrete structure destroyed
40	PSI	Lungs damaged or collapsed
45	PSI	Eardrum rupture 99% of the time
65	PSI	Death 99% of the time.
220	PSI	Loss of limbs

Special Safety Considerations for Breach Teams

Calculated stand-off distances are based upon protection from overpressure and not fragmentation, heat, or noise. Hearing protection also helps against hearing and eardrum damage. Earplugs however make it more difficult to communicate in a tactical operation.

It is best to limit your team to overpressure exposure of 3.4 PSI without hearing protection, or up to 4 PSI with hearing protection. Note also that any breaching indoors will require an extended standoff adjustment due to the increased overpressure based upon how enclosed the indoor space is. This adjustment is typically at least three times the Net Explosives Weight.

Two important things to remember: One is watch for flying debris from the breach itself. This includes parts of the door, jam and flying doorknobs and hardware.

Second, your team may have to adjust your stand-off distance further back if you decide not to wear hearing protection or if you are breaching indoors.

Calculating Breaching Stand-off Distances

The following formula is used to calculate the ***Minimum Safe Distance, MSD*** to an explosives breach charge. This is critical so a breach team leader does not expose their team to additional harm by placing personnel too close to the charge.

While determining the amount of explosive materials for a breach is sometimes more of an art than a science, determining the safe offset is a specific mathematical equation based upon first determining the ***Net Explosive Weight, NEW*** with an adjustment to the RE factor of 1.0 also known as the ***TNT Equivalent***.

Acronyms and Terms you must understand to calculate Breaching Standoff Distances:

K Factor

A number used in connection with a level of overpressure measured by PSI. For example, the safety baseline is 4 PSI which has a K Factor of 18

MSD

The Minimum Safe Distance is the standoff requirement based upon a safe level of exposure to blast overpressure.

NEW

The Net Explosive Weight used in a breaching charge based upon an adjustment to pounds that are equivalent to TNT which has the RE Factor of 1.0.

RE Factor –TNT Equivalent

The RE Factor is how the power of an explosive is rated. The term TNT Equivalent is used because TNT is RE 1.0 as the baseline for the RE Factor measuring system.

Step One – Calculating the NEW

Here is the formula:
Quantity x **Weight** x **RE Factor** = **NEW**

If multiple explosives are used, the NEW needs to be evaluated for each material, then added together so the NEW can be determined for the complete charge.

Convert to Pounds if Necessary
If materials are rated in grams or grains per foot, they need to be converted to pounds to finish the NEW equation.

Determining the Grain Amount for Blasting Caps

Commercial Caps	Grains
No. 6	6
No. 8	8
No. 10	10

US Military Caps	Grains
M11	19
M12	13
M13	13
M14 delay	16
M15 delay	18
M16	19
M18 delay	16
M19 dual (two caps)	35
M 21	19
M 23	19

To convert Grams to Pounds: Grams x .0022 = Pounds
To convert Grains to Pounds: Grains ÷ 7,000 = Pounds
To convert Grains per foot to Pounds: (Feet x Grains/Per Foot) ÷ 7,000 = Pounds

RE Factors for Common Breaching Materials

Blasting Caps	1.60
Boosters (RDX)	1.60
Boosters (PETN)	1.66
Datasheet (C-2, PETN)	1.66
C-4 M112	1.34
C-4 M186	1.14
Detonating cord (PETN)	1.66

Dynamite (Nitroglycerin 60%)	0.92
TNT (the baseline for RE)	1.0

Step Two - Multiplying the Amounts for NEW

Pounds x RE Factor for each explosive material.

<u>Examples for Explosive Products:</u>
Blasting cap, Number 10, ten grain
2 caps, 20 grains ÷ 7,000 x 1.60 = .0045 lb at RE 1.0

Booster, 20 grams x 15.4 (to convert to lb) x 1.66
20 x .0022 x 1.66 = .073 pounds based upon RE 1.0

C-4 M112 block, 1.25 pounds x RE Factor of 1.34
1.25 x 1.34 = 1.675 pounds based upon RE 1.0

C-4 M186 block, 1 pound x RE Factor of 1.14
1 x 1.14 = 1.14 pounds based upon RE 1.0

Detonating cord, feet x grains x 1.66 =
50 gr per foot x 1 foot ÷ 7,000 = .0071
X 1.66 = .0118 of a pound at RE 1.0

Dynamite Stick, .5 pound X RE Factor of .92
.5 x .92 = .46 of a pound based upon RE 1.0

Linear Shaped Charge, RDX in Copper, 125 gains per ft
4 ft section, 4 x 125 ÷ 7,000 = .0714 x 1.60 x .114 lb RE 1.0

Sheet explosives, convert wt to lbs x 1.66 =
200 grams x .0022 = .44 x 1.66 = .73 pound RE 1.0
Note: Check packaging, most sheets are rated for 1 to 1.5 grams per square inch.

Step Three – Understanding the K Factor

The K Factor provides a number used in connection with a level of blast overpressure measured by PSI. For example, the safety baseline is 4 PSI which has a K Factor of 18. The higher the K Factor number the less overpressures. For example, K Factor 30 = 2 PSI.

K Factor Conversion Chart

Overpressure PSA Pounds	K Factor	
0.07	300.02	
0.10	250	
0.50	75	
1	45	
2	30	
3	20	
4	18	Baseline
5	15	
6	14	
7	13	
8	12	
9	11	
10	10	
15	8	
20	7	
30	6	
40	5	
60	4	
100	3.5	
200	3	

Step Four – Calculating the Minimum Safe Distance

Formula: The MSD = the K Factor x the cubed root of the NEW: ***MSD = $\sqrt[3]{}$ NEW * K factor or MSD = K x W⅓***

Don't want to take up mag pouch with a scientific calculator? It is easier to look up the MSD by determining the NEW and looking it up on the following Minimum Safe Distance chart. The MSD is measured in feet in the two right hand columns.

Minimum Safe Distance Chart, K Factor 18

NEW	Cube root	Safe distance w/o shield		w/shield	
0.01	0.215443469	03.877982448		4	2
0.02	0.271441762	04.885951716		5	3
0.03	0.310723251	05.593018517	6	3	
0.05	0.368403150	06.631256704	7	4	
0.08	0.430886938	07.755964891	8	4	

0.12	0.493242415	08.878363474	9	5
0.17	0.553965826	09.971384868	10	5
0.22	0.603681074	10.866259330	11	6
0.29	0.661910595	11.914390710	12	6
0.37	0.717905435	12.922297840	13	7
0.47	0.777498010	13.994964180	14	7
0.57	0.829134434	14.924419820	15	8
0.70	0.887904002	15.982272030	16	8
0.84	0.943538796	16.983698330	17	9
1.00	1.000000000	18.000000000	18	9
1.17	1.053728243	18.967108370	19	10
1.37	1.110640541	19.991529740	20	10
1.58	1.164713284	20.964839120	21	11
1.82	1.220929150	21.976724690	22	11
2.08	1.276500859	22.977015470	23	12
2.37	1.333263885	23.998749930	24	12
2.67	1.387300109	24.971401960	25	13
3.01	1.443850292	25.989305260	26	13
3.37	1.499258893	26.986660070	27	14
3.76	1.554996019	27.989928340	28	14
4.18	1.610863572	28.995544290	29	15
4.62	1.665510308	29.979185550	30	15
5.00	1.709975946	30.779567020	31	16

The MSD without shielding is the Safe Distance number rounded up to the nearest whole number. Shielding reduces the distances by half. For example, one pound of NEW requires 18 feet or 9 feet shielded. It is also important to note that this calculation is for overpressure and does not consider fragmentation, heat and noise.

Protect your team from fragmentation! Also, for indoor or contained area breaching determine your MSD based upon a NEW X 3.

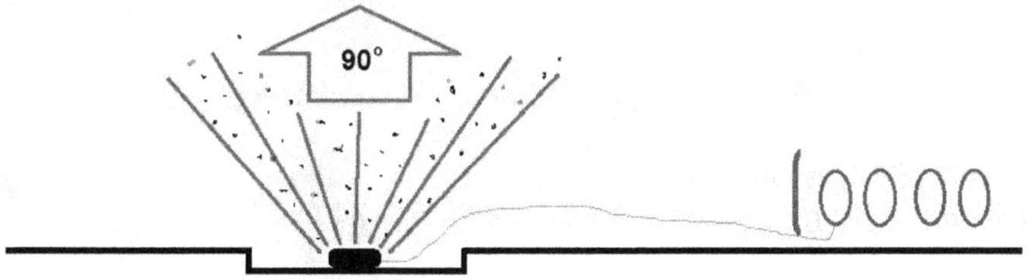

The majority of the blast overpressure and fragmentation projects from the blast at a 90° angle. The team is staged and stacked behind a shield near the wall to help protect them.

Shielding protects against fragmentation and heat, reduced the stand-off by half.

Examples to Calculate the NEW and Standoff

<u>**Example 1. Calculate the Standoff**</u>

Materials: 5 feet of 50 grain per foot of det cord
1 foot of 50 grain per foot of det cord
M11 military blasting cap, 19 grain

Calculate the grains in the det cord and blasting cap:
{(Length in feet [F] x gr per ft) x RE} ÷ 7,000 = NEW
5 ft x 50 x 1.66 = 415 grains at RE 1.0
1 ft x 50 x 1.66 = 83 grains at RE 1.0
1 x 19 x 1.60 = 30.4 grains at RE 1.0
415 + 83 + 30.4 = 528.4 grains at RE 1.0

Convert grains to pounds:
528.4 ÷ 7,000 = .0754 NEW, round up: .08 NEW at RE 1.0

Look up .08 NEW on MSD Chart
Or do the math: (root x K Factor).43 x 18 = 7.74 (round to 8 ft)

Standoff = 8 feet without shielding; 4 feet with shielding

<u>**Example 2. Calculate the standoff**</u>

Materials: 2 feet of 50 grain det cord
1 M112 C-4 block
1 M11 blasting cap

Calculate the grains in the det cord and blasting cap:
{(Length in feet [F] x gr per ft) x RE} ÷ 7,000 = NEW
2 ft x 50 x 1.66 = 166 grains at RE 1.0
1 x 19 x 1.60 = 30.4 grains at RE 1.0
166 + 30.4 = 196.4 grains at RE 1.0

Convert grains to pounds:
196.4 ÷ 7,000 = .028 NEW, round up: .03 NEW at RE 1.0

Convert M112 block
1.25 x 1.34 = 1.67 pounds NEW at RE 1.0
Add together: .028 + 1.67 = 1.70 pounds NEW at RE 1.0

Look up 1.7 NEW on MSD Chart, (round up to 1.82)
Or do the math: (root x K Factor) 1.22 x 18 = 21.96

Standoff = 22 feet without shielding; 11 feet with shielding

Breacher's Report Writing

Completing a ***Breacher's Report*** or ***Breacher's Brief*** is important for two reasons. One, it is a way to document the structure, the explosive amount and the results. This is a critical test and training tool to hone breaching skills. Second, it should be suspected that any breaching action could be heavily scrutinized by the legal defense team, and it certainly could be scrutinized by all parties if the breach action results in any type of wrongful injury or death circumstances.

Breaching operations are the ultimate example of leadership under pressure and teamwork. If the team does not work together during training, they will probably not work together under the pressure of some of the most extreme conditions any law enforcement officer can face.

The breach team leader must have the experience to make good decisions under pressure and lead by example. The leader sets the tone and the pace, as his fellow teammates will follow by example. This begins with the communication skills needed to train and inform the team of all the information they need to help inspire confidence and to ensure that each mission will conclude as a safe and successful one.

The following information and considerations should be addressed through training with the relevant information being documented within a report:

Primary Target
What is the primary target such as a door or window, and where is it located in relation to the building structure. What are the exterior characteristics that could give information to the materials needed for the breach and what is the acceptable method of approach to reach it?

Alternate target
In the event the Primary Target is blocked or booby trapped, determine if there is an acceptable alternative in the building structure. What is the signal to abort the primary and to pursue the alternative and what will be the method of approach to do so?

Charges, Tools, and Techniques
What type of breaching charges will be used on the targets, (primary, alternate, and any interior charges)? What is the blasting cap and fire system for each breach? What signal or notice that is used prior to, (hand signals and/or verbal), and at detonation so everyone knows when the charge is initiated?

NEW and MSD Standoff
What is the total NEW for each charge? Calculate the MSD standoff and communicate the safe distance and how all teammates should be position themselves prior to blast.

Location of the Breacher and Assistants and Roles
Who is and where will the lead breacher and his assistants be located within the team?
What will their specific roles be during the breaching process from making the device, loading, hanging, priming, spooling out line and firing? Who will assume their rolls if they become injured?

Location of Equipment Within the Team
Who will carry what equipment and explosive materials and where they will be positioned within the team?

The Charge Placement and Firing
Where the breacher and assistant will be during the placement the breach charge? Where will the charge be placed and how will the charge be secured or hung on the obstacle? Where will the breacher and the assistant be when the charge is fired?

Conditions Expected During the Breach

Are there any special conditions that the team needs to be aware of prior to and during the breach? Ensure the team knows how many charges will be in use and the firing systems for each.

Post Blast Conditions

What are the conditions in the area of the breach that the team members can expect to encounter or are there any special fragmentation hazards? How long does the team wait before they reach and enter the breach point? Estimate the potential damage to the obstacle (such as the condition of the door and if it is still on the hinges), and what is the best approach to enter?

Communication Considerations

What is the protocol for mission communication, (hand and verbal)? What is the signal to set, fire, abort or move to the alternative target? Who makes the signals that allow the team to understand the criteria of how these actions are taken? Will the team wear ear plugs?

Security

What is the team's SOPs for security during movement, placing the charge, and during detonation? What security role will what teammates play, and will there be someone assigned to overwatch?

Encountering Booby Traps and IEDs

Each team member must understand the SOPs and actions taken when encountering these circumstances.
All team members must be hyper aware of such possibilities and the lead breaching must understand they will probably be the first to encounter such a device.

Misfire Procedures

What is the SOP in the event of a misfire where the charge does not detonate? Will the team carry back up materials and equipment to place and initiate a backup charge?

Failed Breach

What alternative breaching methods are available if the initial breach fails? Who on the team will serve as a backup with mechanical, thermal, or ballistic equipment needed to continue the breach allowing the completion of the mission?

Breaching entry teams are the ultimate example of leadership and teamwork as LEOs work making life and death decisions in the most demanding and extreme conditions possible.

Post Beach Event Brief

Did the charge successfully breach the door or obstacle? For future reference, does a NEW adjustment need to be made for more or less materials basted upon its construction and strength? How did the team perform? Did anyone get injured?
Is there any action that can be considered to allow the next breach operation to go smoother, safer and more efficient?

Breacher's Report Example

The following is an example of a real breacher's report from a training mission conducted by the co-author, Duane Mattson for the *Washington State Police*.

Page one provides the introductory information such as if this report is for training or an incident. Then the date, breacher and location of the operation. It then provides the details and a diagram of the Primary Target.

Page two breaks down the explosive materials used and their conversion to NEW based upon the TNT equivalent. Next is the calculation of the MSD based upon the K Factor of 18, providing the stand-off distance.

Page three starts with a calculation for a confined or indoor breach, which this one was not. The diagram indicates where the breach charge was placed and the location of the breach entry team. Note the stand-off is 7.9 feet, but for training, 20 feet was used.

Page four is the brief the reviews the target, the NET and standoff. Next is the expected blast conditions (watch out for ceiling tiles). Next is the priming, firing and breach placement information as well as operational information including communication and placement of the breacher in the line. Finally, the outcome, a successful breach.

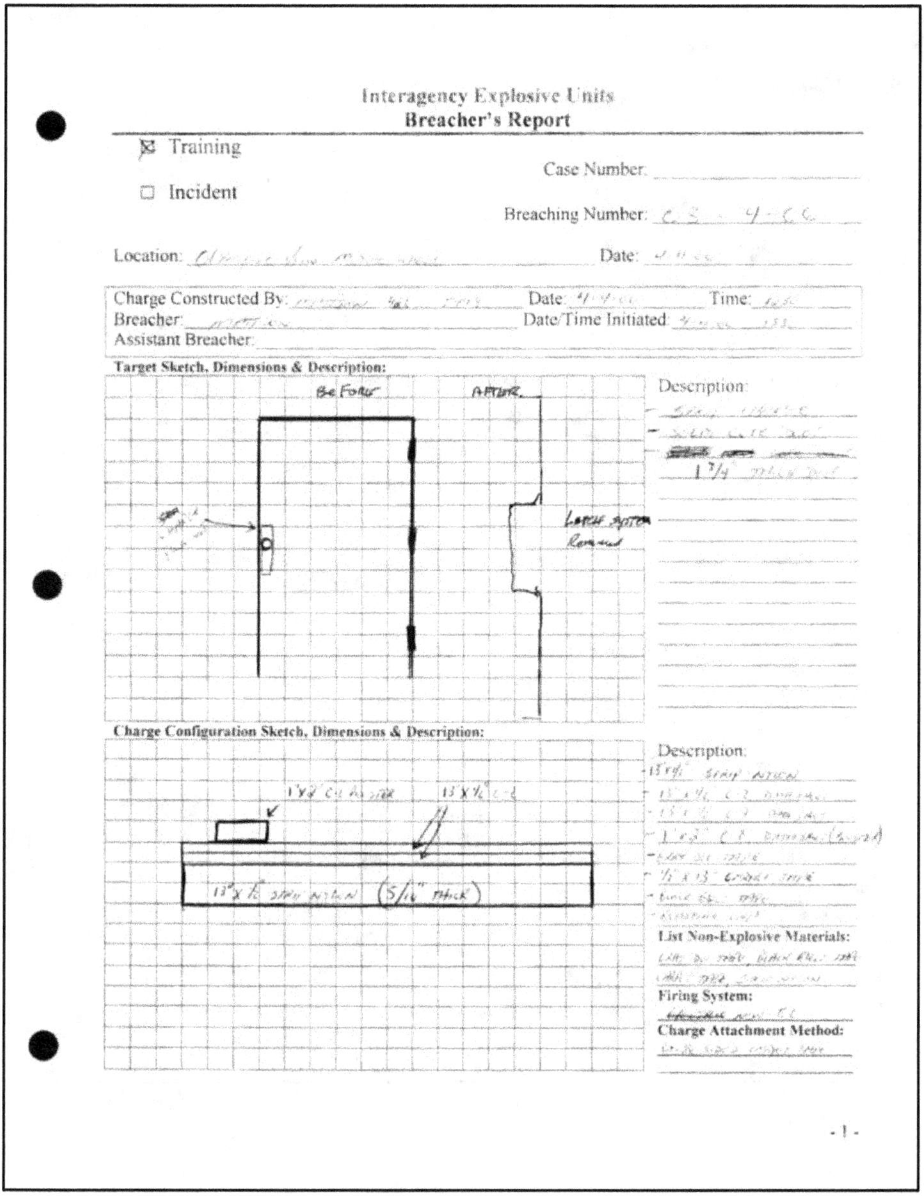

Interagency Explosive Units
Breacher's Report

☒ Training

☐ Incident

Case Number:

Breaching Number:

Location:

Date:

Charge Constructed By:

Date:

Time:

Breacher:

Date/Time Initiated:

Assistant Breacher:

Target Sketch, Dimensions & Description:

Description:

1¾"

Charge Configuration Sketch, Dimensions & Description:

Description:

List Non-Explosive Materials:

Firing System:

Charge Attachment Method:

- 1 -

Interagency Explosive Units
Breacher's Report

List of Explosives:

EXPLOSIVE TYPE & AMOUNT	GRAINS/GRAMS OF EXPLOSIVES	RELATIVE EFFECTIVENESS	GRAINS/GRAMS OF TNT EXPLOSIVE EQUIVALENT	OUNCES OF EXPLOSIVES
1/2" x 15" 1/2" x 15" C-2	26 grams	X 1.14	29.64 grams	GRAMS X .0352 = ~~GRAINS ÷ 437.5 =~~ 1.044
1" x 2" C-2	4 grams	X 1.14	4.56 grams	GRAMS X .0352 = ~~GRAINS ÷ 437.5 =~~ .161
Blasting Cap	15 grams	X 1.66	24.9 grams	~~GRAMS X .0352 =~~ GRAINS ÷ 437.5 = .057
		X		GRAMS X .0352 = GRAINS ÷ 437.5 =
		X		GRAMS X .0352 = GRAINS ÷ 437.5 =
		X		GRAMS X .0352 = GRAINS ÷ 437.5 =

Total Net Explosive Weight, (N.E.W.) in Ounces (TNT) = 1.262

Total N.E.W. in Ounces (TNT) = 1.262 ÷ 16 = .079 Pounds of (TNT)

List of Relative Effectiveness of Explosives:

Deta/Prima Sheet (RDX & PETN	X 1.14	Det Cord (PETN)	X 1.66	ECT (Demex200)	X 1.25
Detacabes & RBC	X 1.50	Detaprime Booster	X 1.19	Detonator (PETN)	X 1.66

Minimum Safe Distance Calculated at 4 P.S.I. The "K" value is 18:

18 ("K" value) Times the Cube Root ($\sqrt[3]{x}$) of the N.E.W. pounds (TNT) equal the minimum safe distance for personnel who are unprotected and in the open.

18 x 3√ .079 (Insert N.E.W. pounds (TNT))

18 x .43 (Cube Root of N.E.W. pounds (TNT))

Minimum Safe Distance in Feet is 7' 9" Calculated at 4 P.S.I.

The use of a shield will reduce the pressure immediately behind the shield by approximately 50 percent.

- 2 -

Interagency Explosive Units
Breacher's Report

Interior Residual Over Pressure:

Rule of thumb for internal charges for calculating safe distance to personnel in confined geometric shapes is to increase the net explosive weight TNT equivalent by three times then calculate the safe distance.

[{N.E.W pounds (TNT) divided by the volume of the room}, to the power of .72(x^y)] times 2410 = inside P.S.I.

Insert N.E.W. pounds (TNT) __________ ÷ __________ the volume of the room:
(Length________ x Width________ x Height________)

= __________ to the power of .072 (x^y) or [__________(x^y) .72]

= __________ x 2410

= __________ P.S.I.

The interior residual overpressure for the room = __________ P.S.I.

This formula does not take into account windows or doorways that could vent pressure. (Calculation gives a worst-case perdition.)

Aerial View Sketch, Dimensions, Description, Stack and Charge Location:

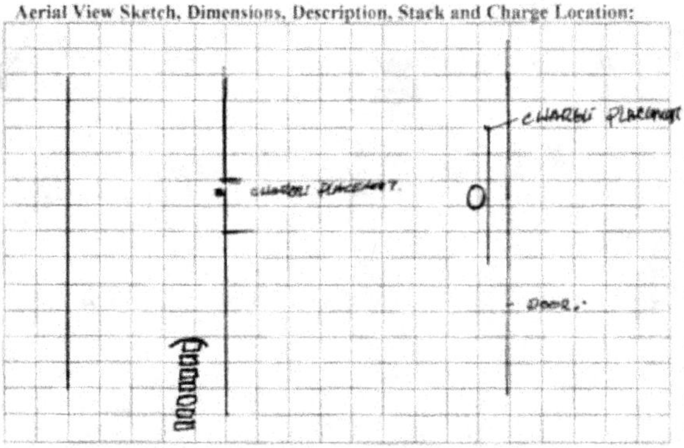

Description:
STRIP CHARGE PLACED ON IN OPENING DOOR WAY.

CHARGE DESIGNED TO ATTACK LATCHING SYSTEM.

Solid CORE COMMERCIAL DOOR.

LATCHES REMOVED FROM DOOR ALLOWING ENTRY.

Additional Information: TEAM STAND OFF 2.9 FEET, TRAINING STAND OFF 2.0 FEET. Shield used No Problems.

- 3 -

Interagency Explosive Units
Breacher's Report

Briefing:

- ☒ Primary Target: Solid core Door
- ☐ Alternate Target:
- ☒ Charges/Tools for each Target: [illegible]
- ☒ N.E.W Lbs. (TNT): .077 LBS
- ☒ Safe Standoff Distance: 7.9 FeeT
- ☒ Expected Blast Conditions: (Smoke) Fire Debris Other: Possible ceiling Tile Falling
- ☒ Priming system for each Charge: NoneL shock Tube.
- ☒ Location of Equipment within Team: 4th BACK IN STICK NEAR T.L.
- ☒ Location of Breacher/Breacher Assistant during:
  - Movement to Target: 4th BACK NEAR T.L
  - Charge Placement: PLACE CHARGE WITH COVER [illegible]
  - Firing Charge: NoneL shock TUBE [illegible]
  - During the Assault: WITH ENTRY.
- ☒ Charge Placement: BETWEEN DOOR KNOB, 3 CASING, CENTER ON DOOR
- ☒ Abort/Alternate Breach signal: HAND SIGNAL, No Go.
- ☒ Misfire Procedures: Disable charge, move to alternate
- ☒ Actions Upon Encountering Booby Trap/s / IED/s: clear By Pass.
- ☐ Other Information:
  DOOR LATCH Removed, clean. very effective transfer of energy.
- ☒ Date & Time Briefing was completed: 04-04-06 1630 hrs
- ☒ Approval for Breaching Technique: (Name & Rank) SGT PORTER KCSO

Breacher's Name & Signature: [signature] DUANE MATTSON

Enrty Team Leader's Name & Signature:

- 4 -

22. IED BOMB WATER DISRUPTERS

Chapter Topics:

- Understand the different types and use for an IED water disrupter.
- Learn how to use the *Dragon* IED water disrupter.

An IED water disrupter is a critical option for bomb techs to use to render an IED safe. The idea is simple, but effective based upon the idea of fighting fire with fire. An explosive charge is used to tear apart a bomb. But in the case of a water disrupter, a jet of water from the disrupter's internal charge 'disrupts' the bomb by tearing apart the components preventing the IED's explosive charge to detonate.

The advantage of using a disrupter is that the water jet can tear a bomb apart without destroying it. This preserves the evidence that will be critical to the investigative team. This includes the bomb's triggering device, like the cell phone keypad and sim card, even finger prints.

Different Forms of IED Disrupters

IED water disrupters come in four different styles including our own design:

PAN Disrupter

The PAN system is a 12-gauge barrel that can shoot a water charge or any other 12-gauge shotgun round. This system can be manually placed by an EOD tech or deployed from an EOD robot. The advantage is that it shoots a very precise blast that is idea for knocking a bomb apart, such as blowing the blasting cap out of the explosives material.

This system has obvious advantages, especially when being used inside buildings where it can be used without a high yield detonation. The disadvantage is that the charge may simply be too small to breach the bomb's case or the bomb components themselves. Or, if the bomb is in a pack or case were the components cannot be seen to aim the PAN barrel to a critical area. Another disadvantage is that this is a one-shot system. Once the barreled is fired, it must be manually reloaded.

Briefcase-Style Disrupters

This style of disrupter uses a sheet of Datasheet plastic explosive material between two chambers of water.

The design is based upon the ***Misznay-Schardin*** effect where the explosive energy is directed to the front and rear of the device.
The advantage is that these are small, neatly self-contained devices in plastic cases that make them easy to deploy manually or by robot. The disadvantage is that because the explosive energy is roughly equally split between the front and back, that may not have the force needed to breach the IED packaging and device. They can be made more efficient by placing sandbags behind the device to direct more energy forward, but this takes more time and gives more exposure to the bomb tech.

Omnidirectional Disrupters

These are round barrels jugs filled with water with a cylinder down the center to be filled with explosive materials. This is the least efficient style because the explosive energy is dispersed equally in a 360° radius. They are heavy and awkward to deploy, but more importantly, due to their lack of direction, more explosive materials need to be used for the same effect, producing a larger, messier explosion to get the job done.

The DRAGON™ IED Water Disrupter

We have designed our own IED disrupter based upon shaped charge technology. This is important because the explosive energy is focused to the front instead of front and rear or in all directions.
The benefit is that by aiming the DRAGON at the target, less explosive material can be used while still doing more damage to the IED.

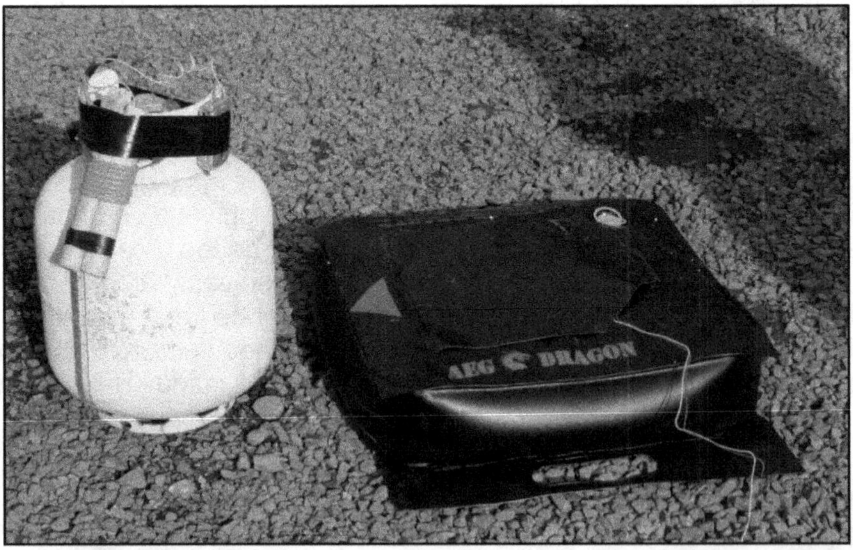

Our new AEG Dragon water impulse shaped charge.

The DRAGON is made from a soft vinyl material. Once filled up with approximately six gallons of water, the shaped charge pocket can be filled with any soft explosive material such as C-4 or even unwrapped dynamite or slurry sticks.

We have found that an *Austin Powder one-pound Rock Crusher* RDX shaped charge is ideal. The RDX is more powerful than C-4 and much easier to insert considering it is already in the correct cone shape. An inner 42° shaped charge cavity is provided, made from Plexiglas (for soft targets) or copper (for hard targets).

Its square design allows it to be used horizontally or vertically.
It can also breach heavy or steel doors with the advantage of not needing to hang anything on the door, just place it in front which is less exposure to tactical officers.

The IED water disrupter rips open the propane tank and dislodges the cell phone, blasting cap and dynamite before it can explode.

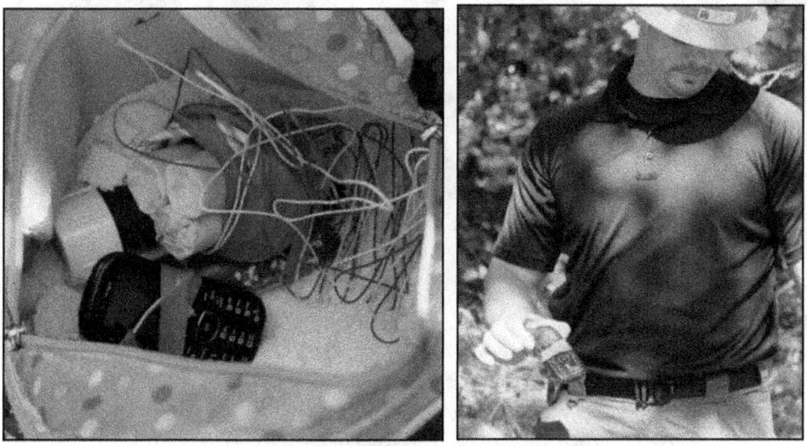

In another test SWAT team member finds the cell phone after the IED disrupter blast.

Once the explosives are set and capped, the *DRAGON* is ready to deploy by carrying it into place using the heavy handles. Unfortunately, its soft bladder design and weight might make it difficult to deploy by robot. It can also be raised in the air, like for shooting through a car door through an optional aluminum plate and inexpensive photo tripod.

The bladder is filled with approximately six gallons of water.

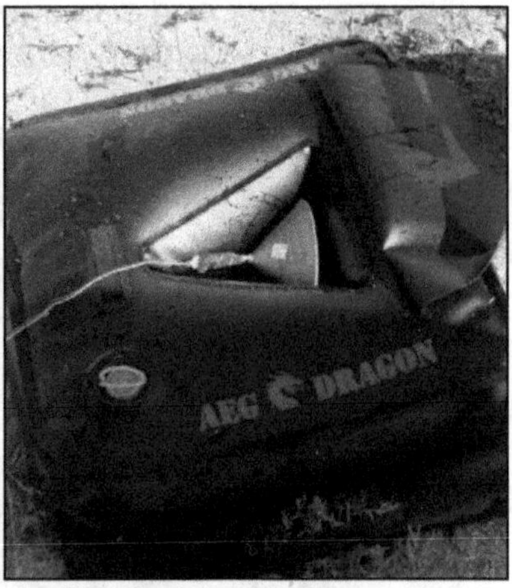

The shaped charge pocket is filled with plastic or any soft explosive. An Austin Powder one-pound RDX Rock Crusher works perfectly.

After the blast, carefully search through the debris field for pieces of the bomb. The majority of the pieces should be within a 10-meter perimeter.

After a quick search, vital parts of the cell phone are located.

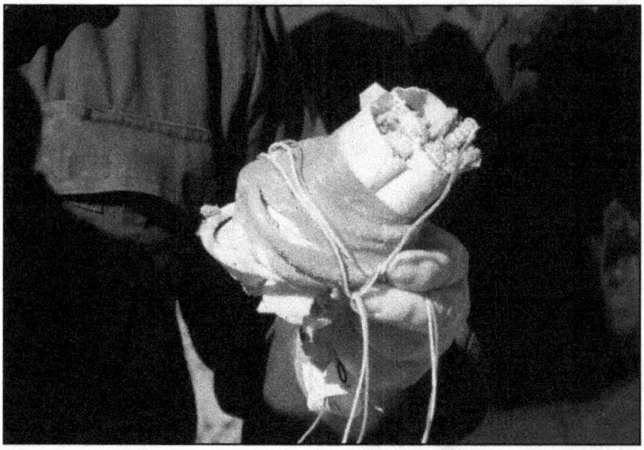

Materials are found with the blasting cap still in place, but the cap's wires were ripped to prevent the bomb from detonating.

... search the debris field for pieces of ... could be within a 10-meter ...

23. INDEX

1.1 Hazmat, 34, 35, 44, 50
1.2 Hazmat, 35, 44, 101
1.3 Hazmat, 34, 35, 44
1.4 Hazmat, 34, 35, 44, 97
1.5 Hazmat, 35, 44, 93, 130, 243
1.6 Hazmat, 34, 35, 44
500-Gram Cake Firworks, 182
Acetone, 75, 76, 83, 84, 85, 86, 143, 145, 147, 158, 159, 162
Active Shooter, 168, 169, 176, 177, 179, 186
AEG Dragon, 219, 266
AEG Dragon Tail, 216, 218
Alcohol, 15, 16, 75, 135, 267, 275
Al-Qaeda, 12
Al-Shabaab, 12
Aluminum Flake Powder, 37, 64, 75, 77, 80, 81, 95, 101, 145
Amatol, 64, 73, 267
Ammonal, 73, 77, 267
Ammonium Nitrate, 27, 31, 33, 37, 42, 43, 48, 51, 52, 53, 64, 78, 207, 208, 267, 270, 271
ANFO, 19, 21, 37, 41, 42, 44, 48, 50, 51, 52, 53, 78, 88, 89, 108, 143, 146, 159, 267
Anti-Opening Switch, 152
Anti-Probe Switch, 152
Armstrong's Mixture, 79
ASMCTE, 179
ATF, 9, 12, 14, 15, 16, 17, 18, 19, 20, 21, 23, 24, 27, 28, 30, 31, 32, 33, 34, 35, 36, 37, 50, 52, 53, 135, 136, 267, 275
Backpack, 167
Ballistic, 210
Ballistic Blankets, 190
Baratol, 64, 73, 267
Barometric Switch, 153
Barotrauma, 239
Binary, 20, 48, 49, 50, 53, 75, 145
Black Match, 97
Black Powder, 20, 41, 42, 43, 53, 54, 79, 80, 146, 158, 159, 161, 162, 199 205, 267
Black-Market, 183
Blast Area, 134
Blast Emergency Plan, 134
Blast Mats, 135
Blaster-in-Charge, 110, 111, 112, 116, 122, 123, 133
Blasting Agents, 9, 15, 27, 31, 39, 48, 49, 51, 60, 267
Blasting Cap, 31, 89, 90, 92, 94, 104, 108, 109, 112, 115, 158, 267
Blasting Machine, 93, 94, 109, 110, 111, 112, 115, 117, 134, 135
Blasting Signals, 134
Blown in Place, 141, 193
Bomb Casings, 161
Bomb Containment Vessels, 193, 194
Bomb Makers, 143
Bomb Suit, 138
Bomb Techs, 164, 185, 187, 188, 191, 192
Booby Traps, 249
Booster, 37, 48, 49, 51, 53, 61, 71, 104, 108, 151, 159, 200, 208, 243
Boston Marathon, 12, 80, 198, 199
Breacher's Report, 247, 250
Breaching, 66, 132, 208, 209, 210, 211, 212, 216, 220, 221, 222, 224, 226, 238, 239, 240, 241, 242, 245, 247, 248, 249
Breaching Bags, 211
Brisance, 39
Bureau of Alcohol, Tobacco, Firearms and Explosives ATF, 15, 16, 135, 275
Burning Fuse, 98, 99, 112, 115, 161
Bypass, 209
C Charge Breach, 214
C-4, 41, 42, 54, 55, 56, 62, 65, 66, 67, 72, 87, 107, 114, 128, 130, 131, 146, 214, 219, 220, 221, 226, 228, 230, 231, 232, 233, 235, 236, 242, 243, 246, 256
Cakes Fireworks, 182

Canada, 13, 20, 21
Cap Sensitive, 37, 48, 50, 60, 88, 89, 267, 272, 273
Capping Explosives, 104
Casually Collection Points, 179
CBRNE, 149
Cell Phone, 151, 153, 163
Centennial Olympic Park, 205
Chlorine, 76, 145
Citric Acid, 80, 81
Clock, 163
Code of Federal Regulations
  CFR, 15
Collapsing Relay Circuit, 154
Command Wire, 149, 151, 163, 187
Commercial Truck Drivers, 33
Composition 4
  C4, 54, 65, 67
Composition A, 64, 268
Composition B, 65, 73, 268
Composition C-3, 65
Contact Team, 179
Containment, 190, 194
Counter Force, 230, 234
Crimping Pliers, 114
Cutting Steel, 230
Cutting Timber, 232
Cyclotrimethylenetrinitramine
  RDX, 62, 268
Daily Summary Transaction Sheet, 23
Date-Shift-Code, 23, 24, 46
Day Boxes, 28
Deadman Switch, 154
Deflagration, 37, 53
Deflagration to Detonation Transition, 38
Delay System, 120, 122
Deliberate Breach, 209
Demolitions, 16, 54, 65, 86, 88, 132, 277
Density, 39
Det Cord, Detonation Cord, 56, 58, 61, 62, 67, 105, 108, 119, 123, 124, 214, 225, 234
Detasheet, 69
Detonation, 31, 37, 38, 40, 42, 51, 53, 55, 56, 62, 66, 72, 78, 80, 87, 97, 104, 111, 114, 115, 116, 120, 140, 161, 189, 190, 192, 193, 204, 206, 223, 228, 229, 230, 247, 249, 255
Detonator, 158, See Blasting Cap
Diamond Pattern, 229
Display Fireworks, 27
Disrupters, 9, 189, 254, 255, 256
Doorknob Charges, 212
Drug Labs, 142, 143, 146
Drugs, 76, 143
Dynamic Pressure, 239
Dynamite, 41, 42, 43, 49, 58, 59, 69, 105, 131, 242, 243, 268
Electric Blasting Cap. See
Electrical Wire, 109
Electronic Squibs, 31
Emulsions, 48
EOD, 3, 11, 137, 138, 139, 140, 141, 187, 190, 192, 193, 255
Erythritol Tetranitrate, 41, 42
Ethyl Ketone, 84
Explosive Detection, 147
Explosive Energy, 126
Explosive Trains, 108
Federal Motor Carrier Safety Administration
  FMCSA, 34
Federal Transfer Receipt, 21, 23
Figure of Insensitivity
  F of I, 42
Fill Material, 162
Fireworks, 12, 16, 17, 31, 32, 33, 38, 43, 44, 54, 97, 98, 101, 102, 176, 268, 272
Firing Sequence, 109, 112, 115
First Responders, 11, 176, 184
Flagging, 222
Flash Powder, 80, 81, 90, 146, 158, 159, 162
Flyrock, 135
Fragmentation, 223, 239, 240
Fuel, 27, 37, 38, 48, 49, 51, 52, 53, 60, 78, 79, 87, 207, 267, 270, 272
Fuse, 43, 89, 90, 94, 98, 99, 100, 102, 108, 112, 151, 186
Galvanometer, 117
Gasoline, 75, 145, 159, 186

Glycol, 76, 81
Grains to Pounds, 242
Hartford Consensus 2013, 177
Hasty Breach Charge, 224
Hasty Charge, 124, 235
Hazard Class, 44
Hazardous Materials, 34, 275
HazMat Classification Numbers, 35
Heavy Acid, 75, 80
Hemorrhage Control, 177, 178
Hemostatic bandages, 178, 179
Hexamethylene Triperoxide Diamine
HMTD, 81
Hexamine, 76, 81, 82, 83, 145
High Explosives, 17, 27, 37, 38, 44
High Order Detonation, 141, 193
HMTD, 80, 81, 82, 270
HMX, 41, 42, 70, 95, 101, 128, 146, 268, 270, 271
Home Borne, 149
Homemade Explosive, 48, 75, 82
Hot Warm and Cold Zone, 180
Hydrochloric Acid
HCl, 83
Hydrogen Peroxide, 75, 76, 81, 83, 84, 145
Hygroscopicity, 40
IED, 9, 13, 78, 137, 139, 141, 148, 149, 151, 159, 161, 164, 166, 167, 168, 169, 184, 186, 187, 188, 189, 192, 194, 195, 200, 202, 255, 256, 257
IED Scenarios, 166
Igniter Cord, 98
Improvised Biological Device, 150
Improvised Chemical Device, 150
Improvised Incendiary Device, 150
Improvised Nuclear Device, 151
Improvised Radioactive Device, 151
Initiator, 89, 108, 115, 158, See Blasting Cap
Institute of the Makers of Explosives
IME, 46
In-Stride Breach, 209
ISIS, 12, 195, 198
Joules, 42, 43
K Factor, 9, 241, 243, 244, 246, 250, 274
Kicker Charge, 233
Licensing, 16, 20
Linear Shaped Charge, 56, 128
Low Explosives, 27, 28, 31, 32, 34, 38, 39, 161, 162
Low Order Detonation, 141, 193
M112 block, 66, 220, 243, 246
M186 block, 243
Magazine Storage, 23, 33
Magnetic Switch, 155
Manufacturer of High Explosives, 17
Martin Luther King Day Parade, 200
Mass Casualty Terrorist Events, 186
Mechanical, 210
MEK Methyl, 84
MEKP, 83, 84
Mercury Fulminate, 84, 85, 158
Military, 7, 11, 37, 42, 62, 64, 65, 69, 71, 73, 86, 88, 99, 114, 138, 149, 192, 206, 211, 235, 246
Mine Safety and Health Administration
MSHA, 16
Misfire, 112, 113, 115, 117, 121, 122, 133, 249
Molotov cocktails, 183
Mortar Firworks, 183
Motion Sensor, 163
Motion Switch, 151
Mouse Hole, 225
MSD, 9, 240, 241, 244, 245, 246, 248, 250
Muriatic Acid, 76, 83
Murrah Federal Building, 206
NA numbers, 36, 44
Negative Pressure, 239
NEW, 241, 242, 244, 245, 246, 248, 249, 250, 274
NFPA, 33, 176, 179, 186, 187
Nitrate, 37, 48, 50, 52, 53, 60, 75, 76, 77, 78, 79, 88, 89, 145, 146, 147, 160, 186, 270
Nitric Acid, 84, 86, 88, 145
Nitro Methane, 75

Nitrocellulose, 69, 146, 271
Nitroglycerin, 37, 41, 42, 58, 59, 69, 81, 85, 86, 130, 146, 242 270
Nonel Blasting Caps, 89, 115, 118, 120, 122
Nonel Shocktube, 115
Nuclear, 42, 151
Occupational Safety and Health Administration
OSHA, 16
Octal, 70
Octogen HMX, 70, 270, 271
Ohm's Law, 118
Orange Book, 15, 17, 18, 27, 30, 52
Overpressure, 223, 239, 240, 243
Oxidizer, 37, 39, 48, 49, 79, 87, 101, 207, 273
PAN Disrupter, 189, 190, 191, 255
Parallel Circuit, 116
PE 4, 67, 71
Pentaerythritol
PETN, 61, 86
Pentolite, 71, 73, 271
PETN, 41, 42, 61, 62, 69, 71, 86, 87, 89, 128, 143, 204, 242, 271
Petroleum Fuels, 75, 145, 159
Photoelectric Switch, 155
Pipe Bomb, 161, 185, 198
Placard Sign, 35
Plastic Explosive, 54, 65, 106
Point of Breach, 210
Potassium Chlorate, 75, 79, 87, 145, 146, 162
Potassium Perchlorate, 76, 80, 81
Power/Performance, 40
Precursors, 75, 144, 145
Prils, 78
Primary Charge, 159
Propane, 75, 145, 159, 186, 200
Pyrotechnics, 181
Radio Controlled, 149, 156
Radio Frequency Jammers, 141, 191
Radio Signal, 163
Radio Signals, 151
RC Servos, 151
RDX, 37, 41, 42, 51, 54, 62, 63, 64, 65, 66, 69, 70, 71, 82, 86, 87, 104, 128, 129, 146, 242, 243, 256, 258, 268, 269, 272
RE Factor, 41, 51, 53, 54, 55, 56, 60, 62, 63, 64, 65, 66, 68, 70, 71, 73, 232, 233, 241, 242, 243
Red Phosphorus, 79
Riots, 176, 180-184, 196
Risk Management, 135
Room Clearing, 221
RTF, 179, 186
Rule of 7000, 56, 68
Safe Detonation Area, 141, 193
Safety, 8, 9, 10, 15, 16, 34, 90, 94, 98, 99, 100, 112, 115, 133, 223, 240, 272, 275
Safety Fuse, 90, 94
Safety Fuses, 27
San Bernardino Shooting, 197
Sandbags, 127, 132, 190, 225, 256
Securing Explosive Materials, 136
Security, 7, 11, 72, 133, 136, 167, 168, 184, 201, 222, 249
Security, 9, 33, 34, 134, 135, 136, 147, 164, 185, 206, 248
Semtex, 41, 42, 61, 67, 71, 72, 86, 87, 146
Sensitivity, 40
Series Circuit, 116
Shaped Charge, 126, 225, 243
Shaped Charges, 127, 129
Shock Tube, 91, 101, 105, 108, 115, 116, 121, 122, 123, 221
Shrapnel, 151, 160
Slurries, 48
Small Arms Ammunition, 20
Smokeless Powder, 37, 53, 54, 147
Sodium Nitrate, 60
Sound Activated Switch, 156
Spider Hole, 225
Stability, 40
Standoff, 9, 238, 246, 248
Stand-off Distances, 240
Sugar, 75, 76, 145
Sulfur, 53, 79, 147
Sulfuric acid, 85
Table of Distance, 27, 29, 30, 31
Taggant, 54, 66, 72
Taliban, 12
Tamping, 131

Tannerite, 3, 50
TATP, 76, 81, 143, 145, 204, 272
TEMS, 180
Terrorism, 166, 276
Terrorists, 10, 11, 13, 86, 89, 133, 136, 140, 147, 148, 150, 197, 198
Tetryl, 42, 65, 146, 272
The Shoe Bomber, 77, 147
The Unabomber, 204
Theft or Loss of Explosive, 135
Thermal, 210
Thermite, 87, 88
Time Square IED, 202, 203
Timing Switch, 157
TNT, 37, 41, 42, 43, 64, 65, 69, 70, 71, 72, 73, 85, 104, 146, 232, 233, 241, 242, 250, 270, 271, 273
Tourniquets, 178, 179
Transportation, 9, 15, 16, 33, 34, 36, 43
Triacetone, Triperoxide
  TATP, 76
Trigger, 151, 161, 162
Trinitrotoluene
  TNT, 43, 72, 77
Trip Wire, 151
U.S. Department of Transportation
  USDOT, 16, 34, 36, 44, 275
UN Numbers, 35, 43
Under Vehicle, 149
Underwear Bomber, 203
United Nations, 35, 43, 44
Urea, 76, 88, 89, 145, 273
Urine, 78, 88
UXO, 139, 140
Vehicle Borne, 149
Velocity of Detonation
  VOD, 42
Victim Operated, 149
Visco fuse, 102, 158
Visual signs, 164
Volatility, 41
Water Disrupter, 141, 189, 255, 257
Water Gels, 27, 48
Water Impulse Charge, 132, 211, 216, 217
Weapons, 149, 150, 222
WMD, 149, 150
WME, 150
World Trade Center, 78, 207, 208
X-Ray, 188

Appendix A

VIDEO QR CODE LINKS

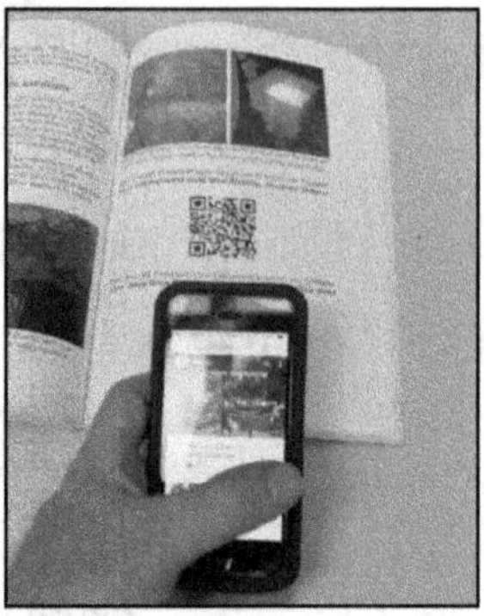

Download a free QR code scanner on your phone to watch our Public Safety related Youtube videos.

Class Video,
Explosive Device Recognition for First Responders.

Class Video
B-TEAM, Breaching, Teambuilding Explosives & Motivation

Product Video
AEG DRAGON Water Disrupter

Homeland Security Conf.
Jack speaking on the Top 10 things First Responders need to know about IEDs & Terrorism

Appendix B

ATF LIST OF EXPLOSIVES

A list of explosive materials and chemicals as provided by the Bureau of Alcohol Tobacco, Firearms and Explosives.

A

Acetylides of heavy metals.
Aluminum containing polymeric propellant.
Aluminum ophorite explosive.
Amatex.
Amatol.
Ammonal.
Ammonium nitrate explosive mixtures (cap sensitive).
*Ammonium nitrate explosive mixtures (non-cap sensitive).
Ammonium perchlorate composite propellant.
Ammonium perchlorate explosive mixtures.
Ammonium picrate [picrate of ammonia, Explosive D].
Ammonium salt lattice with isomorphously substituted inorganic salts.
*ANFO [ammonium nitrate-fuel oil].
Aromatic nitro-compound explosive mixtures.
Azide explosives.

B

Baranol.
Baratol.
BEAF [1, 2-bis (2, 2-difluoro-2-nitroacetoxyethane)].
Black powder.
Black powder based explosive mixtures.
*Blasting agents, nitro-carbo-nitrates, including non-cap sensitive slurry and water gel explosives.
Blasting caps.
Blasting gelatin.
Blasting powder.
BTNEC [bis (trinitroethyl) carbonate].
BTNEN [bis (trinitroethyl) nitramine].
BTTN [1,2,4 butanetriol trinitrate].
Bulk salutes.
Butyl tetryl.

C

Calcium nitrate explosive mixture.
Cellulose hexanitrate explosive mixture.
Chlorate explosive mixtures.

Composition A and variations.
Composition B and variations.
Composition C and variations.
Copper acetylide.
Cyanuric triazide.
Cyclonite [RDX].
Cyclotetramethylenetetranitramine [HMX].
Cyclotol.
Cyclotrimethylenetrinitramine [RDX].

D
DATB [diaminotrinitrobenzene].
DDNP [diazodinitrophenol].
DEGDN [diethyleneglycol dinitrate].
Detonating cord.
Detonators.
Dimethylol dimethyl methane dinitrate composition.
Dinitroethyleneurea.
Dinitroglycerine [glycerol dinitrate].
Dinitrophenol.
Dinitrophenolates.
Dinitrophenyl hydrazine.
Dinitroresorcinol.
Dinitrotoluene-sodium nitrate explosive mixtures.
DIPAM [dipicramide; diaminohexanitrobiphenyl].
Dipicryl sulfone.
Dipicrylamine.
Display fireworks.
DNPA [2,2-dinitropropyl acrylate].
DNPD [dinitropentano nitrile].
Dynamite.

E
EDDN [ethylene diamine dinitrate].
EDNA [ethylenedinitramine].
Ednatol.
EDNP [ethyl 4,4-dinitropentanoate].
EGDN [ethylene glycol dinitrate].
Erythritol tetranitrate explosives.
Esters of nitro-substituted alcohols.
Ethyl-tetryl.
Explosive conitrates.
Explosive gelatins.
Explosive liquids.
Explosive mixtures containing oxygen-releasing inorganic salts and

hydrocarbons.
Explosive mixtures containing oxygen-releasing inorganic salts and nitro bodies.
Explosive mixtures containing oxygen-releasing inorganic salts and water insoluble fuels.
Explosive mixtures containing oxygen-releasing inorganic salts and water soluble fuels.
Explosive mixtures containing sensitized nitromethane.
Explosive mixtures containing tetranitromethane (nitroform).
Explosive nitro compounds of aromatic hydrocarbons.
Explosive organic nitrate mixtures.
Explosive powders.

F

Flash powder.
Fulminate of mercury.
Fulminate of silver.
Fulminating gold.
Fulminating mercury.
Fulminating platinum.
Fulminating silver.

G

Gelatinized nitrocellulose.
Gem-dinitro aliphatic explosive mixtures.
Guanyl nitrosamino guanyl tetrazene.
Guanyl nitrosamino guanylidene hydrazine.
Guncotton.

H

Heavy metal azides.
Hexanite.
Hexanitrodiphenylamine.
Hexanitrostilbene.
Hexogen [RDX].
Hexogene or octogene and a nitrated N-methylaniline.
Hexolites.
HMTD [hexamethylenetriperoxidediamine].
HMX [cyclo-1,3,5,7-tetramethylene 2,4,6,8-tetranitramine; Octogen].
Hydrazinium nitrate/hydrazine/aluminum explosive system.
Hydrazoic acid.

I

Igniter cord.
Igniters.
Initiating tube systems.

K
KDNBF [potassium dinitrobenzo-furoxane].
L
Lead azide.
Lead mannite.
Lead mononitroresorcinate.
Lead picrate.
Lead salts, explosive.
Lead styphnate [styphnate of lead, lead trinitroresorcinate].
Liquid nitrated polyol and trimethylolethane.
Liquid oxygen explosives.

M
Magnesium ophorite explosives.
Mannitol hexanitrate.
MDNP [methyl 4,4-dinitropentanoate].
MEAN [monoethanolamine nitrate].
Mercuric fulminate.
Mercury oxalate.
Mercury tartrate.
Metriol trinitrate.
Minol-2 [40% TNT, 40% ammonium nitrate, 20% aluminum].
MMAN [monomethylamine nitrate]; methylamine nitrate.
Mononitrotoluene-nitroglycerin mixture.
Monopropellants.

N
NIBTN [nitroisobutametriol trinitrate].
Nitrate explosive mixtures.
Nitrate sensitized with gelled nitroparaffin.
Nitrated carbohydrate explosive.
Nitrated glucoside explosive.
Nitrated polyhydric alcohol explosives.
Nitric acid and a nitro aromatic compound explosive.
Nitric acid and carboxylic fuel explosive.
Nitric acid explosive mixtures.
Nitro aromatic explosive mixtures.
Nitro compounds of furane explosive mixtures.
Nitrocellulose explosive.
Nitroderivative of urea explosive mixture.
Nitrogelatin explosive.

Nitrogen trichloride.
Nitrogen tri-iodide.
Nitroglycerine [NG, RNG, nitro, glyceryl trinitrate, trinitroglycerine].
Nitroglycide.
Nitroglycol [ethylene glycol dinitrate, EGDN].
Nitroguanidine explosives.
Nitronium perchlorate propellant mixtures.
Nitroparaffins Explosive Grade and ammonium nitrate mixtures.
Nitrostarch.
Nitro-substituted carboxylic acids.
Nitrourea.

O
Octogen [HMX].
Octol [75 percent HMX, 25 percent TNT].
Organic amine nitrates.
Organic nitramines.

P
PBX [plastic bonded explosives].
Pellet powder.
Penthrinite composition.
Pentolite.
Perchlorate explosive mixtures.
Peroxide based explosive mixtures.
PETN [nitropentaerythrite, pentaerythrite tetranitrate, pentaerythritol tetranitrate].
Picramic acid and its salts.
Picramide.
Picrate explosives.
Picrate of potassium explosive mixtures.
Picratol.
Picric acid (manufactured as an explosive).
Picryl chloride.
Picryl fluoride.
PLX [95% nitromethane, 5% ethylenediamine].
Polynitro aliphatic compounds.
Polyolpolynitrate-nitrocellulose explosive gels.
Potassium chlorate and lead sulfocyanate explosive.
Potassium nitrate explosive mixtures.
Potassium nitroaminotetrazole.
Pyrotechnic compositions.
PYX [2,6-bis(picrylamino)]-3,5-dinitropyridine.

R

RDX [cyclonite, hexogen, T4, cyclo-1,3,5,-trimethylene-2,4,6,-trinitramine; hexahydro-1,3,5-trinitro-S-triazine].

S

Safety fuse.
Salts of organic amino sulfonic acid explosive mixture.
Salutes (bulk).
Silver acetylide.
Silver azide.
Silver fulminate.
Silver oxalate explosive mixtures.
Silver styphnate.
Silver tartrate explosive mixtures.
Silver tetrazene.
Slurried explosive mixtures of water, inorganic oxidizing salt, gelling agent, fuel, and sensitizer (cap sensitive).
Smokeless powder.
Sodatol.
Sodium amatol.
Sodium azide explosive mixture.
Sodium dinitro-ortho-cresolate.
Sodium nitrate explosive mixtures.
Sodium nitrate-potassium nitrate explosive mixture.
Sodium picramate.
Special fireworks.
Squibs.
Styphnic acid explosives.

T

Tacot [tetranitro-2,3,5,6-dibenzo- 1,3a,4,6a tetrazapentalene].
TATB [triaminotrinitrobenzene].
TATP [triacetonetriperoxide].
TEGDN [triethylene glycol dinitrate].
Tetranitrocarbazole.
Tetrazene [tetracene, tetrazine, 1(5-tetrazolyl)-4-guanyl tetrazene hydrate].
Tetryl [2,4,6 tetranitro-N-methylaniline].
Tetrytol.
Thickened inorganic oxidizer salt slurried explosive mixture.
TMETN [trimethylolethane trinitrate].
TNEF [trinitroethyl formal].
TNEOC [trinitroethylorthocarbonate].
TNEOF [trinitroethylorthoformate].
TNT [trinitrotoluene, trotyl, trilite, triton].

Torpex.
Tridite.
Trimethylol ethyl methane trinitrate composition.
Trimethylolthane trinitrate-nitrocellulose.
Trimonite.
Trinitroanisole.
Trinitrobenzene.
Trinitrobenzoic acid.
Trinitrocresol.
Trinitro-meta-cresol.
Trinitronaphthalene.
Trinitrophenetol.
Trinitrophloroglucinol.
Trinitroresorcinol.
Tritonal.

U
Urea nitrate.

W
Water-bearing explosives having salts of oxidizing acids and nitrogen bases, sulfates, or sulfamates (cap sensitive).
Water-in-oil emulsion explosive compositions.

X
Xanthamonas hydrophilic colloid explosive mixture.

Appendix C

MINIMUM SAFE DISTANCE CHART, K FACTOR 18

Determine your Net Explosive Weight based upon RE 1.0, then match the amount on left column to look up standoff on right.

NEW	Cube root	Safe distance	w/o shield	w/shield
0.010	.215443469	03.877982448	4	2
0.020	.271441762	04.885951716	5	3
0.030	.310723251	05.593018517	6	3
0.050	.368403150	06.631256704	7	4
0.080	.430886938	07.755964891	8	4
0.120	.493242415	08.878363474	9	5
0.170	.553965826	09.971384868	10	5
0.220	.603681074	10.866259330	11	6
0.290	.661910595	11.914390710	12	6
0.370	.717905435	12.922297840	13	7
0.470	.777498010	13.994964180	14	7
0.570	.829134434	14.924419820	15	8
0.700	.887904002	15.982272030	16	8
0.840	.943538796	16.983698330	17	9
1.001	.000000000	18.000000000	18	9
1.171	.053728243	18.967108370	19	10
1.371	.110640541	19.991529740	20	10
1.581	.164713284	20.964839120	21	11
1.821	.220929150	21.976724690	22	11
2.081	.276500859	22.977015470	23	12
2.371	.333263885	23.998749930	24	12
2.671	.387300109	24.971401960	25	13
3.011	.443850292	25.989305260	26	13
3.371	.499258893	26.986660070	27	14
3.761	.554996019	27.989928340	28	14
4.181	.610863572	28.995544290	29	15
4.621	.665510308	29.979185550	30	15
5.001	.709975946	30.779567020	31	16

These amounts do not consider fragmentation, triple the standoff distance for indoor on confined spaces.

Appendix D

IMPORTANT CONTACT INFORMATION

U.S. Bureau of Alcohol, Tobacco, Firearms and Explosives

ATF 24-Hour Hotline 800 800-3855
Bomb Data Center 800 461-8841
Stolen Explosives Hotline 888 283-2662
(After hours, weekends) .... (888-ATF-BOMB)
Distribution Center 877 283-3352

Main Website .... www.atf.gov
ATF Forms .... http://www.atf.gov/forms/dcof/

ATF U.S. Bomb Data Center (Repository)
P.O. Box 50980, Washington, D.C. 20091

ATF Explosives Industry Programs Branch (EIPB)
650 Massachusetts Avenue NW, Room 5000
Washington, D.C. 20226

ATF Distribution Center
7943 Angus Court, Springfield, Virginia 22153

U.S. Department of Transportation

Telephone 202-366-4433
HAZMAT transport information line 800 467-4922
Website .... http://www.dot.gov/

Pipeline and Hazardous Materials Safety Administration
East Building, 2nd Floor, 1200 New Jersey Ave., SE
Washington, DC 20590

State Numbers

State Fire Marshall ________________________________
State Police ________________________________

Appendix E

ABOUT THE AUTHORS

Duane R. 'Matt' Mattson

Instructor and Special Explosives/Anti-Terrorism Consultant

Matt travels the world as an explosives and anti-terrorism specialist and trainer. His credentials are longer than we can list here, but they include; U.S. Army Ranger and Special Forces with a specialty in demolition and engineering, Washington State Inter-Agency Bomb Squad, SWAT and Explosive Breacher. He is also a former Police Officer and commercial blasting company owner.

Matt A. Byers

Instructor & Demolition Specialist

Matt is an explosvies specialist from Florida with 15 years of experence in explosive demolitions.

Tyson Krieger

Vice President and Instructor
American Explosives Group, Inc.

Tyson is an explosives and fire science specialist who is also the Fire Chief of the Gold Beach, Oregon Fire Department.

Jack W. Peters

President and Founder
American Explosives Group, Inc.

Jack is an explosives specialist as well as a business speaker, instructor, and author. Jack is also the blaster and treasure hunter in Discovery Channel's *Treasure Quest* series filmed in Bolivia, South America, released in 2018.

Thank you purchasing the book and we wish you a safe and successful explosives career!

Jack W. Peters, President

www.ingramcontent.com/pod-product-compliance
Lightning Source LLC
Chambersburg PA
CBHW071734270326
41928CB00013B/2672